C-591   CAREER EXAMINATION SERIES

This is your
PASSBOOK for...

Plumber

Test Preparation Study Guide
Questions & Answers

NATIONAL LEARNING CORPORATION®

COPYRIGHT NOTICE

This book is SOLELY intended for, is sold ONLY to, and its use is RESTRICTED to individual, bona fide applicants or candidates who qualify by virtue of having seriously filed applications for appropriate license, certificate, professional and/or promotional advancement, higher school matriculation, scholarship, or other legitimate requirements of education and/or governmental authorities.

This book is NOT intended for use, class instruction, tutoring, training, duplication, copying, reprinting, excerption, or adaptation, etc., by:

1) Other publishers
2) Proprietors and/or Instructors of "Coaching" and/or Preparatory Courses
3) Personnel and/or Training Divisions of commercial, industrial, and governmental organizations
4) Schools, colleges, or universities and/or their departments and staffs, including teachers and other personnel
5) Testing Agencies or Bureaus
6) Study groups which seek by the purchase of a single volume to copy and/or duplicate and/or adapt this material for use by the group as a whole without having purchased individual volumes for each of the members of the group
7) Et al.

Such persons would be in violation of appropriate Federal and State statutes.

PROVISION OF LICENSING AGREEMENTS – Recognized educational, commercial, industrial, and governmental institutions and organizations, and others legitimately engaged in educational pursuits, including training, testing, and measurement activities, may address request for a licensing agreement to the copyright owners, who will determine whether, and under what conditions, including fees and charges, the materials in this book may be used them. In other words, a licensing facility exists for the legitimate use of the material in this book on other than an individual basis. However, it is asseverated and affirmed here that the material in this book CANNOT be used without the receipt of the express permission of such a licensing agreement from the Publishers. Inquiries re licensing should be addressed to the company, attention rights and permissions department.

All rights reserved, including the right of reproduction in whole or in part, in any form or by any means, electronic or mechanical, including photocopying, recording, or by any information storage and retrieval system, without permission in writing from the Publisher.

Copyright © 2024 by
National Learning Corporation

212 Michael Drive, Syosset, NY 11791
(516) 921-8888 • www.passbooks.com
E-mail: info@passbooks.com

PUBLISHED IN THE UNITED STATES OF AMERICA

PASSBOOK® SERIES

THE *PASSBOOK® SERIES* has been created to prepare applicants and candidates for the ultimate academic battlefield – the examination room.

At some time in our lives, each and every one of us may be required to take an examination – for validation, matriculation, admission, qualification, registration, certification, or licensure.

Based on the assumption that every applicant or candidate has met the basic formal educational standards, has taken the required number of courses, and read the necessary texts, the *PASSBOOK® SERIES* furnishes the one special preparation which may assure passing with confidence, instead of failing with insecurity. Examination questions – together with answers – are furnished as the basic vehicle for study so that the mysteries of the examination and its compounding difficulties may be eliminated or diminished by a sure method.

This book is meant to help you pass your examination provided that you qualify and are serious in your objective.

The entire field is reviewed through the huge store of content information which is succinctly presented through a provocative and challenging approach – the question-and-answer method.

A climate of success is established by furnishing the correct answers at the end of each test.

You soon learn to recognize types of questions, forms of questions, and patterns of questioning. You may even begin to anticipate expected outcomes.

You perceive that many questions are repeated or adapted so that you can gain acute insights, which may enable you to score many sure points.

You learn how to confront new questions, or types of questions, and to attack them confidently and work out the correct answers.

You note objectives and emphases, and recognize pitfalls and dangers, so that you may make positive educational adjustments.

Moreover, you are kept fully informed in relation to new concepts, methods, practices, and directions in the field.

You discover that you are actually taking the examination all the time: you are preparing for the examination by "taking" an examination, not by reading extraneous and/or supererogatory textbooks.

In short, this PASSBOOK®, used directedly, should be an important factor in helping you to pass your test.

PLUMBER

WHAT THE JOB INVOLVES:
Plumbers, under supervision, perform work relating to the installation, alteration, maintenance, and repair of piping of gas, potable water, plumbing and drainage systems. They install, maintain and repair piping of all kinds for water, gas, storm, waste, soil and vent systems; set, maintain and repair plumbing fixtures, equipment and appurtenances; when necessary, determine and requisition job materials while work is in progress; supervise and are responsible for the work of Plumber's Helpers; in the temporary absence of the supervisor, may perform the duties of that position; and operate a motor vehicle. All Plumbers perform related work.

When assigned as a licensed plumber, Plumbers obtain written building permits for plumbing work to be performed; conduct and/or witness tests on plumbing and gas piping systems; prepare applications, reports, notices and other documents; and prepare sketches, drawings and layouts which may be required.

THE TEST:
The multiple-choice test is designed to assess the extent to which candidates have certain knowledge and abilities determined to be important to the performance of the tasks of a Plumber. Task areas to be tested are as follows: repairs and installation; tools and materials; and administrative duties.

The multiple-choice test may include questions on the knowledge plumbing techniques, methodology, materials, tools, equipment, and practices; pertinent parts of the Building Code and other related codes including interpretation of plans and specifications; safe work practices; job-related math; standards of proper employee ethical conduct; and other related areas.

The multiple-choice test may also include questions requiring the use of any of the following abilities:
Analytical Thinking: Analyzing information and using logic to address specific work-related issues and problems; involves the identification of problems, not implementation of solutions. Example: A Plumber analyzes the whereabouts and solutions of water leaks.
Planning & Organizing: Establishing a method of execution to accomplish a specific goal over an extended period of time; determining appropriate assignments and allocation of resources. Example: A Plumber plans, organizes, and prioritizes their work orders.
Written Comprehension: Understanding English words and sentences. Example: A Plumber reads and understands work orders pertaining to the Building Code.
Written Expression: Using English words or sentences in writing so that others will understand. Example: A Plumber writes reports free of grammatical errors. Certain questions may need to be answered on the basis of documents or other information supplied to the candidates on the date of the multiple-choice test.

HOW TO TAKE A TEST

I. YOU MUST PASS AN EXAMINATION

A. *WHAT EVERY CANDIDATE SHOULD KNOW*

Examination applicants often ask us for help in preparing for the written test. What can I study in advance? What kinds of questions will be asked? How will the test be given? How will the papers be graded?

As an applicant for a civil service examination, you may be wondering about some of these things. Our purpose here is to suggest effective methods of advance study and to describe civil service examinations.

Your chances for success on this examination can be increased if you know how to prepare. Those "pre-examination jitters" can be reduced if you know what to expect. You can even experience an adventure in good citizenship if you know why civil service exams are given.

B. *WHY ARE CIVIL SERVICE EXAMINATIONS GIVEN?*

Civil service examinations are important to you in two ways. As a citizen, you want public jobs filled by employees who know how to do their work. As a job seeker, you want a fair chance to compete for that job on an equal footing with other candidates. The best-known means of accomplishing this two-fold goal is the competitive examination.

Exams are widely publicized throughout the nation. They may be administered for jobs in federal, state, city, municipal, town or village governments or agencies.

Any citizen may apply, with some limitations, such as the age or residence of applicants. Your experience and education may be reviewed to see whether you meet the requirements for the particular examination. When these requirements exist, they are reasonable and applied consistently to all applicants. Thus, a competitive examination may cause you some uneasiness now, but it is your privilege and safeguard.

C. *HOW ARE CIVIL SERVICE EXAMS DEVELOPED?*

Examinations are carefully written by trained technicians who are specialists in the field known as "psychological measurement," in consultation with recognized authorities in the field of work that the test will cover. These experts recommend the subject matter areas or skills to be tested; only those knowledges or skills important to your success on the job are included. The most reliable books and source materials available are used as references. Together, the experts and technicians judge the difficulty level of the questions.

Test technicians know how to phrase questions so that the problem is clearly stated. Their ethics do not permit "trick" or "catch" questions. Questions may have been tried out on sample groups, or subjected to statistical analysis, to determine their usefulness.

Written tests are often used in combination with performance tests, ratings of training and experience, and oral interviews. All of these measures combine to form the best-known means of finding the right person for the right job.

II. HOW TO PASS THE WRITTEN TEST

A. NATURE OF THE EXAMINATION

To prepare intelligently for civil service examinations, you should know how they differ from school examinations you have taken. In school you were assigned certain definite pages to read or subjects to cover. The examination questions were quite detailed and usually emphasized memory. Civil service exams, on the other hand, try to discover your present ability to perform the duties of a position, plus your potentiality to learn these duties. In other words, a civil service exam attempts to predict how successful you will be. Questions cover such a broad area that they cannot be as minute and detailed as school exam questions.

In the public service similar kinds of work, or positions, are grouped together in one "class." This process is known as *position-classification*. All the positions in a class are paid according to the salary range for that class. One class title covers all of these positions, and they are all tested by the same examination.

B. FOUR BASIC STEPS

1) Study the announcement

How, then, can you know what subjects to study? Our best answer is: "Learn as much as possible about the class of positions for which you've applied." The exam will test the knowledge, skills and abilities needed to do the work.

Your most valuable source of information about the position you want is the official exam announcement. This announcement lists the training and experience qualifications. Check these standards and apply only if you come reasonably close to meeting them.

The brief description of the position in the examination announcement offers some clues to the subjects which will be tested. Think about the job itself. Review the duties in your mind. Can you perform them, or are there some in which you are rusty? Fill in the blank spots in your preparation.

Many jurisdictions preview the written test in the exam announcement by including a section called "Knowledge and Abilities Required," "Scope of the Examination," or some similar heading. Here you will find out specifically what fields will be tested.

2) Review your own background

Once you learn in general what the position is all about, and what you need to know to do the work, ask yourself which subjects you already know fairly well and which need improvement. You may wonder whether to concentrate on improving your strong areas or on building some background in your fields of weakness. When the announcement has specified "some knowledge" or "considerable knowledge," or has used adjectives like "beginning principles of..." or "advanced ... methods," you can get a clue as to the number and difficulty of questions to be asked in any given field. More questions, and hence broader coverage, would be included for those subjects which are more important in the work. Now weigh your strengths and weaknesses against the job requirements and prepare accordingly.

3) Determine the level of the position

Another way to tell how intensively you should prepare is to understand the level of the job for which you are applying. Is it the entering level? In other words, is this the position in which beginners in a field of work are hired? Or is it an intermediate or advanced level? Sometimes this is indicated by such words as "Junior" or "Senior" in the class title. Other jurisdictions use Roman numerals to designate the level – Clerk I, Clerk II, for example. The word "Supervisor" sometimes appears in the title. If the level is not indicated by the title, check the description of duties. Will you be working under very close supervision, or will you have responsibility for independent decisions in this work?

4) Choose appropriate study materials

Now that you know the subjects to be examined and the relative amount of each subject to be covered, you can choose suitable study materials. For beginning level jobs, or even advanced ones, if you have a pronounced weakness in some aspect of your training, read a modern, standard textbook in that field. Be sure it is up to date and has general coverage. Such books are normally available at your library, and the librarian will be glad to help you locate one. For entry-level positions, questions of appropriate difficulty are chosen -- neither highly advanced questions, nor those too simple. Such questions require careful thought but not advanced training.

If the position for which you are applying is technical or advanced, you will read more advanced, specialized material. If you are already familiar with the basic principles of your field, elementary textbooks would waste your time. Concentrate on advanced textbooks and technical periodicals. Think through the concepts and review difficult problems in your field.

These are all general sources. You can get more ideas on your own initiative, following these leads. For example, training manuals and publications of the government agency which employs workers in your field can be useful, particularly for technical and professional positions. A letter or visit to the government department involved may result in more specific study suggestions, and certainly will provide you with a more definite idea of the exact nature of the position you are seeking.

III. KINDS OF TESTS

Tests are used for purposes other than measuring knowledge and ability to perform specified duties. For some positions, it is equally important to test ability to make adjustments to new situations or to profit from training. In others, basic mental abilities not dependent on information are essential. Questions which test these things may not appear as pertinent to the duties of the position as those which test for knowledge and information. Yet they are often highly important parts of a fair examination. For very general questions, it is almost impossible to help you direct your study efforts. What we can do is to point out some of the more common of these general abilities needed in public service positions and describe some typical questions.

1) General information

Broad, general information has been found useful for predicting job success in some kinds of work. This is tested in a variety of ways, from vocabulary lists to questions about current events. Basic background in some field of work, such as sociology or economics, may be sampled in a group of questions. Often these are principles which have become familiar to most persons through exposure rather than through formal training. It is difficult to advise you how to study for these questions; being alert to the world around you is our best suggestion.

2) Verbal ability

An example of an ability needed in many positions is verbal or language ability. Verbal ability is, in brief, the ability to use and understand words. Vocabulary and grammar tests are typical measures of this ability. Reading comprehension or paragraph interpretation questions are common in many kinds of civil service tests. You are given a paragraph of written material and asked to find its central meaning.

3) Numerical ability

Number skills can be tested by the familiar arithmetic problem, by checking paired lists of numbers to see which are alike and which are different, or by interpreting charts and graphs. In the latter test, a graph may be printed in the test booklet which you are asked to use as the basis for answering questions.

4) Observation

A popular test for law-enforcement positions is the observation test. A picture is shown to you for several minutes, then taken away. Questions about the picture test your ability to observe both details and larger elements.

5) Following directions

In many positions in the public service, the employee must be able to carry out written instructions dependably and accurately. You may be given a chart with several columns, each column listing a variety of information. The questions require you to carry out directions involving the information given in the chart.

6) Skills and aptitudes

Performance tests effectively measure some manual skills and aptitudes. When the skill is one in which you are trained, such as typing or shorthand, you can practice. These tests are often very much like those given in business school or high school courses. For many of the other skills and aptitudes, however, no short-time preparation can be made. Skills and abilities natural to you or that you have developed throughout your lifetime are being tested.

Many of the general questions just described provide all the data needed to answer the questions and ask you to use your reasoning ability to find the answers. Your best preparation for these tests, as well as for tests of facts and ideas, is to be at your physical and mental best. You, no doubt, have your own methods of getting into an exam-taking mood and keeping "in shape." The next section lists some ideas on this subject.

IV. KINDS OF QUESTIONS

Only rarely is the "essay" question, which you answer in narrative form, used in civil service tests. Civil service tests are usually of the short-answer type. Full instructions for answering these questions will be given to you at the examination. But in case this is your first experience with short-answer questions and separate answer sheets, here is what you need to know:

1) Multiple-choice Questions

Most popular of the short-answer questions is the "multiple choice" or "best answer" question. It can be used, for example, to test for factual knowledge, ability to solve problems or judgment in meeting situations found at work.

A multiple-choice question is normally one of three types—
- It can begin with an incomplete statement followed by several possible endings. You are to find the one ending which *best* completes the statement, although some of the others may not be entirely wrong.
- It can also be a complete statement in the form of a question which is answered by choosing one of the statements listed.

- It can be in the form of a problem – again you select the best answer.

Here is an example of a multiple-choice question with a discussion which should give you some clues as to the method for choosing the right answer:

When an employee has a complaint about his assignment, the action which will *best* help him overcome his difficulty is to
   A. discuss his difficulty with his coworkers
   B. take the problem to the head of the organization
   C. take the problem to the person who gave him the assignment
   D. say nothing to anyone about his complaint

In answering this question, you should study each of the choices to find which is best. Consider choice "A" – Certainly an employee may discuss his complaint with fellow employees, but no change or improvement can result, and the complaint remains unresolved. Choice "B" is a poor choice since the head of the organization probably does not know what assignment you have been given, and taking your problem to him is known as "going over the head" of the supervisor. The supervisor, or person who made the assignment, is the person who can clarify it or correct any injustice. Choice "C" is, therefore, correct. To say nothing, as in choice "D," is unwise. Supervisors have and interest in knowing the problems employees are facing, and the employee is seeking a solution to his problem.

2) True/False Questions

The "true/false" or "right/wrong" form of question is sometimes used. Here a complete statement is given. Your job is to decide whether the statement is right or wrong.

SAMPLE: A roaming cell-phone call to a nearby city costs less than a non-roaming call to a distant city.

This statement is wrong, or false, since roaming calls are more expensive.

This is not a complete list of all possible question forms, although most of the others are variations of these common types. You will always get complete directions for answering questions. Be sure you understand *how* to mark your answers – ask questions until you do.

V. RECORDING YOUR ANSWERS

Computer terminals are used more and more today for many different kinds of exams.

For an examination with very few applicants, you may be told to record your answers in the test booklet itself. Separate answer sheets are much more common. If this separate answer sheet is to be scored by machine – and this is often the case – it is highly important that you mark your answers correctly in order to get credit.

An electronic scoring machine is often used in civil service offices because of the speed with which papers can be scored. Machine-scored answer sheets must be marked with a pencil, which will be given to you. This pencil has a high graphite content which responds to the electronic scoring machine. As a matter of fact, stray dots may register as answers, so do not let your pencil rest on the answer sheet while you are pondering the correct answer. Also, if your pencil lead breaks or is otherwise defective, ask for another.

Since the answer sheet will be dropped in a slot in the scoring machine, be careful not to bend the corners or get the paper crumpled.

The answer sheet normally has five vertical columns of numbers, with 30 numbers to a column. These numbers correspond to the question numbers in your test booklet. After each number, going across the page are four or five pairs of dotted lines. These short dotted lines have small letters or numbers above them. The first two pairs may also have a "T" or "F" above the letters. This indicates that the first two pairs only are to be used if the questions are of the true-false type. If the questions are multiple choice, disregard the "T" and "F" and pay attention only to the small letters or numbers.

Answer your questions in the manner of the sample that follows:

32. The largest city in the United States is
    A. Washington, D.C.
    B. New York City
    C. Chicago
    D. Detroit
    E. San Francisco

1) Choose the answer you think is best. (New York City is the largest, so "B" is correct.)
2) Find the row of dotted lines numbered the same as the question you are answering. (Find row number 32)
3) Find the pair of dotted lines corresponding to the answer. (Find the pair of lines under the mark "B.")
4) Make a solid black mark between the dotted lines.

VI. BEFORE THE TEST

Common sense will help you find procedures to follow to get ready for an examination. Too many of us, however, overlook these sensible measures. Indeed, nervousness and fatigue have been found to be the most serious reasons why applicants fail to do their best on civil service tests. Here is a list of reminders:

- Begin your preparation early – Don't wait until the last minute to go scurrying around for books and materials or to find out what the position is all about.
- Prepare continuously – An hour a night for a week is better than an all-night cram session. This has been definitely established. What is more, a night a week for a month will return better dividends than crowding your study into a shorter period of time.
- Locate the place of the exam – You have been sent a notice telling you when and where to report for the examination. If the location is in a different town or otherwise unfamiliar to you, it would be well to inquire the best route and learn something about the building.
- Relax the night before the test – Allow your mind to rest. Do not study at all that night. Plan some mild recreation or diversion; then go to bed early and get a good night's sleep.
- Get up early enough to make a leisurely trip to the place for the test – This way unforeseen events, traffic snarls, unfamiliar buildings, etc. will not upset you.
- Dress comfortably – A written test is not a fashion show. You will be known by number and not by name, so wear something comfortable.

- Leave excess paraphernalia at home – Shopping bags and odd bundles will get in your way. You need bring only the items mentioned in the official notice you received; usually everything you need is provided. Do not bring reference books to the exam. They will only confuse those last minutes and be taken away from you when in the test room.
- Arrive somewhat ahead of time – If because of transportation schedules you must get there very early, bring a newspaper or magazine to take your mind off yourself while waiting.
- Locate the examination room – When you have found the proper room, you will be directed to the seat or part of the room where you will sit. Sometimes you are given a sheet of instructions to read while you are waiting. Do not fill out any forms until you are told to do so; just read them and be prepared.
- Relax and prepare to listen to the instructions
- If you have any physical problem that may keep you from doing your best, be sure to tell the test administrator. If you are sick or in poor health, you really cannot do your best on the exam. You can come back and take the test some other time.

VII. AT THE TEST

The day of the test is here and you have the test booklet in your hand. The temptation to get going is very strong. Caution! There is more to success than knowing the right answers. You must know how to identify your papers and understand variations in the type of short-answer question used in this particular examination. Follow these suggestions for maximum results from your efforts:

1) Cooperate with the monitor

The test administrator has a duty to create a situation in which you can be as much at ease as possible. He will give instructions, tell you when to begin, check to see that you are marking your answer sheet correctly, and so on. He is not there to guard you, although he will see that your competitors do not take unfair advantage. He wants to help you do your best.

2) Listen to all instructions

Don't jump the gun! Wait until you understand all directions. In most civil service tests you get more time than you need to answer the questions. So don't be in a hurry. Read each word of instructions until you clearly understand the meaning. Study the examples, listen to all announcements and follow directions. Ask questions if you do not understand what to do.

3) Identify your papers

Civil service exams are usually identified by number only. You will be assigned a number; you must not put your name on your test papers. Be sure to copy your number correctly. Since more than one exam may be given, copy your exact examination title.

4) Plan your time

Unless you are told that a test is a "speed" or "rate of work" test, speed itself is usually not important. Time enough to answer all the questions will be provided, but this does not mean that you have all day. An overall time limit has been set. Divide the total time (in minutes) by the number of questions to determine the approximate time you have for each question.

5) Do not linger over difficult questions

If you come across a difficult question, mark it with a paper clip (useful to have along) and come back to it when you have been through the booklet. One caution if you do this – be sure to skip a number on your answer sheet as well. Check often to be sure that you have not lost your place and that you are marking in the row numbered the same as the question you are answering.

6) Read the questions

Be sure you know what the question asks! Many capable people are unsuccessful because they failed to *read* the questions correctly.

7) Answer all questions

Unless you have been instructed that a penalty will be deducted for incorrect answers, it is better to guess than to omit a question.

8) Speed tests

It is often better NOT to guess on speed tests. It has been found that on timed tests people are tempted to spend the last few seconds before time is called in marking answers at random – without even reading them – in the hope of picking up a few extra points. To discourage this practice, the instructions may warn you that your score will be "corrected" for guessing. That is, a penalty will be applied. The incorrect answers will be deducted from the correct ones, or some other penalty formula will be used.

9) Review your answers

If you finish before time is called, go back to the questions you guessed or omitted to give them further thought. Review other answers if you have time.

10) Return your test materials

If you are ready to leave before others have finished or time is called, take ALL your materials to the monitor and leave quietly. Never take any test material with you. The monitor can discover whose papers are not complete, and taking a test booklet may be grounds for disqualification.

VIII. EXAMINATION TECHNIQUES

1) Read the general instructions carefully. These are usually printed on the first page of the exam booklet. As a rule, these instructions refer to the timing of the examination; the fact that you should not start work until the signal and must stop work at a signal, etc. If there are any *special* instructions, such as a choice of questions to be answered, make sure that you note this instruction carefully.

2) When you are ready to start work on the examination, that is as soon as the signal has been given, read the instructions to each question booklet, underline any key words or phrases, such as *least, best, outline, describe* and the like. In this way you will tend to answer as requested rather than discover on reviewing your paper that you *listed without describing*, that you selected the *worst* choice rather than the *best* choice, etc.

3) If the examination is of the objective or multiple-choice type – that is, each question will also give a series of possible answers: A, B, C or D, and you are called upon to select the best answer and write the letter next to that answer on your answer paper – it is advisable to start answering each question in turn. There may be anywhere from 50 to 100 such questions in the three or four hours allotted and you can see how much time would be taken if you read through all the questions before beginning to answer any. Furthermore, if you come across a question or group of questions which you know would be difficult to answer, it would undoubtedly affect your handling of all the other questions.

4) If the examination is of the essay type and contains but a few questions, it is a moot point as to whether you should read all the questions before starting to answer any one. Of course, if you are given a choice – say five out of seven and the like – then it is essential to read all the questions so you can eliminate the two that are most difficult. If, however, you are asked to answer all the questions, there may be danger in trying to answer the easiest one first because you may find that you will spend too much time on it. The best technique is to answer the first question, then proceed to the second, etc.

5) Time your answers. Before the exam begins, write down the time it started, then add the time allowed for the examination and write down the time it must be completed, then divide the time available somewhat as follows:
    - If 3-1/2 hours are allowed, that would be 210 minutes. If you have 80 objective-type questions, that would be an average of 2-1/2 minutes per question. Allow yourself no more than 2 minutes per question, or a total of 160 minutes, which will permit about 50 minutes to review.
    - If for the time allotment of 210 minutes there are 7 essay questions to answer, that would average about 30 minutes a question. Give yourself only 25 minutes per question so that you have about 35 minutes to review.

6) The most important instruction is to *read each question* and make sure you know what is wanted. The second most important instruction is to *time yourself properly* so that you answer every question. The third most important instruction is to *answer every question*. Guess if you have to but include something for each question. Remember that you will receive no credit for a blank and will probably receive some credit if you write something in answer to an essay question. If you guess a letter – say "B" for a multiple-choice question – you may have guessed right. If you leave a blank as an answer to a multiple-choice question, the examiners may respect your feelings but it will not add a point to your score. Some exams may penalize you for wrong answers, so in such cases *only*, you may not want to guess unless you have some basis for your answer.

7) Suggestions
    a. Objective-type questions
        1. Examine the question booklet for proper sequence of pages and questions
        2. Read all instructions carefully
        3. Skip any question which seems too difficult; return to it after all other questions have been answered
        4. Apportion your time properly; do not spend too much time on any single question or group of questions

5. Note and underline key words – *all, most, fewest, least, best, worst, same, opposite,* etc.
6. Pay particular attention to negatives
7. Note unusual option, e.g., unduly long, short, complex, different or similar in content to the body of the question
8. Observe the use of "hedging" words – *probably, may, most likely,* etc.
9. Make sure that your answer is put next to the same number as the question
10. Do not second-guess unless you have good reason to believe the second answer is definitely more correct
11. Cross out original answer if you decide another answer is more accurate; do not erase until you are ready to hand your paper in
12. Answer all questions; guess unless instructed otherwise
13. Leave time for review

b. Essay questions
1. Read each question carefully
2. Determine exactly what is wanted. Underline key words or phrases.
3. Decide on outline or paragraph answer
4. Include many different points and elements unless asked to develop any one or two points or elements
5. Show impartiality by giving pros and cons unless directed to select one side only
6. Make and write down any assumptions you find necessary to answer the questions
7. Watch your English, grammar, punctuation and choice of words
8. Time your answers; don't crowd material

8) Answering the essay question

Most essay questions can be answered by framing the specific response around several key words or ideas. Here are a few such key words or ideas:

M's: manpower, materials, methods, money, management
P's: purpose, program, policy, plan, procedure, practice, problems, pitfalls, personnel, public relations

a. Six basic steps in handling problems:
1. Preliminary plan and background development
2. Collect information, data and facts
3. Analyze and interpret information, data and facts
4. Analyze and develop solutions as well as make recommendations
5. Prepare report and sell recommendations
6. Install recommendations and follow up effectiveness

b. Pitfalls to avoid
1. *Taking things for granted* – A statement of the situation does not necessarily imply that each of the elements is necessarily true; for example, a complaint may be invalid and biased so that all that can be taken for granted is that a complaint has been registered

2. *Considering only one side of a situation* – Wherever possible, indicate several alternatives and then point out the reasons you selected the best one
3. *Failing to indicate follow up* – Whenever your answer indicates action on your part, make certain that you will take proper follow-up action to see how successful your recommendations, procedures or actions turn out to be
4. *Taking too long in answering any single question* – Remember to time your answers properly

IX. AFTER THE TEST

Scoring procedures differ in detail among civil service jurisdictions although the general principles are the same. Whether the papers are hand-scored or graded by machine we have described, they are nearly always graded by number. That is, the person who marks the paper knows only the number – never the name – of the applicant. Not until all the papers have been graded will they be matched with names. If other tests, such as training and experience or oral interview ratings have been given, scores will be combined. Different parts of the examination usually have different weights. For example, the written test might count 60 percent of the final grade, and a rating of training and experience 40 percent. In many jurisdictions, veterans will have a certain number of points added to their grades.

After the final grade has been determined, the names are placed in grade order and an eligible list is established. There are various methods for resolving ties between those who get the same final grade – probably the most common is to place first the name of the person whose application was received first. Job offers are made from the eligible list in the order the names appear on it. You will be notified of your grade and your rank as soon as all these computations have been made. This will be done as rapidly as possible.

People who are found to meet the requirements in the announcement are called "eligibles." Their names are put on a list of eligible candidates. An eligible's chances of getting a job depend on how high he stands on this list and how fast agencies are filling jobs from the list.

When a job is to be filled from a list of eligibles, the agency asks for the names of people on the list of eligibles for that job. When the civil service commission receives this request, it sends to the agency the names of the three people highest on this list. Or, if the job to be filled has specialized requirements, the office sends the agency the names of the top three persons who meet these requirements from the general list.

The appointing officer makes a choice from among the three people whose names were sent to him. If the selected person accepts the appointment, the names of the others are put back on the list to be considered for future openings.

That is the rule in hiring from all kinds of eligible lists, whether they are for typist, carpenter, chemist, or something else. For every vacancy, the appointing officer has his choice of any one of the top three eligibles on the list. This explains why the person whose name is on top of the list sometimes does not get an appointment when some of the persons lower on the list do. If the appointing officer chooses the second or third eligible, the No. 1 eligible does not get a job at once, but stays on the list until he is appointed or the list is terminated.

X. HOW TO PASS THE INTERVIEW TEST

The examination for which you applied requires an oral interview test. You have already taken the written test and you are now being called for the interview test – the final part of the formal examination.

You may think that it is not possible to prepare for an interview test and that there are no procedures to follow during an interview. Our purpose is to point out some things you can do in advance that will help you and some good rules to follow and pitfalls to avoid while you are being interviewed.

What is an interview supposed to test?

The written examination is designed to test the technical knowledge and competence of the candidate; the oral is designed to evaluate intangible qualities, not readily measured otherwise, and to establish a list showing the relative fitness of each candidate – as measured against his competitors – for the position sought. Scoring is not on the basis of "right" and "wrong," but on a sliding scale of values ranging from "not passable" to "outstanding." As a matter of fact, it is possible to achieve a relatively low score without a single "incorrect" answer because of evident weakness in the qualities being measured.

Occasionally, an examination may consist entirely of an oral test – either an individual or a group oral. In such cases, information is sought concerning the technical knowledges and abilities of the candidate, since there has been no written examination for this purpose. More commonly, however, an oral test is used to supplement a written examination.

Who conducts interviews?

The composition of oral boards varies among different jurisdictions. In nearly all, a representative of the personnel department serves as chairman. One of the members of the board may be a representative of the department in which the candidate would work. In some cases, "outside experts" are used, and, frequently, a businessman or some other representative of the general public is asked to serve. Labor and management or other special groups may be represented. The aim is to secure the services of experts in the appropriate field.

However the board is composed, it is a good idea (and not at all improper or unethical) to ascertain in advance of the interview who the members are and what groups they represent. When you are introduced to them, you will have some idea of their backgrounds and interests, and at least you will not stutter and stammer over their names.

What should be done before the interview?

While knowledge about the board members is useful and takes some of the surprise element out of the interview, there is other preparation which is more substantive. It *is* possible to prepare for an oral interview – in several ways:

1) Keep a copy of your application and review it carefully before the interview

This may be the only document before the oral board, and the starting point of the interview. Know what education and experience you have listed there, and the sequence and dates of all of it. Sometimes the board will ask you to review the highlights of your experience for them; you should not have to hem and haw doing it.

2) Study the class specification and the examination announcement

Usually, the oral board has one or both of these to guide them. The qualities, characteristics or knowledges required by the position sought are stated in these documents. They offer valuable clues as to the nature of the oral interview. For example, if the job involves supervisory responsibilities, the announcement will usually indicate that knowledge of modern supervisory methods and the qualifications of the candidate as a supervisor will be tested. If so, you can expect such questions, frequently in the form of a hypothetical situation which you are expected to solve. NEVER go into an oral without knowledge of the duties and responsibilities of the job you seek.

3) Think through each qualification required

Try to visualize the kind of questions you would ask if you were a board member. How well could you answer them? Try especially to appraise your own knowledge and background in each area, *measured against the job sought*, and identify any areas in which you are weak. Be critical and realistic – do not flatter yourself.

4) Do some general reading in areas in which you feel you may be weak

For example, if the job involves supervision and your past experience has NOT, some general reading in supervisory methods and practices, particularly in the field of human relations, might be useful. Do NOT study agency procedures or detailed manuals. The oral board will be testing your understanding and capacity, not your memory.

5) Get a good night's sleep and watch your general health and mental attitude

You will want a clear head at the interview. Take care of a cold or any other minor ailment, and of course, no hangovers.

What should be done on the day of the interview?

Now comes the day of the interview itself. Give yourself plenty of time to get there. Plan to arrive somewhat ahead of the scheduled time, particularly if your appointment is in the fore part of the day. If a previous candidate fails to appear, the board might be ready for you a bit early. By early afternoon an oral board is almost invariably behind schedule if there are many candidates, and you may have to wait. Take along a book or magazine to read, or your application to review, but leave any extraneous material in the waiting room when you go in for your interview. In any event, relax and compose yourself.

The matter of dress is important. The board is forming impressions about you – from your experience, your manners, your attitude, and your appearance. Give your personal appearance careful attention. Dress your best, but not your flashiest. Choose conservative, appropriate clothing, and be sure it is immaculate. This is a business interview, and your appearance should indicate that you regard it as such. Besides, being well groomed and properly dressed will help boost your confidence.

Sooner or later, someone will call your name and escort you into the interview room. *This is it.* From here on you are on your own. It is too late for any more preparation. But remember, you asked for this opportunity to prove your fitness, and you are here because your request was granted.

What happens when you go in?

The usual sequence of events will be as follows: The clerk (who is often the board stenographer) will introduce you to the chairman of the oral board, who will introduce you to the other members of the board. Acknowledge the introductions before you sit down. Do not be surprised if you find a microphone facing you or a stenotypist sitting by. Oral interviews are usually recorded in the event of an appeal or other review.

Usually the chairman of the board will open the interview by reviewing the highlights of your education and work experience from your application – primarily for the benefit of the other members of the board, as well as to get the material into the record. Do not interrupt or comment unless there is an error or significant misinterpretation; if that is the case, do not hesitate. But do not quibble about insignificant matters. Also, he will usually ask you some question about your education, experience or your present job – partly to get you to start talking and to establish the interviewing "rapport." He may start the actual questioning, or turn it over to one of the other members. Frequently, each member undertakes the questioning on a particular area, one in which he is perhaps most competent, so you can expect each member to participate in the examination. Because time is limited, you may also expect some rather abrupt switches in the direction the questioning takes, so do not be upset by it. Normally, a board member will not pursue a single line of questioning unless he discovers a particular strength or weakness.

After each member has participated, the chairman will usually ask whether any member has any further questions, then will ask you if you have anything you wish to add. Unless you are expecting this question, it may floor you. Worse, it may start you off on an extended, extemporaneous speech. The board is not usually seeking more information. The question is principally to offer you a last opportunity to present further qualifications or to indicate that you have nothing to add. So, if you feel that a significant qualification or characteristic has been overlooked, it is proper to point it out in a sentence or so. Do not compliment the board on the thoroughness of their examination – they have been sketchy, and you know it. If you wish, merely say, "No thank you, I have nothing further to add." This is a point where you can "talk yourself out" of a good impression or fail to present an important bit of information. Remember, *you close the interview yourself*.

The chairman will then say, "That is all, Mr. _____, thank you." Do not be startled; the interview is over, and quicker than you think. Thank him, gather your belongings and take your leave. Save your sigh of relief for the other side of the door.

How to put your best foot forward

Throughout this entire process, you may feel that the board individually and collectively is trying to pierce your defenses, seek out your hidden weaknesses and embarrass and confuse you. Actually, this is not true. They are obliged to make an appraisal of your qualifications for the job you are seeking, and they want to see you in your best light. Remember, they must interview all candidates and a non-cooperative candidate may become a failure in spite of their best efforts to bring out his qualifications. Here are 15 suggestions that will help you:

1) Be natural – Keep your attitude confident, not cocky

If you are not confident that you can do the job, do not expect the board to be. Do not apologize for your weaknesses, try to bring out your strong points. The board is interested in a positive, not negative, presentation. Cockiness will antagonize any board member and make him wonder if you are covering up a weakness by a false show of strength.

2) Get comfortable, but don't lounge or sprawl

Sit erectly but not stiffly. A careless posture may lead the board to conclude that you are careless in other things, or at least that you are not impressed by the importance of the occasion. Either conclusion is natural, even if incorrect. Do not fuss with your clothing, a pencil or an ashtray. Your hands may occasionally be useful to emphasize a point; do not let them become a point of distraction.

3) Do not wisecrack or make small talk

This is a serious situation, and your attitude should show that you consider it as such. Further, the time of the board is limited – they do not want to waste it, and neither should you.

4) Do not exaggerate your experience or abilities

In the first place, from information in the application or other interviews and sources, the board may know more about you than you think. Secondly, you probably will not get away with it. An experienced board is rather adept at spotting such a situation, so do not take the chance.

5) If you know a board member, do not make a point of it, yet do not hide it

Certainly you are not fooling him, and probably not the other members of the board. Do not try to take advantage of your acquaintanceship – it will probably do you little good.

6) Do not dominate the interview

Let the board do that. They will give you the clues – do not assume that you have to do all the talking. Realize that the board has a number of questions to ask you, and do not try to take up all the interview time by showing off your extensive knowledge of the answer to the first one.

7) Be attentive

You only have 20 minutes or so, and you should keep your attention at its sharpest throughout. When a member is addressing a problem or question to you, give him your undivided attention. Address your reply principally to him, but do not exclude the other board members.

8) Do not interrupt

A board member may be stating a problem for you to analyze. He will ask you a question when the time comes. Let him state the problem, and wait for the question.

9) Make sure you understand the question

Do not try to answer until you are sure what the question is. If it is not clear, restate it in your own words or ask the board member to clarify it for you. However, do not haggle about minor elements.

10) Reply promptly but not hastily

A common entry on oral board rating sheets is "candidate responded readily," or "candidate hesitated in replies." Respond as promptly and quickly as you can, but do not jump to a hasty, ill-considered answer.

11) Do not be peremptory in your answers

A brief answer is proper – but do not fire your answer back. That is a losing game from your point of view. The board member can probably ask questions much faster than you can answer them.

12) Do not try to create the answer you think the board member wants

He is interested in what kind of mind you have and how it works – not in playing games. Furthermore, he can usually spot this practice and will actually grade you down on it.

13) Do not switch sides in your reply merely to agree with a board member

Frequently, a member will take a contrary position merely to draw you out and to see if you are willing and able to defend your point of view. Do not start a debate, yet do not surrender a good position. If a position is worth taking, it is worth defending.

14) Do not be afraid to admit an error in judgment if you are shown to be wrong

The board knows that you are forced to reply without any opportunity for careful consideration. Your answer may be demonstrably wrong. If so, admit it and get on with the interview.

15) Do not dwell at length on your present job

The opening question may relate to your present assignment. Answer the question but do not go into an extended discussion. You are being examined for a *new* job, not your present one. As a matter of fact, try to phrase ALL your answers in terms of the job for which you are being examined.

Basis of Rating

Probably you will forget most of these "do's" and "don'ts" when you walk into the oral interview room. Even remembering them all will not ensure you a passing grade. Perhaps you did not have the qualifications in the first place. But remembering them will help you to put your best foot forward, without treading on the toes of the board members.

Rumor and popular opinion to the contrary notwithstanding, an oral board wants you to make the best appearance possible. They know you are under pressure – but they also want to see how you respond to it as a guide to what your reaction would be under the pressures of the job you seek. They will be influenced by the degree of poise you display, the personal traits you show and the manner in which you respond.

ABOUT THIS BOOK

This book contains tests divided into Examination Sections. Go through each test, answering every question in the margin. We have also attached a sample answer sheet at the back of the book that can be removed and used. At the end of each test look at the answer key and check your answers. On the ones you got wrong, look at the right answer choice and learn. Do not fill in the answers first. Do not memorize the questions and answers, but understand the answer and principles involved. On your test, the questions will likely be different from the samples. Questions are changed and new ones added. If you understand these past questions you should have success with any changes that arise. Tests may consist of several types of questions. We have additional books on each subject should more study be advisable or necessary for you. Finally, the more you study, the better prepared you will be. This book is intended to be the last thing you study before you walk into the examination room. Prior study of relevant texts is also recommended. NLC publishes some of these in our Fundamental Series. Knowledge and good sense are important factors in passing your exam. Good luck also helps. So now study this Passbook, absorb the material contained within and take that knowledge into the examination. Then do your best to pass that exam.

EXAMINATION SECTION

EXAMINATION SECTION
TEST 1

DIRECTIONS: Each question or incomplete statement is followed by several suggested answers or completions. Select the one that BEST answers the question or completes the statement. *PRINT THE LETTER OF THE CORRECT ANSWER IN THE SPACE AT THE RIGHT.*

1. Of the following valves and fittings, the one that offers the LEAST resistance to the flow of water under similar conditions is a

    A. 45° standard ell
    B. 90° standard ell
    C. globe valve
    D. angle valve

    1.____

2. A fitting having a 1/16th bend has an angle of MOST NEARLY

    A. 5 5/8°   B. 11 1/4°   C. 22 1/2°   D. 30°

    2.____

3. Roof tanks from which water is furnished for drinking and domestic purposes are required to be emptied and thoroughly cleaned at least a minimum of once every

    A. week
    B. three months
    C. six months
    D. year

    3.____

4. The hypochlorite solution that is used for disinfecting the inside surface of a domestic water supply tank usually contains a minimum amount of available chlorine of approximately _____ parts per million.

    A. 10   B. 15   C. 20   D. 25

    4.____

5. If a set of sanitary plans are drawn to a scale of 1 1/2" = 1 foot, the plans can be said to be _____ size.

    A. one-sixteenth
    B. one-eighth
    C. one-quarter
    D. half

    5.____

6. Assume that the pressure in a pneumatically operated potable water tank is 45 p.s.i. Neglecting friction loss, this pressure will elevate the water to a height above the tank of APPROXIMATELY _____ feet.

    A. 34   B. 45   C. 94   D. 104

    6.____

7. In the event of a stoppage in a natural gas line, the RECOMMENDED gas to use to remove the stoppage is

    A. oxygen   B. nitrogen   C. argon   D. hydrogen

    7.____

Questions 8-11.

DIRECTIONS: Questions 8 through 11 are to be answered in accordance with the following sketch.

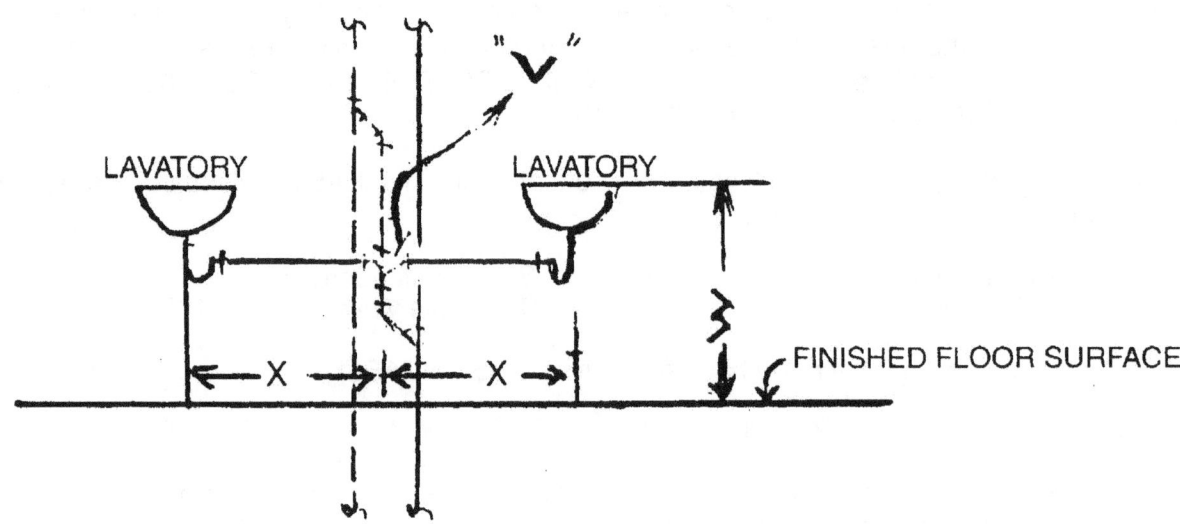

8. In the above sketch, the name of the type of vent used is called a _____ vent.

   A. blind
   B. continuous
   C. unit
   D. revent

9. In the above sketch, in order to install the lavatories as shown, the distance X should not exceed

   A. 2'   B. 3'   C. 4'   D. 5'

10. In the above sketch, the fitting Y designates a _____ turn double TY.

    A. 1 1/2" long
    B. 1 1/2" x 1 1/4" reducing short
    C. 2" short
    D. 1 1/2" x 1 1/4" reducing long

11. In the above sketch, the distance W should be MOST NEARLY

    A. 26"   B. 31"   C. 36"   D. 39"

12. The gas pressure in a domestic gas line after it leaves the gas meter is USUALLY at least _____ of water column.

    A. 1"   B. 2"   C. 3"   D. 4"

13. The use of wall carriers is generally recommended when the walls are constructed of

    A. metal lath and plaster
    B. hollow tile
    C. wood lath and plaster
    D. plywood

14. If a trench is excavated 3'0" wide by 5'6" deep and 50 feet long, the total number of cubic yards of earth removed is MOST NEARLY

    A. 30   B. 90   C. 150   D. 825

15. The insulation of a hot water riser from a cold water riser is USUALLY not required when the distance between the two risers is

    A. 3 1/2"   B. 4"   C. 5"   D. 6"

Questions 16-19.

DIRECTIONS: Questions 16 through 19 are to be answered in accordance with the following sketch.

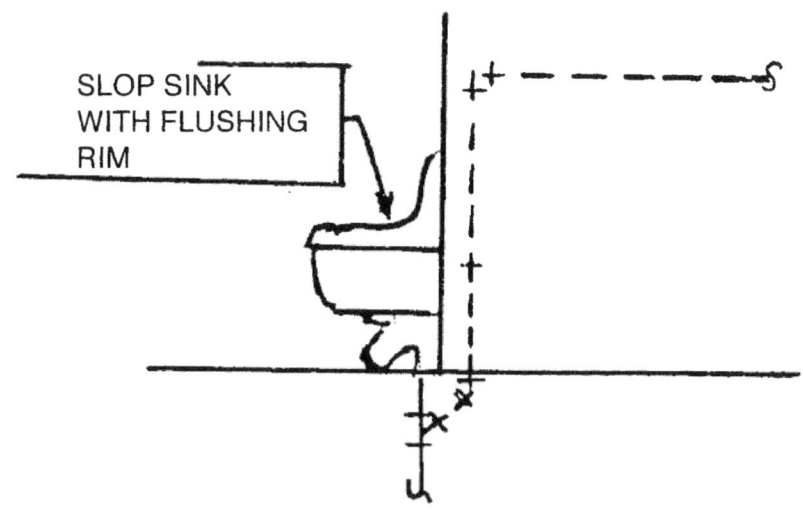

16. The total number of fixture units for the above fixture is
    A. 1 B. 3 C. 6 D. 7

17. In the above sketch, assuming that the developed length of the vent piping does not exceed 25 feet, the size of the vent piping that would usually be used is MOST NEARLY
    A. 1" B. 1 1/2" C. 2" D. 2 1/2"

18. In the above sketch, the size of the waste piping should be MOST NEARLY
    A. 1 1/2" B. 2" C. 2 1/2" D. 3"

19. In the above sketch, the type of trap that is shown is GENERALLY known as a(n) _____ trap.
    A. S B. P C. 1/2S D. running

20. The total number of pounds of caulking lead needed to properly caulk 40 lengths of 6" diameter cast iron soil pipe is MOST NEARLY
    A. 240 B. 180 C. 120 D. 60

21. Of the following statements, the one which is CORRECT is that the number of threads per inch on a pipe
    A. increases as the diameter of pipe increases
    B. decreases as the diameter of pipe increases
    C. remains constant for all diameters of pipe
    D. depends upon the total length of thread cut on the pipe

22. Of the following screwed pipe fittings, the one that is made of wrought iron is the
    A. 90° elbow B. cross C. coupling D. tee

23. The disadvantage of using yellow brass pipe for hot water lines and hot water circulating lines is that the yellow brass has a tendency to become

   A. flexible   B. soft   C. coated   D. fragile

24. If 300 pounds of lead are required for properly caulking a specific number of cast iron joints, the amount of oakum needed for the same number of joints is MOST NEARLY _____ pounds.

   A. 17   B. 32   C. 47   D. 60

25. The minimum depth of cement mortar or asphaltic compound required in making up joints in vitrified clay sewer pipe is MOST NEARLY

   A. 2 3/8"   B. 1 3/4"   C. 1"   D. 3/4"

26. Assume that the waste discharge from a certain number of fixtures through one waste pipe is at the rate of 360 gallons per minute.
   The rate at which the drainage is carried by the pipe in terms of fixture units is MOST NEARLY

   A. 90   B. 75   C. 50   D. 35

Questions 27-28.

DIRECTIONS: Questions 27 and 28 are to be answered in accordance with the sketch below.

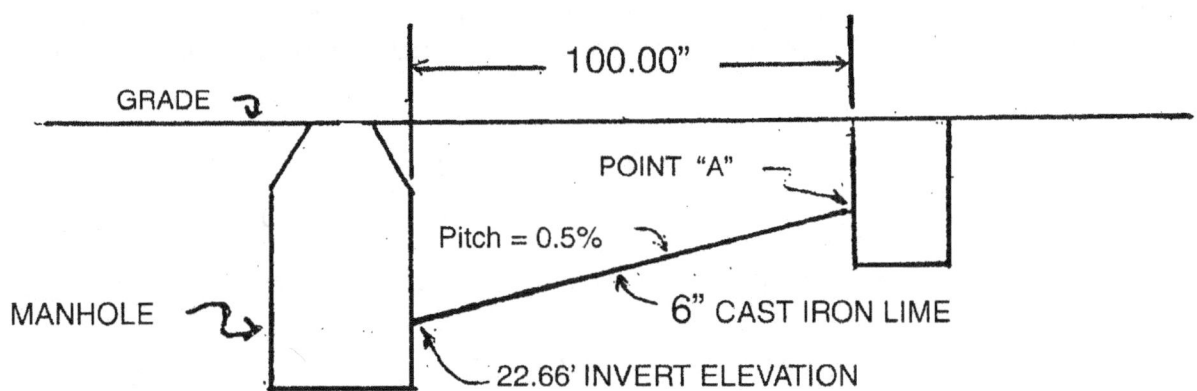

27. In the above sketch, the number of standard lengths of 6" cast iron pipe required to install the line is MOST NEARLY

   A. 9   B. 10   C. 13   D. 21

28. In the above sketch, if the invert of the 6" cast iron sewer line entering the manhole is at elevation 22.66' and the pitch of the line is equal to 0.5%, the invert elevation at point A is MOST NEARLY

   A. 27.66'   B. 23.16'   C. 22.16'   D. 17.66'

29. The proper size of pipe wrench that should generally be used to make up 3/4" or 1" diameter pipe is

   A. 6"   B. 8"   C. 10"   D. 18"

30. Gas outlets from concealed piping should usually extend through the finished ceiling or wall a distance of NOT LESS THAN

    A. 1/2" B. 3/4" C. 1" D. 1 1/4"

31. The minimum size of water closet trap permitted in large metropolitan cities is _____ diameter.

    A. 2" B. 2 1/2" C. 3" D. 4"

32. Assume that pure lead will melt at 620°F and pure tin will melt at 450°F. A (50-50) mixture of the two will MOST likely melt at an approximate temperature of _____ °F.

    A. 1070 B. 535 C. 425 D. 185

33. Of the following factors, the one that is NOT used for determining the size of a gas pipe is the

    A. length of pipe and number of fittings
    B. maximum gas consumption to be provided
    C. specific gravity of the gas
    D. type of pipe material

34. The minimum diameter of the fresh air inlet pipe for a 4" cast iron house drain trap is MOST NEARLY

    A. 2" B. 2 1/2" C. 3" D. 4"

35. The minimum number of fixture units allowed by the Code for a bathroom group containing one (1) water closet, one (1) lavatory, one (1) bathtub, and one (1) shower is MOST NEARLY

    A. 5 B. 6 C. 7 D. 10

36. A plumber ordering pipe made of *Muntz metal* would actually be ordering a type of _____ pipe.

    A. brass   B. cast iron
    C. galvanized   D. ferrous

37. Of the following statements concerning a house trap and fresh air inlet for a pneumatic sewage ejector, the one that is MOST correct is that the house trap and fresh air inlet are usually

    A. required when the ejector forms a trap
    B. placed on the outlet side of the ejector
    C. placed on the inlet side of the ejector
    D. connected to the house sewer above the crown level of the city sewer

38. Of the following types of insulation for piping, the type that is usually used for insulating cold water lines is

    A. wool-felt and tar paper lining
    B. wool-felt alone
    C. asbestos air-cell
    D. magnesia

39. The minimum distance of the water supply branch to a urinal with a flush valve and vacuum breaker is

    A. 1/2"   B. 5/8"   C. 3/4"   D. 1"

Questions 40-42.

DIRECTIONS: Questions 40 through 42 are to be answered in accordance with the sketch shown below.

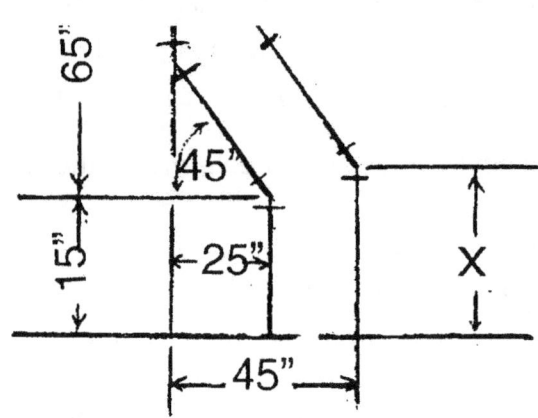

TWO PIPES 45° OFF SET
NOT TO SCALE

40. The *rise* in the above sketch is equal to

    A. 12.5"   B. 20"   C. 25"   D. 35"

41. In the above sketch, the *spread* distance is equal to

    A. 45"   B. 32"   C. 25"   D. 20"

42. If, in the above sketch, the constant for the rise is equal to 0.414, then the length of dimension *x* is MOST NEARLY

    A. 17"   B. 23"   C. 33"   D. 43"

43. The recommended number and sizes of brass branches that can be supplied from a 1 1/2" brass main (running full) is MOST NEARLY

    A. one - 1 1/4" and two - 3/4"
    B. one - 1 1/2" and two - 1 1/4"
    C. two - 1 1/2" and two - 1 1/4"
    D. two - 1 1/2"

44. In accordance with good practice, hangers for supporting 3/8" or 1/2" diameter pipe are usually spaced approximately _____ feet apart.

    A. 4   B. 7   C. 13   D. 15

45. The minimum diameter recommended for water riser lines in pluribing systems made from material other than lead, copper, or brass is

   A. 3/8"   B. 1/2"   C. 3/4"   D. 1"

46. The diameter of the overflow pipe for a gravity roof house supply tank MUST be at least _____ than the supply pipe.

   A. one commercial size smaller
   B. two commercial sizes smaller
   C. one-half commercial size larger
   D. one commercial size larger

47. The MINIMUM diameter of outlets for gas ranges must be

   A. 3/8"   B. 3/4"   C. 1"   D. 1 1/4"

48. Assume that it becomes necessary to cut out a section of gas line in order to repair a leak in the line.
    When making up the line again, it is BEST to use a

   A. ground joint union
   B. union and gasket
   C. right and left coupling
   D. coupling with running threads

49.

   In the above sketch, if the length of the nipple is 5", the distance X will be MOST NEARLY

   A. 7 1/2"   B. 8 3/4"   C. 9 5/8"   D. 10 1/8"

50. The proper size of chain tong to use when making up a 7" diameter iron pipe connection is

   A. 3'   B. 4'   C. 5'   D. 6'

51. In a pipe shop, the length of hacksaw blade that is USUALLY used is

   A. 14"   B. 12"   C. 10"   D. 8"

52. The proper pitch of a hacksaw blade, in teeth per inch, that is recommended for cutting tubing, conduit, and sheet metal work is USUALLY

    A. 14   B. 18   C. 24   D. 32

53. Of the following types of saws, the one that is USUALLY used for cutting lead pipe is the _____ saw.

    A. crosscut   B. rip   C. hack   D. dove-tail

54. *Plumbers soil* is GENERALLY used by plumbers as an aid when

    A. wiping lead joints
    B. backfilling a trench
    C. threading steel pipes
    D. making up flange joints

55. Assume that a 2" diameter cold water galvanized iron pipe is to be replaced with brass pipe.
    According to recommended practice, the proper size of brass pipe that could be substituted for the 2" galvanized line is MOST NEARLY

    A. 1 3/4"   B. 1 1/2"   C. 1 1/4"   D. 1"

56. Standard weight wrought iron pipe with threaded ends is GENERALLY obtained in random lengths of _____ to _____ feet.

    A. 10; 18   B. 12; 19   C. 14; 20   D. 16; 22

57. The PRIMARY difference between a schedule 40 pipe and a schedule 80 pipe, of the same material and size, is that schedule 80 pipe

    A. weighs more per foot
    B. has fewer threads per inch
    C. has a larger inside diameter
    D. has a thinner wall thickness

58. Pipe that is specified as *Red Brass Pipe* and conforms to standard specifications will have AT LEAST 85%

    A. brass   B. copper   C. tin   D. zinc

59. Of the following valves, the one that can BEST be used to throttle a liquid to a fine and minimum flow is the _____ valve.

    A. needle   B. gate   C. globe   D. angle

60. The minimum thickness of a flange that receives a fixture outlet is MOST NEARLY

    A. 1/32"   B. 1/16"   C. 1/8"   D. 3/16"

61. Assume that a plumber earns $43,250 per year.
    If eighteen percent of his pay is deducted for taxes and social security, his net weekly pay will be APPROXIMATELY

    A. $663.00   B. $682.50   C. $718.00   D. $728.75

62. Assume that a plumbing installation is made up of the following fixtures and groups of fixtures: 12 bathroom groups each contaning one W.C., one lavatory, and one bathtub with shower; 12 bathroom groups each containing one W.C., one lavatory, one bathtub, and one shower stall; 24 combination kitchen fixtures; 4 floor drains; 6 slop sinks without flushing rim; and 2 shower stalls (or shower bath).
The total number of fixture unit equivalents for the above plumbing installation is MOST NEARLY

    A. 220　　　B. 230　　　C. 260　　　D. 310

63. The recommended rate of water supply, in gallons per minute, to a water closet equipped with a flush valve is MOST NEARLY

    A. 3-5　　　B. 10-15　　　C. 20-25　　　D. 30-40

64. Of the following chemicals, the one which is LEAST likely to dissolve or attach pure lead is

    A. diluted peat acids
    B. diluted nitric acid
    C. citric acid (in presence of air)
    D. hydrochloric acid

65. Assume that a combined sanitary and storm drainage system is made up of 200 F.U. and 1,000 sq.ft. of drained area. In order to determine the size of the house drain for this system after the point of junction, one should allow 1,000 sq.ft. of drained area plus _____ square feet for the 20 F.U.

    A. 372　　　B. 400　　　C. 430　　　D. 460

66. As a safety precaution, concentrated sulphuric acid should be

    A. diluted by pouring the acid into the water
    B. stored in a metal container lined with a tin coating
    C. stored in a tile container lined with a zinc coating
    D. diluted by pouring cold water into the acid

67. To efficiently accomplish the MOST work within a given period, the plumber, when supervising other men, should

    A. advise his men of the work to be done and leave it up to them to accomplish it
    B. study the work to be done and plan a program to accomplish it
    C. request his men to work overtime
    D. request that additional men be assigned to him .

68. The definition, *The lowest portion of the inside top surface of the channel through the trap*, BEST describes which one of the following plumbing terms?

    A. Dip　　　　　　　　　　B. Crown weir
    C. Crown　　　　　　　　　D. Seal

69. The definition, *A connection between two parallel pipes in the water supply system*, BEST describes which one of the following plumbing terms?

    A. Cross connection　　　　B. Cross
    C. Crossover　　　　　　　　D. Interconnection

70. In taking disciplinary action against one of his helpers, the plumber's PRIMARY obligation is to

    A. discuss the matter with his immediate superior
    B. know what the punishment was in the last similar case
    C. learn all the facts of the case
    D. recommend transfer to another department

Questions 71-75.

DIRECTIONS: Questions 71 through 75 should be answered in accordance with the following paragraph.

The strength of the seal of a trap is closely proportional to the depth of the seal, regardless of the size of the trap. Unfortunately, an increase in the depth of the seal also increases the probability of solids being retained in the trap, and a limit of about a 4" depth of seal for traps that must pass solids has been imposed by some plumbing codes. The depth of seal most commonly found in simple traps is between 1 1/2" and 2". The Hoover Report recommends a minimum depth of 2" as a safeguard against seal rupture and a maximum depth of 4" to avoid clogging, fungus growths, and similar difficulties. Traps in rain-water leaders and other pipes carrying clear-water wastes only, and which are infrequently used, should have seal depths equal to or greater than 4. The increase in the volume of water retained in the trap helps very little in increasing the strength of the seal, but it does materially reduce the velocity of flow through the trap so as to increase the probability of the sedimentation of solids therein.

71. In accordance with the above, it may be said that traps carrying rain water should have a seal of

    A. 5"   B. 3 1/2"   C. 2"   D. 1 1/2"

72. In accordance with the preceding paragraph, which one of the following statements is MOST NEARLY correct?

    A. Simple traps have a depth of seal between 1 1/2" to 4".
    B. A minimum depth of 4" is recommended to avoid seal rupture.
    C. The strength of the seal is proportional to the size of the trap.
    D. The higher the depth of seal, the more chance of collecting solids.

73. In accordance with the above, it may be said that increasing the volume of water retained in a trap may

    A. *greatly* increase the velocity of flow
    B. *slightly* increase the velocity of flow
    C. *greatly* increase the trap seal
    D. *slightly* increase the trap seal

74. Of the following, the title which BEST explains the main idea of this paragraph is

    A. TRAPS SEAL DEPTHS
    B. THE EFFECTS OF SEDIMENTATION ON TRAP SEALS
    C. COMMON TRAP SIZES
    D. TRAP SIZES AND VELOCITY OF FLOW

75. Assume that the strength of a trap seal is indicated by 8 units when the trap depth is 2". In accordance with the above paragraph, increasing the depth of seal to 4" will cause the strength of the trap seal to be MOST NEARLY _____ units.

    A. 2   B. 4   C. 8   D. 16

Questions 76-77.

DIRECTIONS: Questions 76 and 77 refer to the sketch below.

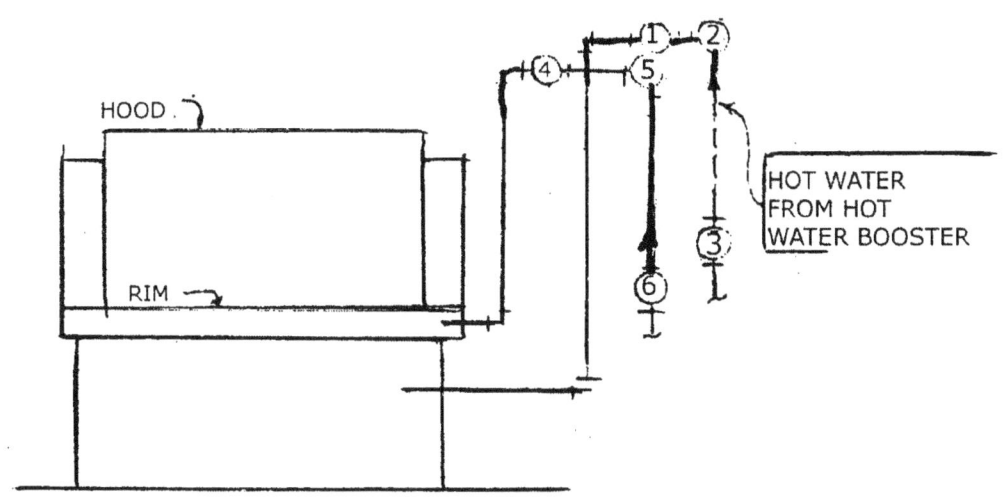

COMMERCIAL DISHWASHING MACHINE

76. The device which is usually installed at point 2 is GENERALLY known as a(n)

    A. dial thermometer
    B. integral stop and check
    C. vacuum breaker
    D. thermostatic mixing valve

77. The device which is usually installed at point 4 is GENERALLY known as a _____ valve.

    A. check   B. gate   C. relief   D. clean-out

78. Of the following hot water temperature ranges, the one which is GENERALLY used for a commercial dishwashing machine is _____ °F.

    A. 95 to 135
    B. 140 to 180
    C. 190 to 210
    D. 212 to 220

79. Of the following drainage and vent piping used within structures, the one that must NOT be buried underground is

    A. galvanized steel
    B. brass
    C. lead
    D. extra heavy cast iron

80. The MAXIMUM developed length of lead pipe (within a structure) that may be used in connection with any one fixture is _____ feet.

    A. 3   B. 4   C. 5   D. 6

KEY (CORRECT ANSWERS)

1. A	21. B	41. D	61. B
2. C	22. C	42. B	62. C
3. D	23. D	43. A	63. D
4. D	24. B	44. B	64. D
5. B	25. C	45. C	65. B
6. D	26. C	46. D	66. A
7. B	27. D	47. B	67. B
8. C	28. B	48. C	68. A
9. A	29. D	49. B	69. C
10. A	30. C	50. D	70. C
11. B	31. B	51. B	71. A
12. D	32. C	52. D	72. D
13. B	33. D	53. A	73. D
14. A	34. C	54. A	74. A
15. D	35. C	55. B	75. D
16. C	36. A	56. D	76. C
17. B	37. C	57. A	77. A
18. D	38. A	58. B	78. B
19. A	39. C	59. A	79. A
20. B	40. C	60. D	80. C

TEST 2

DIRECTIONS: Each question or incomplete statement is followed by several suggested answers or completions. Select the one that BEST answers the question or completes the statement. *PRINT THE LETTER OF THE CORRECT ANSWER IN THE SPACE AT THE RIGHT.*

1. The rate of discharge of a *unit fixture* which determines the total number of fixture units of a fixture is MOST NEARLY

   A. 10 g.p.m.   B. 4 g.p.m.   C. 3 c.f.m.   D. 1 c.f.m.

   1.____

2. Of the following fixtures, the one which is USUALLY taken as the *unit fixture* is the

   A. water closet   B. slop sink
   C. lavatory   D. urinal

   2.____

3. Of the following plumbing piping, the one in which hoarfrost USUALLY occurs is the _____ pipe.

   A. soil   B. vent   C. waste   D. water

   3.____

4. The discharge from an oil separator which collects liquid waste including oil from a garage floor may be connected DIRECTLY to the

   A. house side of the house trap
   B. storm water main
   C. public sewer
   D. sanitary branch

   4.____

5. If 500 feet of pipe weighs 800 lbs., the number of pounds that 120 feet will weigh is MOST NEARLY

   A. 190   B. 210   C. 230   D. 240

   5.____

6. Pneumatic tools are operated by the use of

   A. electricity   B. steam
   C. compressed air   D. oil under pressure

   6.____

7. Of the following materials used for water or gas connections, the one which cannot be welded, in accordance with the Plumbing Code, is _____ pipe.

   A. galvanized   B. brass
   C. black wrought iron   D. black steel

   7.____

8. When braxing standard brass pipe fittings to copper or brass pipe, the silver braxing alloy used should have a melting point of

   A. less than 400°F   B. less than 600°F
   C. less than 800°F   D. greater than 1000°F

   8.____

9. Of the following combinations of metals, the one which, when added to silver, becomes an alloy known as silver solder is

   A. lead and tin   B. copper and zinc
   C. tin and antimony   D. aluminum and copper

   9.____

10. Clean outs on horizontal soil lines should be of the same nominal size as the pipes for diameters up to 4 inches. For pipes larger than 4 inches, the clean out should be not less than

    A. 4"   B. 6"   C. 8"   D. 10"

11. The purpose of a vacuum breaker used with an automatic self-metering flush valve is to

    A. limit the flow of water to the fixture
    B. control the water pressure to the fixture
    C. equalize the water pressure
    D. prevent pollution of the water supply

12. Flush valves installed on fixtures are usually connected to a water supply that will maintain a minimum flushing pressure of NOT LESS THAN _____ psi.

    A. 2   B. 5   C. 10   D. 20

13. A one-sixteenth bend is equivalent to a fitting having an angle of

    A. 60°   B. 45°   C. 22 1/2°   D. 11 1/4°

14. The vertical distance between the crown weir and the dip of a trap is called the

    A. jumpover   B. air gap
    C. seal depth D. diameter of the trap

15. Of the following types of water closets, the one which is prohibited in the East is the _____ type.

    A. siphon action   B. hopper
    C. washout   D. siphon jet

16. The composition of general purpose *wiping solder* is USUALLY _____ tin and _____ lead.

    A. 70; 30   B. 60; 40   C. 50; 50   D. 35; 65

17. In making a vertical caulked joint on cast iron soil pipe, the tools and material required are usually oakum,

    A. solder, hammer, and inside and outside irons
    B. swab, scraper, trowel, and cement
    C. lead, pouring rope, hammer, and inside and outside irons
    D. lead, hammer, and inside and outside irons

18. A joint between a china fixture and a wall, floor, or other china fixture or parts is USUALLY filled with a _____ mix.

    A. plaster of paris   B. cement-plaster
    C. portland cement-sand D. lime-sand

Questions 19-20.

DIRECTIONS: Questions 19 and 20 refer to the sketches for screwed pipe fittings and valves shown below.

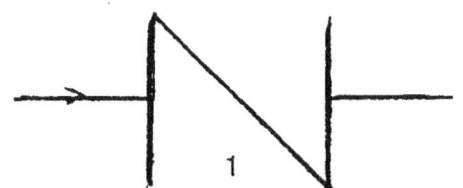

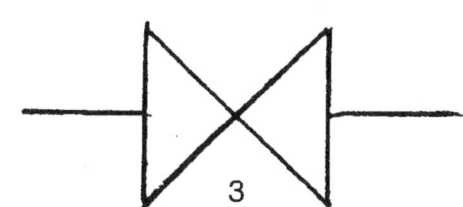

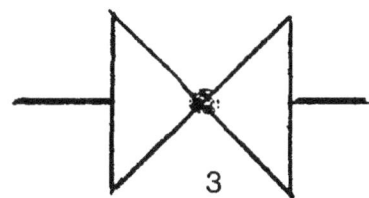

19. Of the above sketches, the one representing a gate valve is numbered 19.____
    A. 1   B. 2   C. 3   D. 4

20. Of the above sketches, the one representing a check valve is numbered 20.____
    A. 1   B. 2   C. 3   D. 4

21. To compensate for the expansion of hot water pipes on a long horizontal run, it is USUALLY necessary to install 21.____

    A. insulation
    B. anchors only
    C. swivel offsets
    D. iron pipe clamps only

22. Of the following wrenches, the one which is BEST suited for use on screwed valves and fittings have hexagonal shape connections is the _____ wrench. 22.____

    A. pipe   B. monkey   C. open-end   D. strap

Questions 23-25.

DIRECTIONS: Questions 23 through 25 refer to the following sketch.

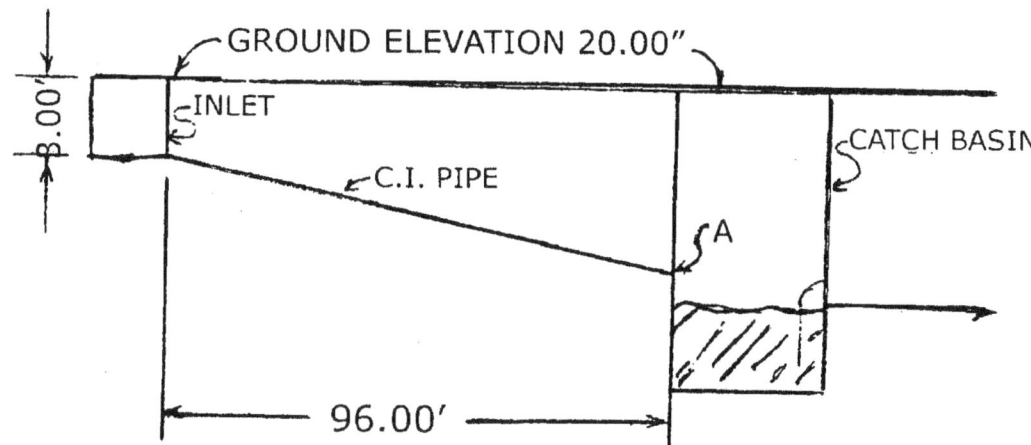

23. If the pitch of the C.I. pipe is 1/4" per foot, the elevation of the pipe at point A is MOST NEARLY _____ feet.

   A. 9.00   B. 12.00   C. 15.00   D. 18.00

24. If the pitch of the C.I. pipe is changed from 1/4" per foot to 1% per foot, the elevation of the pipe at point A would be MOST NEARLY _____ feet.

   A. 19.00   B. 16.00   C. 15.00   D. 11.00

25. Of the following plumbing drainage systems, the one which BEST describes the sketch above is _____ system.

   A. sanitary   B. storm water
   C. combined   D. acid waste

26. If a sheet lead pan fitted into a shower measures 12 square feet, the minimum total weight of this lead, allowed by the code, is MOST NEARLY _____ lbs.

   A. 24   B. 36   C. 48   D. 60

27. Vacuum breakers installed in water supplies to sanitary fixtures are USUALLY

   A. furred-in
   B. exposed
   C. on the inlet side of the control valve
   D. hidden below the fixture

28. A cast iron coupling that has one end threaded for screwed pipe and the other end hubbed to receive the spigot end of a pipe is known as a

   A. union coupling   B. tucker fitting
   C. socket pipe   D. normandy joint

29. The installation of the plumbing supply and drainage pipes in a building under construction is known as

   A. furring-in   B. roughing-in
   C. finishing   D. setting-in

30. Pipe joint cement performs two valuable functions in the screwing-up of a joint. It fills small spaces between the threads making them water-tight and also

   A. cools the threads while screwing-up
   B. lubricates the threads
   C. hardens the joint
   D. cleans the threads

31. The taper of standard pipe threads is MOST NEARLY _____ to the foot.

   A. 1/8"   B. 1/4"   C. 1/2"   D. 3/4"

32. If a 90° bend is to be made to a 2" diameter brass pipe, the RECOMMENDED radius to use is between _____ to _____ times the inside pipe diameter.

   A. 1.0; 2.0   B. 2.5; 3.0   C. 3.5; 4.0   D. 4.5; 5.0

33. The tool that holds the dies when threading pipe is GENERALLY called a   33._____

   A. yoke   B. vise   C. stock   D. swedge

34. Of the following statements concerning the use of wicking on threaded brass joints, the one which is MOST NEARLY correct is that this   34._____

   A. eliminates the use of pipe compound
   B. indicates best modern day practice
   C. strengthens the joints
   D. suggests possible existence of an imperfect thread

35. When threading pipe with properly adjusted and correctly made pipe dies, the PROPER thread is obtained when   35._____

   A. three threads protrude the die
   B. five non-taper threads are made
   C. the pipe end is flush with the face of the dies
   D. the thread length is approximately twice the diameter of the pipe

36. The type of thread that is used on standard i.p.s. brass pipe is known as the   36._____

   A. Whitworth Standard   B. Briggs Standard
   C. British Association   D. Standard Acme

37. Standard brass fittings are USUALLY designed for working pressures up to _____ psi.   37._____

   A. 50   B. 75   C. 100   D. 125

38. For plumbing work in the East, the MINIMUM percent of copper in threaded brass pipe should be   38._____

   A. 40%   B. 50%   C. 60%   D. 85%

39. The CORRECT procedure in making-up a threaded pipe joint would be to screw the pipe into the fitting   39._____

   A. until 1 or 2 threads are left exposed on the pipe
   B. a distance equal to the diameter of the pipe
   C. until no threads are showing on the pipe
   D. a distance equal to twice the length of the fitting thread

40. The cross fitting in the sketch shown at the right is GENERALLY specified as a   40._____
   A. 4" x 3" x 2" x 1 1/2"
   B. 3" x 4" x 1 1/2" x 2"
   C. 1 1/2" x 2" x 3" x 4"
   D. 2" x 1 1/2" x 4" x 3"

41. The one of the following types of traps that is used in a storm water catch basin to prevent sewer gas from flowing back into the street area is the _____ trap.   41._____

   A. P   B. house   C. bell   D. S

42. Of the following types of traps, the one that can be floor mounted, supports the fixture, and has the waste outlet extending down the floor is a 3" cast iron _____ trap.

    A. P B. S C. bell D. running

43. Joints in vitrified clay sewer pipe are properly made by packing joints with oakum of hemp and applying mortar or asphaltic compound to a depth of AT LEAST

    A. 1" B. 3/4" C. 1/2" D. 1/4"

44. Any part of a piping system that extends horizontally at a slight grade, with or without lateral or vertical extensions or vertical arms from the main to fixtures on two or less consecutive floors is called a(n)

    A. stack
    B. lateral
    C. interceptor
    D. branch

45. A *chair-carrier* is USUALLY used to support

    A. wall hung fixtures
    B. pedestal type fixtures
    C. several pipes
    D. bathtubs

46. Of the following types of pumps, the one which is NOT used for sewage and drainage is the

    A. piston pump
    B. air displacement pump
    C. centrifugal pump
    D. water or steam ejector

47. The MAIN purpose of a storm water catch basin in an open area is to

    A. act as a combined sewer
    B. collect debris and dirt
    C. facilitate rodding of sewer lines
    D. prevent a back-pressure in the line

48. The difference in area between a 4" *plain round leader* and a 2" x 4" *plain rectangular leader* is MOST NEARLY, in square inches,

    A. 1 1/2 B. 2 1/2 C. 3 1/2 D. 4 1/2

49. Approved type soldering nipples are USUALLY manufactured of

    A. copper
    B. heavy cast brass
    C. pig lead
    D. wrought iron

50. The minimum size piping requirements allowed in the East for a single low-down tank water closet is _____ soil, _____ vent, _____ cold water.

    A. 3"; 1 1/2"; 3/4"
    B. 4"; 2"; 1"
    C. 4"; 0; 1 1/2"
    D. 3"; 1 1/2"; 3/8"

51. In plumbing work, the term *sheathing and bracing* is MOST NEARLY associated with

    A. insulation
    B. excavation
    C. pipe hangers
    D. hot water tank

52. Of the following agents, the one that is GENERALLY used for disinfecting domestic water tanks is

    A. zeolite
    B. hypochlorite
    C. calgon (threshold treatment)
    D. washing soda

53. The connection of the base of all main vent stacks to main soil and waste pipes is USUALLY necessary in order to

    A. anchor the vent stack
    B. prevent evaporation of trap seals
    C. prevent accumulation of rust, scale, or condensation
    D. relieve excessive water pressure

54. Connections to soil and waste stacks should be made with _____ fittings.

    A. double sanitary-tee
    B. sanitary tee and wye
    C. double tee
    D. double hub

55. An *escutcheon* often used in plumbing work is GENERALLY used as a

    A. tool
    B. pipe support
    C. restrictive device
    D. metal collar

56. If a tank contains 8 cubic feet of water at a temperature of approximately 70°F, the weight of the water, in pounds, is MOST NEARLY

    A. 300   B. 500   C. 600   D. 700

57. A rectangular tank contains water to a height of 4'0". The pressure, in pounds per square inch, on the base of the tank is MOST NEARLY

    A. 0.82   B. 1.50   C. 1.73   D. 2.15

58. Of the following piping systems, the one that is NOT considered a *stack* when run as a vertical main is the _____ piping.

    A. soil   B. waste   C. vent   D. water

59. Type *K* copper tubing is USUALLY classified as _____ hard.

    A. extra-heavy
    B. heavy
    C. standard
    D. light

60. You are directed to cut 4 pieces of pipe, one each of the following length: 2'6 1/4", 3'9 3/8", 4'7 5/8", and 5'8 7/8". The total length of these 4 pieces is MOST NEARLY

    A. 15'7 1/4"   B. 15'9 3/8"   C. 16'5 7/8"   D. 16'8 1/8"

61. The PROPER type of covering to use on cold water pipe lines to prevent sweating is

    A. hair felt covering
    B. 85% magnesia
    C. moisture-resisting asbestos
    D. asbestos-sponge insulation

62. The MAIN purpose of the refill tube in a low-down W.C. is to

    A. re-establish the seal in the closet trap
    B. break the seal of the tank ball valve
    C. clean the overflow tube
    D. flush out the low-down tank

63. The MAXIMUM distance, in feet, between clean-outs in horizontal soil lines should be

    A. 5   B. 25   C. 50   D. 75

64. A CLOSE nipple is defined as a short piece of pipe, threaded at both ends and having _____ shoulder.

    A. a 3/4"   B. a 1/2"   C. a 1/4"   D. no

65. A triangular opening in a wall forms a 30-60 degree right triangle.
    If the longest side measures 12'0", then the shortest side will measure MOST NEARLY

    A. 3'0"   B. 4'0"   C. 6'0'   D. 8'0"

66. The MOST successful trap in keeping itself from being clogged is the _____ trap.

    A. ball   B. bell   C. drum   D. S

67. The size of the fresh air inlet is GENERALLY based on the size of the

    A. house drain   B. city sewer
    C. building   D. storm sewer

68. Of the following materials, the group that is used to make up a threaded joint between cast iron and wrought iron pipe is

    A. lead wool, lampwick, and sulphur
    B. sal ammonia, sulphur, and lead wool
    C. bituminous and lampwick
    D. graphite, lead compounds, and lampwick

69. Cutting brass pipe with a conventional three-wheel cutter equipped with thin blades will

    A. speed up the cutting time and increase the size of the burr
    B. slow down the cutting time without forming a pronounced burr
    C. speed up the cutting time and decrease the size of the burr
    D. slow down the cutting time but form no burrs

70. In making up threaded brass pipe and fittings, the RECOMMENDED practice would be to hold the fitting with a

    A. monkey wrench, turn pipe first by hand into the fitting, and then tighten with a strap wrench
    B. stillson wrench, turn pipe first by hand into the fitting, and tighten with a friction wrench
    C. pipe vise and tighten with a stillson wrench
    D. friction clamp in a vise, turn pipe first by hand into the fitting, and tighten with a chain wrench

9 (#2)

71. A pipe that has a high percentage of silicon is GENERALLY used for _____ waste.   71._____

   A. sanitary   B. acid   C. storm   D. kitchen

72. Of the following types of joints, the one which is used on lead pipes is the _____ joint.   72._____

   A. flange
   C. mechanical
   B. wiped
   D. sisson

73. Caulking ferrules are GENERALLY used as a connection between _____ pipe.   73._____

   A. lead and cast iron
   C. brass and wrought iron
   B. cast iron and brass
   D. steel and wrought iron

74. Siphonage may result in a hot water storage tank when the main water supply pipe is   74._____

   A. under excessive city water pressure
   B. shut-off and a faucet on the supply line is opened in the basement
   C. tapped for mixing with the hot water circulating line
   D. oversized and excessive in length

75. A device for regulating or stopping the flow in a pipe, made by a taper plug that may be rotated in a body having ports corresponding to those in the plug, is known as a   75._____

   A. check valve
   C. stop cock
   B. gate valve
   D. globe valve

76. *A thorough working knowledge of arithmetic is necessary if the plumber is to be able to make the many calculations that are used in the plumbing trade as well as in everyday life. Skill in arithmetic comes readily with practice. No special talent is needed.*
   This conclusion BEST supports the statement that   76._____

   A. a knowledge of arithmetic is valuable in everyday life
   B. few plumbers have a special talent for arithmetic
   C. it is less necessary for the plumber to be good in arithmetic than the average citizen
   D. most plumbers have little opportunity to make calculations

Questions 77-78.

DIRECTIONS: Questions 77 and 78 are based upon the following paragraph.

One of the most common and objectionable difficulties occurring in a drainage system is trap seal loss. This failure can be attributed directly to inadequate ventilation of the trap and the subsequent negative and positive pressures which occur. A trap seal may be lost either by siphonage and/or back pressure. Loss of the trap seal by siphonage is the result of a negative pressure in the drainage system. The seal content of the trap is forced by siphonage into the waste piping of the drainage system through exertion of atmospheric pressure on the fixture side of the trap seal.

77. According to the above paragraph, a positive pressure is a direct result of   77._____

   A. siphonage
   C. poor ventilation
   B. unbalanced trap seal
   D. atmospheric pressure

78. According to the above paragraph, the water in the trap is forced into the drain pipe by   78.___

   A. atmospheric pressure
   B. back pressure
   C. negative pressure
   D. back pressure on fixture side of seal

Questions 79-80.

DIRECTIONS: Questions 79 and 80 are based on the following paragraph.

In determining the size of a storm drain, a number of factors must be taken into consideration. One factor which makes sizing the storm drain difficult is the matter of predicting rainfall over a given period. Using a maximum estimate of about 1 inch of rain in a 10 minute interval, the approximate volume of water that will fall on a roof or surface in one minute's time can be determined readily. Another factor is the pitch and material of a roof or surface upon which the rain falls. A surface that has a pitch and smooth surface would increase the flow of water into a drain pipe.

79. According to the above paragraph, the statement which includes all factors needed to determine the size of a drain pipe is the   79.___

   A. maximum rainfall on a surface
   B. pitch and surface of the area
   C. amount of water to be piped in a definite time interval
   D. area of the surface

80. A roof that has a 45° pitch would PROBABLY have a drain pipe size   80.___

   A. smaller than a roof with no pitch
   B. larger than a roof with no pitch
   C. equal to that of a flat roof
   D. equal to the amount of water falling in ten minutes

KEY (CORRECT ANSWERS)

1.	D	21.	C	41.	C	61.	A
2.	C	22.	B	42.	B	62.	A
3.	B	23.	C	43.	A	63.	C
4.	C	24.	B	44.	D	64.	D
5.	A	25.	B	45.	A	65.	C
6.	C	26.	C	46.	A	66.	D
7.	A	27.	B	47.	B	67.	A
8.	D	28.	B	48.	D	68.	D
9.	B	29.	B	49.	B	69.	C
10.	A	30.	B	50.	D	70.	A
11.	D	31.	D	51.	B	71.	B
12.	B	32.	B	52.	B	72.	B
13.	C	33.	C	53.	C	73.	A
14.	C	34.	D	54.	B	74.	B
15.	C	35.	C	55.	D	75.	C
16.	D	36.	B	56.	B	76.	A
17.	D	37.	D	57.	C	77.	C
18.	C	38.	C	58.	D	78.	A
19.	C	39.	A	59.	A	79.	C
20.	A	40.	A	60.	D	80.	B

EXAMINATION SECTION
TEST 1

DIRECTIONS: Each question or incomplete statement is followed by several suggested answers or completions. Select the one that BEST answers the question or completes the statement. *PRINT THE LETTER OF THE CORRECT ANSWER IN THE SPACE AT THE RIGHT.*

Questions 1-4.

DIRECTIONS: Questions 1 through 4 relate to the sketch shown below.

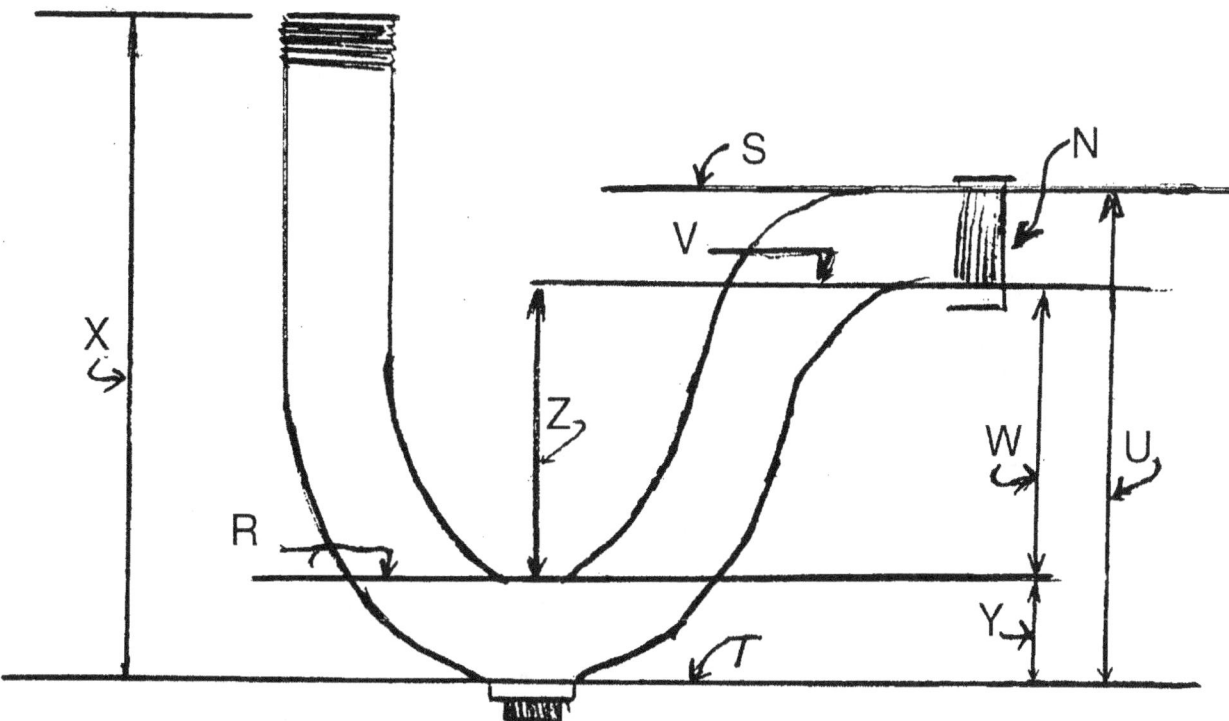

1. The trap shown in the sketch is COMMONLY known as a(n) 1.____

   A. S trap B. running trap
   C. P trap D. bottle trap

2. The seal of this trap is the dimension lettered 2.____

   A. W B. X C. Y D. Z

3. The dip of the trap is the level lettered 3.____

   A. R B. S C. T D. V

4. The crown weir is the level lettered 4.____

   A. N B. S C. T D. V

25

5. Offsets in C.I. drainage piping can be made with any of several fittings. If the constant 2.613 is used to compute the developed length of the offset piping (the center line offset is known), then the fittings used to make the offset must be

   A. 1/4 bends
   B. 1/8 bends
   C. 1/16 bends
   D. L.T.T.Y.s

6. The one of the following definitions relating to plumbing terms which is MOST NEARLY CORRECT is that the term

   A. *branch* shall mean that part of a piping system which extends from the main to fixtures on three or less consecutive floors
   B. *dead end* shall mean a branch which is terminated at a developed length of two feet by a fitting not used for admitting liquids to the pipe
   C. *developed length* of a pipe shall mean the length along the bottom line of the pipe
   D. *leader* shall mean any line of storm water piping

7. The one of the following definitions relating to plumbing terms which is MOST NEARLY CORRECT is that the term

   A. *soil pipe* shall mean any pipe made of cast iron and which conveys to the house drain the discharge of fixtures receiving human waste
   B. *stack* shall mean any line of soil, vent, or waste piping
   C. *sub-house drain* shall mean that portion of a drainage system which is positioned below the first floor level
   D. *indirect waste pipe* shall mean a waste pipe which fails to connect directly with a house drain or a soil or a waste shack

8. The one of the following statements relative to a private sewage disposal system which is MOST NEARLY CORRECT is that a

   A. septic tank is basically a treatment tank to which chemicals must be added from time to time
   B. cesspool is a covered pit with open-jointed or perforated lining into which raw sewage is discharged
   C. distribution box is a chamber from which raw sewage is discharged to the septic tank
   D. seepage pit is an open pit with a perforated lining into which septic tank effluent is discharged

9. In checking out some drainage lead pipe which has been collapsed in shipment, it is found that one lineal foot weighs 6 lbs. If it is assumed that this pipe does comply with the minimum requirements of weight set forth in C26-1232.0a, then its *caliber* is

   A. 1 1/2"   B. 2"   C. 3"   D. 4"

10. A lead shower safe weighs 54 pounds. It is 3'-0" x 3'-0" with a 4" standing lip and with ears forming the corners to assure tightness. If the sheet lead used in making this safe conforms to the minimum code requirements, then it has a thickness of *most nearly*

    A. 1/32"   B. 1/16"   C. 3/16"   D. 1/4"

11. In a comparison of the specifications for threaded and unthreaded brass pipe, it can be CORRECTLY stated that

    A. size for size, the wall thickness of the unthreaded pipe is generally less than that of the threaded pipe
    B. the minimum copper content of the threaded pipe is generally greater
    C. the unthreaded pipe, though intended for use with approved silver-brazed joints, may be threaded and properly used with threaded fittings
    D. size for size, the weight per linear foot is the same for both threaded and unthreaded pipe

12. In running a cast iron waste, it is necessary to run and caulk 6-4" joints, 8-2" joints, and 8-1 1/2" joints. The minimum poundage of lead which must be used to properly secure these joints is *most nearly*

    A. 26   B. 39   C. 52   D. 78

13. A full-wiped joint is made between 4" lead pipe (drainage lead) and a 4" brass ferrule. The MINIMUM dimensions (length and diameter at the thickest part) of this wiped joint shall be

    A. 1 1/4" long x 4 1/4" diameter
    B. 1 3/4" long x 4 1/2" diameter
    C. 2" long x 4 3/4" diameter
    D. 1 1/2" long x 5" diameter

14. According to the code, the maximum height of structures in which vertical lines may be installed without providing means for taking care of the expansion and contraction of these lines is

    A. 150'   B. 125'   C. 100'   D. 75'

15. The one of the following statements with respect to water seals in traps that is MOST NEARLY CORRECT is that a

    A. slop sink (with flushing rim) shall be provided with a trap which has a minimum seal of at least 3"
    B. basin shall be provided with a trap which has a seal of at least 2"
    C. running trap in a leader line shall be provided with trap which has a seal of at least 2 1/2"
    D. house trap shall have a minimum seal of at least 3 1/2"

16. A pressure tank set in the basement of a 12 story building is intended to deliver at 5 lbs. per square inch at the control valve of a fixture set on the 12th story. The elevation of this fixture above the tank is 120'. Assume that the overall friction loss at average flow is 15'. Then the minimum pressure in pounds per square inch which must be maintained within the tank for adequate operation is *most nearly*

    A. 66.00   B. 63.00   C. 50.40   D. 45.40

17. An alteration involving the installation of several W.C.'s, urinals, and basins is being made in a remote section of a large building. The main vent for these fixtures is terminated in the mid-section of a metal chimney which is conveniently located. This arrangement is

A. *acceptable* as a considerable cost for piping material is saved
B. *not acceptable* as this piping arrangement is contrary to the sanitary code
C. *acceptable* as the stack effect of the chimney makes the vent work better
D. *not acceptable* as the flue gases in the chimney could readily enter the toilet room

18. The rules of the Board require that a vacuum breaker and check valve be installed in the water supply line to water preheating devices using waste water. The minimum elevation in feet at which the vacuum breaker shall be set above the highest elevation of the preheating apparatus is *most nearly* _____ feet.

    A. 6   B. 5   C. 4   D. 3

19. If it is estimated that the rate of flushing a w.c. is 25 gpm, then the velocity in feet per second at which this flush water is conveyed through a minimum size flush tube from a low tank to a w.c. is *most nearly* _____ feet per second.

    A. 7.2   B. 5.25   C. 2.63   D. 0.8

20. The one of the following types of water closets which is NOT prohibited under the provisions of C26-1277.0 of the code is the _____ type.

    A. plunger   B. pan   C. washout   D. blowout

21. A fixture other than one listed in the F.U. table of C26-1291.0 has a waste connection of 3". If a flow of 1 cubic feet per minute is assumed for each F.U., then the maximum rated flow, in gpm, for this waste connection is *most nearly* _____ gpm.

    A. 226   B. 172   C. 112   D. 60

22. A P and D specification calls for the installation of a local vent piping system. Indications are very evident that condensation will collect in this system and so drip connections are called for. These drips shall be connected to

    A. a leader through a swing check valve
    B. the house side of a fixture trap
    C. the sewer side of the house trap
    D. the drain side of a leader running trap

23. Domestic hot water supply systems shall be installed with a hot water return circulation system when the

    A. building exceeds three stories in height
    B. operating hot water temperature exceeds 180° F
    C. developed length of hot water piping from the source
    D. to the extreme fixture supplied exceeds one hundred feet
    E. the hot water supply line runs parallel to and within 12" of the cold water supply line

24. In a three story dwelling, the minimum size of the water supply riser to flushometer valves to water closets set on each floor is *most nearly*

    A. 1"   B. 1 1/4"   C. 1 1/2"   D. 2"

25. The use of short turn tee wyes fitting is restricted to 25.____

    A. gas piping
    B. horizontal house drains
    C. vertical stacks
    D. uniformly pitched horizontal runs in vent branches

26. The code provides that gas pipe outlets from concealed piping shall extend through the finished wall after first being secured to the wall or stud. This extension should be AT LEAST 26.____

    A. 1"   B. 3/4"   C. 1/2"   D. 1/4"

27. A perforated metal plate fixed in the mouth of a F.A.I. pipe has 75 holes each 3/4" in diameter. If the F.A.I. pipe is of 6" in diameter, then this perforated metal plate is 27.____

    A. more than adequate as it has at least 11 holes more than is required
    B. adequate as it just complies with minimum requirements
    C. inadequate as 9 more holes are required to comply with code requirements
    D. inadequate as 5 more holes are required to comply with code requirements

28. The maximum number of water closets which may be permitted to discharge into a 5" branch soil *is most nearly* 28.____

    A. 40   B. 34   C. 28   D. 11

29. The SMALLEST size of stack which has no limitation with respect to its developed length is 29.____

    A. 5"   B. 6"   C. 8"   D. 10"

30. The one of the following statements relative to overflow pipes for roof-mounted gravity house supply tanks which is MOST NEARLY CORRECT is that these overflow pipes shall 30.____

    A. discharge above and within 12" of the roof
    B. discharge over an open water supplied sink set 4'-6" above the floor
    C. connect through a vacuum breaker to a waste line
    D. connect through a check valve to a leader

31. In an industrial building, fluid for processing chemicals is supplied by a straight horizontal run of wrought iron pipe 200' long. The range of temperature of the pipe is from 60° F to 300° F. 31.____
    If the coefficient of expansion for wrought iron is 0.00000686" per inch per degree F, the total expansion in the run of pipe is *most nearly*

    A. 3"   B. 4"   C. 5"   D. 6"

Questions 32-37.

DIRECTIONS: Questions 32 through 37, inclusive, are to be answered in connection with the information given in the following paragraph.

The acceptor's responsibility - The purpose of commercial standards is to establish for specific commodities, nationally recognized grades or consumer criteria and the benefits therefrom will be measurable in direct proportion to their general recognition and actual use. Instances will occur when it may be necessary to deviate from the standard and the signing of an acceptance does not preclude such departures; however, such signature indicates an intention to follow the commercial standard where practicable, in the production, distribution, or consumption of the article in question.

32. The advantage which may be gained from the establishment of commercial standards is dependent upon the

    A. degree of consumer and manufacturer acceptance
    B. improvement of product quality
    C. degree of change required in the manufacturing process
    D. establishment and use of the highest standards

33. Nationally respected and adopted commercial standards are

    A. *undesirable* as they are a direct benefit to unscrupulous manufacturers
    B. *desirable* as they serve as a yardstick for consumers
    C. *undesirable* as they tend to lower quality
    D. *desirable* as they tend to reduce manufacturing costs

34. The word *preclude* as used in this paragraph means *most nearly*

    A. permit   B. allow   C. include   D. prevent

35. The word *intention* as used in this paragraph means *most nearly*

    A. agreement   B. impulse
    C. objection   D. obstinance

36. The word *recognized* as used in this paragraph means *most nearly*

    A. desirable   B. stable   C. branded   D. accepted

37. The word *criteria* as used in this paragraph means *most nearly*

    A. efforts   B. standards   C. usage   D. costs

38. A flat bottom 10 foot diameter house supply tank located on the roof of a building is also used to hold in reserve the quantity of water required for stand pipe service. The distance, in feet, above the bottom of the tank at which the domestic supply line should be connected is *most nearly*

    A. 4   B. 5   C. 6   D. 7

39. *Hard* water usually contains mineral compounds of

    A. potassium hydroxides   B. sodium hydroxides
    C. calcium and magnesium   D. carbon dioxide and oxygen

40. A device which prevents backflow from a drainage system into a potable water supply system GENERALLY acts as a

    A. siphon breaker   B. crossover
    C. tampion   D. volumeter

41. To make a *rust joint* between two pieces of threaded iron pipe, the BEST thing to use, of the following, is a   41._____

    A. solution of iron filings B. bituminous material
    C. solution of sal ammoniac D. water glass compound

42. To make a *flanged joint* between bronze and wrought iron pipe, the BEST thing to use, of the following, is   42._____

    A. graphite   B. solder
    C. lead wool D. a gasket

43. To make a *bell* and *spigot joint* between vitrified clay pipe and cast iron pipe, the BEST thing to use, of the following, is   43._____

    A. oakum and poured lead   B. graphite and lampwick
    C. lead wire and sal ammoniac D. sulphur and sand

44. Wiping solder for lead pipe USUALLY has a melting range of   44._____

    A. 150 to 250 deg. F B. 251 to 350 deg. F
    C. 360 to 470 deg. F D. 475 to 600 deg. F

45. Of the following, the statement that gives a MAIN advantage of wrought iron pipe over cast iron soil pipe when used as drainage piping is that the wrought iron pipe   45._____

    A. has a cheaper first cost   B. does away with recessed fittings
    C. has fewer joints per unit length D. occupies more space in floors

46. Of the following statements, the one which does NOT cause water hammer is   46._____

    A. admitting water rapidly into a closed tank filled with air
    B. admitting steam into cold water in a closed container
    C. operating a reciprocating water pump too rapidly
    D. the sudden opening of a valve with water at different pressures on each side of the valve

47. The percentage of zinc in threaded yellow brass pipe is GENERALLY   47._____

    A. 35 to 40%   B. 50 to 55%   C. 60 to 65%   D. 70 to 75%

48. A water tank measures 4 feet square and 6 feet high. If the water depth is 5'-6', the total weight of water in the tank is *most nearly*   48._____

    A. 4500#   B. 5500#   C. 6500#   D. 7500#

49. A water tank measures 4 feet in diameter and 8'-0" high. If the water depth is 6'-6", the pressure in pounds per square inch at the bottom of the tank is *most nearly*   49._____

    A. 1.5   B. 1.9   C. 2.4   D. 2.8

50. In order to clear a stoppage in a trap or drain that cannot be cleared by any other means, it is BEST to use, of the following, a solution of   50._____

    A. copper sulphate   B. potassium hydroxide
    C. hydrogen sulphate D. calcium chloride

51. Leadite has a melting point of APPROXIMATELY

    A. 700° F   B. 400° F   C. 250° F   D. 200° F

52. The total length of four pieces of 2" O.D. pipe, whose lengths are 7 ft. 3 1/2 in., 4 ft. 2 3/16 in., 5 ft. 7 5/16 in., and 8 ft. 5 7/8 in., respectively, is *most nearly*

    A. 24 ft. 6 3/4 in.   B. 24 ft. 7 15/16 in.
    C. 25 ft. 5 13/16 in.   D. 25 ft. 6 7/8 in.

Questions 53-57.

DIRECTIONS: Questions 53 through 57 refer to the sketch in Figure I on Page 9...

53. When a vacuum breaker is used in conjunction with the valve shown, it is USUALLY connected to the position numbered

    A. 3   B. 1   C. 6   D. 5

54. The first space within the valve which the water normally enters is numbered

    A. 8   B. 1   C. 6   D. 2

55. The space that fills with water permitting the valve to close is numbered

    A. 4   B. 2   C. 7   D. 1

56. The part that lifts when the water flows through the valve into the fixture is numbered

    A. 9   B. 12   C. 10   D. 13

57. The part that is known as the by-pass is numbered

    A. 4   B. 15   C. 14   D. 1

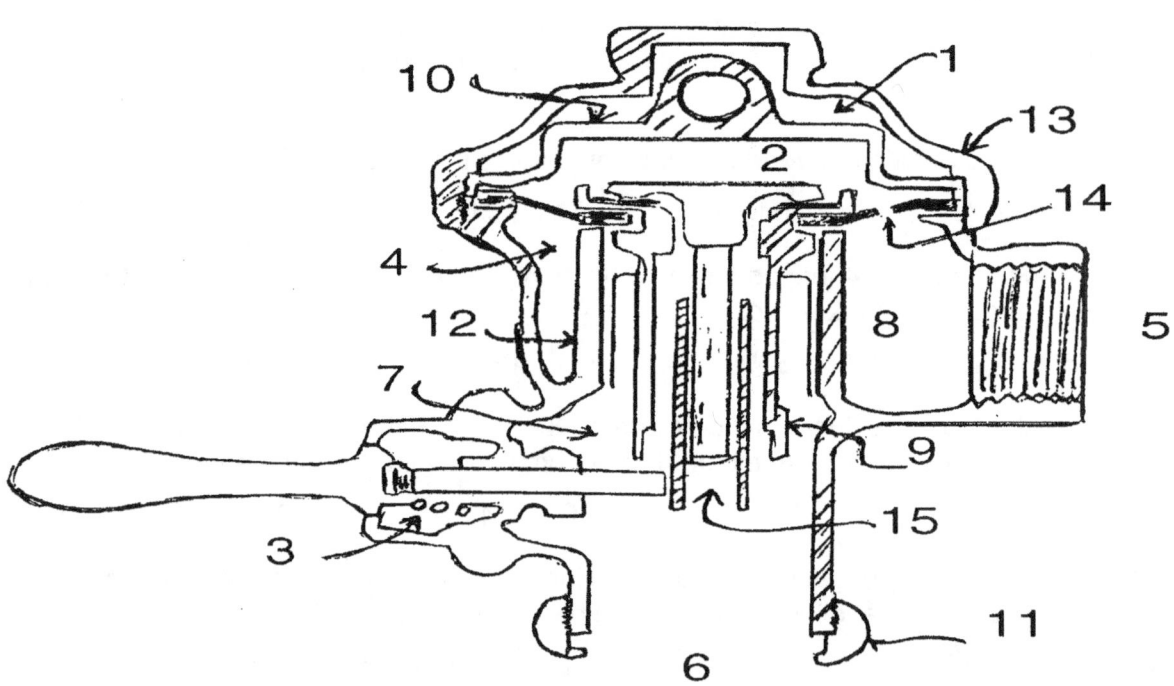

FIGURE I

Questions 58-60.

DIRECTIONS: Questions 58 to 60 refer to the sketch in Figure II on Page 10.

58. The device shown in Figure II is USUALLY known as 58.____
    A. sealing chamber B. venturi
    C. vacuum breaker D. one-way valve

59. The part that moves upward when water flows through the device in Figure II is numbered 59.____
    A. 3   B. 4   C. 6   D. 1

60. The space numbered 7 is for the purpose of admitting 60.____
    A. air B. water
    C. lubricant D. sealing compound

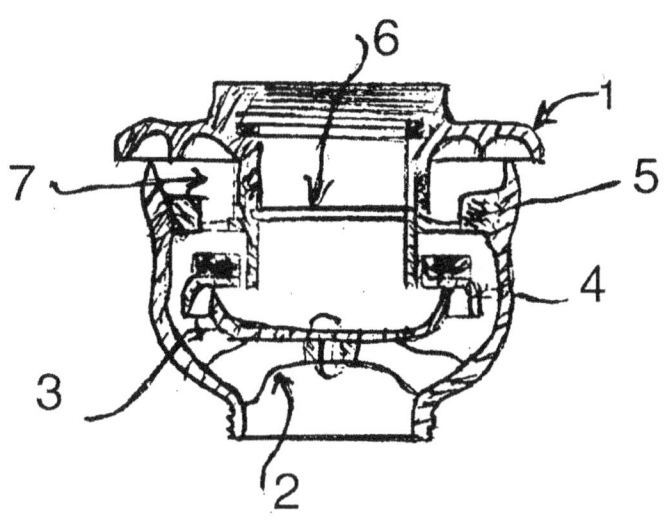

FIGURE II

61. The heating value of natural gas in Btu per cubic foot is *most nearly* 61.____
    A. 600   B. 1100   C. 1400   D. 2000

62. The MAJOR effect of the condensation of moisture from surrounding warm air is to cause uncovered 62.____
    A. cold water pipes to sweat
    B. pipes to expand linearly
    C. hot water pipes to sweat
    D. pipes to contract linearly

63. Under proper conditions, the one of the following groups of pipes that gives the same flow in gallons/minute as one 6" diameter pipe is (neglect friction) 63.____
    A. 3 pipes of 3" dia. each B. 4 pipes of 3" dia. each
    C. 2 pipes of 4" dia. each D. 3 pipes of 4" dia. each

64. A spring loaded pressure regulator has a 70 lb. spring load acting on a 3" diameter diaphragm. The pressure, in pounds per square inch, required to lift this diaphragm is *most nearly*

    A. 27   B. 20   C. 17   D. 10

65. Horizontal swing joints or pipe loops at floor level are GENERALLY employed for the purpose of

    A. nullifying the effect of water hammer in the pipe
    B. allowing for movement of pipe due to temperature changes
    C. providing an easy path for hot liquids
    D. providing a cushion for absorbing mechanical vibrations

66. When water hammer conditions exist in a 2 1/2" water service line, then the recommended minimum length of the air chamber to be installed shall be *most nearly* _____ feet.

    A. 4   B. 5   C. 6   D. 8

67. A corporation cock is USUALLY found on a

    A. service pipe installation
    B. two-pipe jet pump
    C. Bourdon gage line
    D. hydraulic ejector line

68. The amount that water expands when frozen is *most nearly* _____ of its original volume.

    A. 1/3   B. 1/4   C. 1/6   D. 1/12

69. In reference to service hot water systems, the one statement MOST NEARLY CORRECT is that

    A. circulating lines are of greatest importance where the use of hot water is intermittent
    B. air chambers are mainly used to properly vent the hot risers
    C. where hot water lines are not circulated, it is good practice to make the diameter of hot water supply lines larger than usual
    D. constant circulation of hot water reduces heat losses from bare pipes

70. In reference to foot valves, the one statement that is MOST NEARLY CORRECT is that they

    A. are intended only for low pressure service
    B. do not operate the same way as lift check valves
    C. are used primarily to reduce pulsation of water flow
    D. are used to drain the bottom of water risers

71. A centrifugal pump is to be selected to take suction from an open water tank 8 feet below the centerline of the pump and to deliver this water to a pressure tank 32 feet above the centerline of the pump.
    If the pressure tank is to be maintained at a pressure of 20 pounds per square inch, the pump should have a head in feet of *most nearly* (neglecting pipe friction)

    A. 40   B. 60   C. 78   D. 88

72. Assume a certain quantity of 180° F water is mixed with 60° F water in such a proportion that the final temperature of the mixture is 140° F. For a ten gallon tank of mixed water, the amount of 180° F water necessary is *most nearly* _____ gallons.   72._____

   A. 3 B. 4 C. 5 D. 6

73. In reference to the proper use of check valves for various services, the one statement that is MOST NEARLY CORRECT is: 73._____

   A. Where volatile liquids are being handled, swing check valves will prove very effective
   B. Swing check valves should never be used on rapidly pulsating flow
   C. The outside lever and weight of a weighted swing check valve does not assist the operation of the disc
   D. Where check valves are required on steam, air, gas, or general vapor service, it is recommended that the swing check be used in preference to lift checks

74. Properly tapped and recessed threaded drainage ells are used to run a horizontal offset in a vent branch. The developed length of this offset is 12'-0". The difference in elevation from end to end of this offset should be, according to the code provisions, AT LEAST   74._____

   A. 1" B. 1 1/4" C. 1 1/2" D. 1 3/4"

Questions 75-76.

DIRECTIONS: In the figure below, pipes 1 and 2 are parallel vertical pipes. Questions 75 and 76 refer to the figure below.

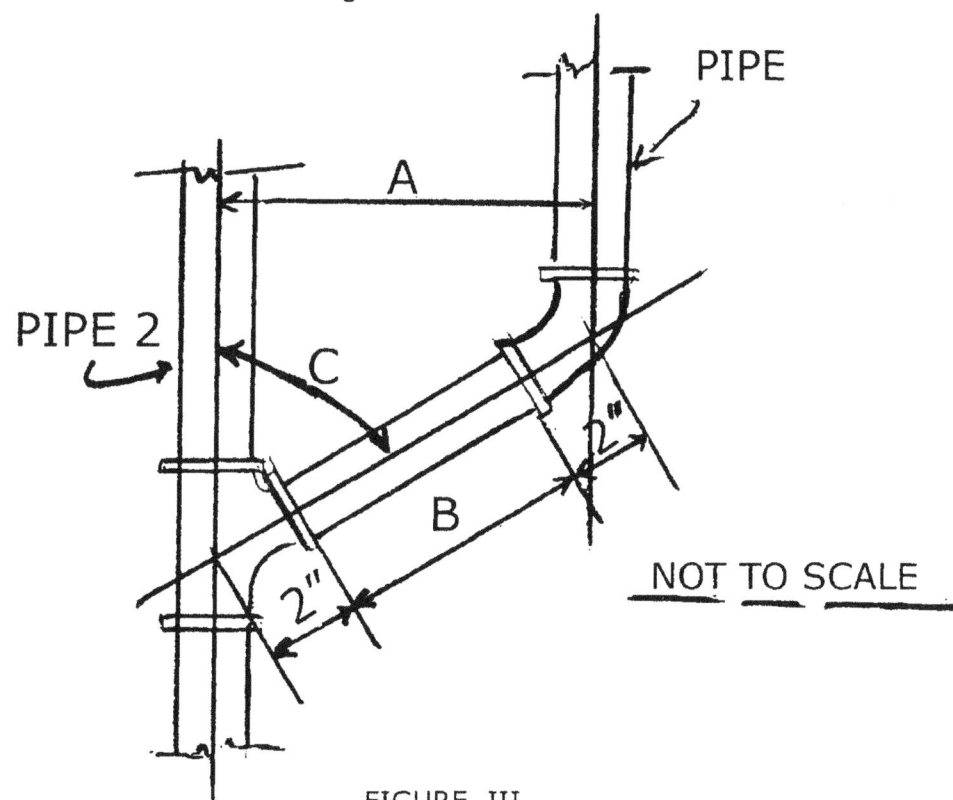

FIGURE III

75. If dimension A in the figure is 24" and two pipes are connected at an angle of 45, the face-to-face dimension B is *most nearly*

   A. 30"   B. 32"   C. 35"   D. 39"

76. If dimension A in the figure is 30" and the angle C is 30°, the face-to-face dimension B is *most nearly*

   A. 45"   B. 48"   C. 56"   D. 64"

77. Under good conditions, your estimate of the journeyman labor required to complete a given job is 7 journeymen working for 15 days.
   If it became necessary to complete this job in 10 days, then the number of journeymen required would be *most nearly* (disregard helper or apprentice labor)

   A. 9   B. 10   C. 12   D. 15

78. In an inspection of a plumbing system, it is noted that a particular fixture trap (laundry trap) is not set true with respect to its water seal. It is tilted downward toward the outlet at an angle of about 10 degrees.
   In operation, it is *most likely* that

   A. the trap would tend to clog rapidly
   B. the depth of seal of the trap would be reduced
   C. a gurgling sound would be heard when discharging waste
   D. the trap would readily become air bound

79. Three main 4" stacks are grouped together at the top of a structure into one combined vent which then extends through the roof.
   The minimum size of this one combined vent should be AT LEAST

   A. 4"   B. 5"   C. 6"   D. 8"

80. Each urinal of a battery of four is floor-mounted and so set as to act as a floor drain. The fixture unit value of this battery is

   A. 8   B. 9   C. 11   D. 12

KEY (CORRECT ANSWERS)

1.	C	21.	C	41.	C	61.	B
2.	A	22.	B	42.	D	62.	A
3.	A	23.	C	43.	D	63.	B
4.	D	24.	C	44.	C	64.	D
5.	C	25.	C	45.	C	65.	B
6.	B	26.	A	46.	D	66.	C
7.	D	27.	A	47.	A	67.	A
8.	B	28.	C	48.	B	68.	D
9.	C	29.	B	49.	D	69.	A
10.	B	30.	D	50.	B	70.	A
11.	A	31.	B	51.	B	71.	D
12.	B	32.	A	52.	D	72.	D
13.	D	33.	B	53.	C	73.	B
14.	A	34.	D	54.	A	74.	C
15.	B	35.	A	55.	B	75.	A
16.	B	36.	D	56.	A	76.	C
17.	B	37.	B	57.	C	77.	A
18.	C	38.	C	58.	C	78.	B
19.	A	39.	C	59.	B	79.	C
20.	D	40.	A	60.	A	80.	D

TEST 2

DIRECTIONS: Each question or incomplete statement is followed by several suggested answers or completions. Select the one that BEST answers the question or completes the statement. *PRINT THE LETTER OF THE COERECT ANSWER IN THE SPACE AT THE RIGHT.*

1. You are working at running and caulking bell and spigot joints on a soil stack. If for any reason the oakum already in a joint should become damp, an acceptable thing to do prior to the first pouring is to

    A. repack the same oakum vigorously
    B. heat the outside lower portion of the bell with a high temperature oxyacteylene welding torch
    C. pour several tablespoons of cutting oil on top of the caulked oakum, wait for a few minutes, and then go ahead with the pouring
    D. reduce the temperature of the lead

    1.____

2. The effect, when vigorously caulking a joint after it has been run with overheated (one or two hours) lead, is MOST LIKELY a(n)

    A. very tight joint
    B. acceptable joint
    C. joint which looks all right but which may or may not pass inspection
    D. unacceptable joint because the lead will crack and chip due to its brittleness

    2.____

3. When installing hot water risers in tall buildings, expansion joints or loops are provided. The pipe which will undergo the GREATEST change in length for a given change in temperature is *most generally*

    A. brass
    B. copper (type B)
    C. wrought iron
    D. galvanized steel

    3.____

4. Under ordinary conditions, a cement mortar which is commonly used to make up tight joints in bell and spigot tile house sewer pipe consists of

    A. one part cement, three parts clean sand, and enough water to make a stiff mortar
    B. one part cement, two parts clean sand, and enough water to make a loose mortar
    C. one part cement, three parts clean sand, four parts small gravel, and enough water to make a stiff mixture
    D. two parts cement, three parts clean sand, and enough water to make a stiff mortar

    4.____

5. *Cut Acid* commonly used as a flux for soldering galvanized iron or steel is made by dissolving in

    A. vitriolic acid as much zinc as it will take
    B. muriatic acid as much zinc as it will take
    C. caustic soda as much zinc as it will take
    D. vitriolic acid as much lead as it will take

    5.____

6. An extensive domestic hot water system is installed with the vertical recirculation manifolding together in the basement with this manifold sloping back to the hot water storage tank.
   The primary purpose for sloping this manifold is *most likely* to

    6.____

A. assist the circulation of hot water
B. allow for unequal expansion
C. allow a tolerance in hanging the manifold
D. allow for complete drainage when necessary

7. A plumbing contract calls for the setting of wrought iron pipe sleeves in concrete floor construction for the passage of water risers.
In order to provide for the passage of a 2" wrought iron water riser, the MINIMUM diameter wrought iron pipe sleeve which should be used for this purpose is *most nearly*

   A. 2 1/2"   B. 3"   C. 4"   D. 5"

8. Bare wrought iron or steel pipe is laid in the cinder fill under a cellar floor. The PROBABLE result of running these lines in this manner is that

   A. the lines will tend to corrode
   B. a protective oxide coating will form on these lines
   C. lines will last just as long as if they were laid in clean dry sand
   D. a protective scale coating will form on these lines in a short time

9. An existing system of plumbing stacks is to be tested by means of the peppermint test. One of the disadvantages relative to the use of this test is that

   A. it must be used with at least 20 gallons of hot water for each two ounces of oil of peppermint
   B. it requires at least twice as many men and more costly equipment than the smoke test
   C. mercury gauges are required because the pressures generated are very high
   D. the fumes of the peppermint diffuse very quickly whenever they make their escape, and this makes it difficult to definitely locate the leak

10. A completed soil stack in a new installation is to be subjected to a water test. The roof (weather protection only and flat) is 55 feet above test tee at the base of the stack and from which point it is being tested.
With this stack full of water, the pressure, in pounds per square inch, at the top of the test tee is *most nearly*

    A. 25.4   B. 23.8   C. 127.0   D. 136.0

11. Slip joints, as used in approved plumbing installations, are MOST generally found only

    A. in the brass bodied clean outs at the house trap
    B. the connection of the F.A.I. line to the perforated plate at the front wall of the building
    C. on the inlet side of several fixture traps
    D. on the outlet side of several fixture traps

12. In the course of doing a specific job, it becomes necessary to join two pieces of block tin together by soldering. The composition of the solder, which is best suited for this job, is *most nearly* _____ lead, _____ tin.

    A. 60%; 40%   B. 50%; 50%   C. 66%; 34%   D. 33%; 67%

13. The MINIMUM diameter of hanger rods set on 8'-0" centers which may be used to carry a single 3" water pipe is *most nearly*

    A. 1/4"   B. 1/2"   C. 3/4"   D. 7/8"

14. The type of trap which is commonly recommended and used for refrigerator waste pipes is _____ Trap.

    A. P   B. Bottle   C. Bag   D. Bell

15. A catch basin receives the flow from several yard and area drains properly installed. The inlets to and in the catch basin should be so set as to be

    A. above the outlet from the catch basin
    B. below the outlet from the catch basin
    C. at same elevation as the outlet from the catch basin
    D. at same elevation as the outlet tail pipe in the catch basin

16. The length of 3/4" pipe which should be allowed for screwing into a 3/4" elbow when laying out a job is *most nearly*

    A. 1/2"   B. 7/8"   C. 1"   D. 1/4"

17. The flushing mechanism in a low tank water closet is so arranged that a fill tube supplies water from the ball cock to the overflow stand pipe for a short interval immediately after the closet is flushed.
    The PRIMARY reason for this is to

    A. finish cleaning the water passages of the closet
    B. properly seal the ball in its seat
    C. renew the seal in the closet trap
    D. scour the flush tube from the tank to the closet

18. The flush mechanism in a low tank water closet is equipped with a copper float. If this float should become perforated and filled with water, the PROBABILITY is that the closet

    A. would flush once and then fail to operate
    B. could be continued in use though water would be wasted
    C. could be continued in use for several days without annoyance or waste
    D. could not be used at all

19. A lavatory is carelessly installed in that its waste is doubletrapped before it is connected to the branch waste. In operation, the PROBABILITY is that

    A. both traps would lose their seal
    B. only the lower trap would lose its seal
    C. only the upper trap would lose its seal
    D. the fixture waste may become air bound

20. The condition in the stack which is created by the discharge of waste from a fixture on an upper floor causes a small part of the water in a fixture trap on a lower floor to be discharged into the stack. Sufficient water remains in the lower fixture trap to fill the outer leg and the lowest portion of the trap when siphonage conditions exist subsequently.
    With respect to the lower fixture trap, it can be said that the trap seal

A. has been weakened
B. has not been weakened
C. may become air bound
D. may be broken more easily by momentum

21. A plumber, when preparing to wipe several lead bends to brass ferrules, skims and discards the dross from his wiping solder when it is molten but before it is at working heat. This action on the part of the plumber is

   A. entirely proper and unwasteful
   B. somewhat wasteful as the dross then contains considerable lead and zinc
   C. somewhat wasteful as the dross then contains tin
   D. entirely proper and unwasteful but should be done with a heated ladle

22. In order to properly conduct the waste from a given receptacle, it is necessary to use rust joints on the bell and spigot cast iron waste pipe.
   To properly make this joint after yarning with oakum, one should use iron filings

   A. mixed with oil and muriatic acid
   B. , powdered sulphur, and sal ammoniac
   C. , sal ammoniac and caustic soda
   D. , powdered sulphur, oil, and "killed" muriatic acid

23. The condition known as *water hammer* in a water supply system in a building is *most likely* brought about by

   A. long straight runs of water supply pipe
   B. short straight runs with many offsets in the water supply system
   C. quickly stopping the flow of water by sudden closing of a self-closing valve
   D. varying pressures in the water supply system

24. The public water supply to many buildings is metered. The type of meter which offers the least resistance to water flow is *most likely* (same water flow)

   A. the disc type
   B. the turbine type (current type)
   C. piston type
   D. wobble disc type

25. A house drain is successively offset by means of a 1/8 bend, 1/16 bend, and a 1/32 bend. The total angular offset of this line is most nearly

   A. 78 3/4°   B. 67 1/2°   C. 56 1/4°   D. 72 3/4°

26. The (siphon-action type) water closets in a building have been protected against freezing by the addition of a quart of kerosene to the water in each water closet trap. Two months pass and then prolonged freezing weather sets in. The PROBABLE result of winterizing as indicated above is that

   A. all the water closets will be in good condition despite the fact that water and kerosene do not mix well
   B. the greater number, if not all, of the water closet bowls will crack
   C. all of the water closet bowls will be in good condition if the *gravity* of the kerosene is low enough
   D. all of the water closet bowls will be in good condition if the *gravity* of the kerosene is greater than 1

27. An adequately designed air chamber is installed on the discharge side of a reciprocating pump. With the pump in operation, the PROBABLE effect of this air chamber is to

    A. increase the capacity of the pump
    B. decrease the head against which the pump is operating
    C. give a more uniform and steady delivery of water from the pump
    D. decrease the power required to operate the pump

28. In a complete plumbing installation, in order to prevent back-siphonage at a lavatory, it is common to make use of a(n)

    A. system of continuous venting
    B. system of yoke venting if the lavatory is one of a group
    C. system of unit venting if the lavatory is one of two set back to back
    D. air gap between the faucet spout and the flood rim level of the fixture

29. A water distribution system in a given public building has two supply risers, one of which is 2" nominal pipe size (2.067" I.D.) and the other is 1" nominal pipe size (1.049" I.D.). Both risers are 92 feet high, and both are fed from a pneumatic tank in the basement. Under the condition of no flow, the pressure at the base of each of these lines due to the water in the risers is *most nearly* 40 p.s.i. for

    A. 2" pipe and 20 p.s.i. for 1" pipe
    B. each riser
    C. 2" pipe and 10 p.s.i. for 1" pipe
    D. 2" pipe and 15 p.s.i. for 1" pipe

30. When comparing standard weight black steel pipe with extra strong galvanized steel pipe of the same nominal pipe size, it can be GENERALLY said that the

    A. internal diameters are the same
    B. weight per foot of one is twice that of the other
    C. external diameters are the same
    D. same threading dies cannot be used for both

31. The type of valve which is GENERALLY used for throttling or controlling the water flow in a plumbing system is

    A. 2 1/2"   B. 2"   C. 3"   D. 2 1/4"

32. The required MINIMUM diameter of a water closet trap shall be

    A. 2 1/2"   B. 2"   C. 3"   D. 2 1/4"

33. For a particular plumbing and drainage system for an office building, the roof and area storm water drains are properly connected to the rear of the main house drain. For this set-up, it can be said that

    A. the house drain and trap will be flushed from time to time
    B. it may become a source of trouble due to its forming a cross-connection
    C. this is entirely satisfactory regardless of the size and capacity of the house drain
    D. the leader trap will lose its seal most frequently because of capillary attraction

34. Of the following chemicals, which one is LEAST likely to dissolve or attack pure lead? 34.____

    A. Diluted peat acids
    B. Diluted nitric acid
    C. Citric acid (in presences of air)
    D. Hydrochloric acid

35. A group of water closets are to be set side by side in a men's room in an office building. In general, the MINIMUM center-to-center distances for these closets (flush valve type) should be *most nearly* 35.____

    A. 3'2"　　B. 3'10"　　C. 2'1"　　D. 2'8"

36. In the plumbing industry, the MOST common use for *inserts* is to 36.____

    A. reduce the I.D. of a pipe in a rush job in the field
    B. provide proper and easy entrance into an existing vent line
    C. provide a means to secure pipe hangers to masonry construction
    D. provide an easy entrance into an existing waste line

37. The MAXIMUM theoretical suction lift of water pumps, expressed in feet of water, for sea level elevation and 60° F water is *most nearly* _____ feet. 37.____

    A. 32　　B. 28　　C. 24　　D. 20

38. A particular hot water line made of copper has a straight horizontal run of 150' and, when installed, is at a temperature of 45° F. In use, its temperature rises to 190° F.
    If the coefficient of expansion for copper is 0.0000095"
    per foot per degree F, the total expansion in the run of pipe is *most nearly* 38.____

    A. 0.21"　　B. 4 1/2"　　C. 2 1/2"　　D. 0.41"

39. In a particular horizontal hot water line, expansion joints are set 50' apart. This line should be well supported an anchored 39.____

    A. at the expansion joints
    B. immediately each side of the expansion joints
    C. midway between the expansion joints
    D. 8' each side of the expansion joints

40. For a hot water storage tank, the cold water supply is introduced through the top of the tank and by means of a tail pipe is carried down and close to the bottom of the tank. To guard against siphonage, a small hole is bored in this cold water supply pipe within and near the top of the tank. The area of this hold should be AT LEAST equal to _____ the area of the cold water supply pipe. 40.____

    A. 1/4　　B. 1/2　　C. 1/8　　D. 3/32

41. In a given plumbing installation, if for some reason the roof extension of a given stack should become completely clogged, the MOST probable result with continued usage of the fixtures connected to this stack would *most likely* be 41.____

    A. ultimate clogging of the stack at the base thereof
    B. a reduction in capacity of the stack

C. probable siphonage of the seal of fixture traps by the discharge from a single water closet on the stack
D. the rapid loss of the seals of the fixture traps due entirely to momentum or evaporation

42. After a flushometer valve has been placed in operation, the force which causes it to close automatically is

   A. the return of the lever handle to the neutral position
   B. a flat helical spring above the diaphragm
   C. the water pressure on the inlet side of the valve which is applied to a space above the relief valve
   D. the springy force in a stainless steel diaphragm

43. Before acid waste may be discharged into a house drain, it should be neutralized. This is generally done in and by a water supplied

   A. cast iron sink with a special partition and the use of lime
   B. soapstone sink having a partition and the use of lime
   C. cast iron sink having a partition and the use of clay
   D. lead-lined sink having a partition and the use of Nessler's solution

44. In a particular plumbing installation, it becomes necessary to trap the vent pipe for a given fixture.
In order to permit continued and proper operation of this fixture, one should

   A. provide an accessible cleanout at the low point of the vent trap
   B. drip the low point of the vent trap into the branch waste from the fixture
   C. provide an automatic siphon to remove any condensation which may collect in the vent trap
   D. wash the vent trap with the discharge from the nearest water closet

45. The solder and flux which is generally recommended for use in brazing cast iron is *most* likely

   A. silfoz and rosin
   B. 60% tin - 40% lead and sperm
   C. silfoz and borax
   D. 60% copper - 40% zinc and borax

46. A particular plumbing specification calls for the installation of a double suction single stage centrifugal type water pump.
This type of pump may be described as having a(n)

   A. suction inlet to each side of the single impeller from a common connection and a single discharge connection from the impeller
   B. suction inlet to one side of each impeller and a combined or common discharge from the impellers
   C. suction inlet to the impeller which is at least three pipe sizes larger than the discharge
   D. open impeller with fairly large clearances

47. Which one of the following statements is MOST NEARLY CORRECT? 47.____
    A. The solubility of tin in potable water is great enough to ultimately cause the breakdown of the public health.
    B. On occasion, the solution of copper in potable water (brass piping system) has been found to be as high as 0.2 to 0.3 parts per million. In this concentration, it is dangerous to the health of the public.
    C. Zinc is sufficiently soluble in potable water to have a slightly injurious effect on the health of the public under unusual conditions.
    D. The presences of iron in water in high concentration is desirable because of its health restoring qualities.

48. The recommended supply flow of water in gallons per minute to a water closet equipped with a flushometer valve is NOT LESS THAN 48.____
    A. 12.5 B. 5.0 C. 8.0 D. 30.0

Questions 49-53.

DIRECTIONS: The following group of 5 questions relate to the materials used and in the manner in which piping in plumbing systems may be joined to form a continuous piping system. For each of the listed (and numbered) combination of pipes in the left-hand column, select the lettered manner of joining in the right-hand column.

49. Galv. steel to bell and spigot C.I.
   A. Yarn, run, and caulk with oakum and pig lead
   49.____

50. Vitrified clay to vitrified clay
   B. Ground union with screwed female ends (pipe dope on male threads)
   50.____

51. Brass to bell and spigot C.I.
   51.____

   C. R-L coupling-screwed (pipe dope on male threads)

52. Unthreaded brass to unthreaded brass
   52.____

   D. Approved welded fittings silver solder

53. Black steel to black steel for gas
   53.____

   E. Yarn and cement mortar

   F. 50-50 solder with streamlined copper fittings

   G. Rust joints

   H. Yarn, run, and caulk with oakum and lead wool

   I. Brass nipples - male threads turned

54. A 4" C.I. soil stack (bell and spigot joints) is 36 feet high. When making a water test, this stack is filled with water. A base sweep set on brick pier is provided at the base of the stack.
The total weight which is transmitted to this brick pier during the water test is *most nearly* (assume 10 joints in this stack and C.I. pipe weights 60# per 5' length) _____ lbs.

   A. 460 B. 660 C. 1320 D. 1120

55. A perforated fresh air inlet plate is to be provided for a 5" diameter cast iron F.A.I, pipe. This line is properly terminated in the front wall of the building. If the holes in the perforated plate are 5/8" in diameter, the total number of holes required is *most nearly*

   A. 100 B. 64 C. 42 D. 32

56. The survey of a building shows that water is to be supplied to a roof tank. The supply risers enter this tank 85' above the center line of the water supply main in the street. The loss through meter and valves is 10 lbs. per square inch, and the piping loss is estimated at 8' per 100' of total and equivalent length of run for the estimated flow. The supply main and riser make up a total and equivalent length of 160'.
The minimum pressure, in pounds per square inch, required at the street main in order to put water into the roof tank without pumping is *most nearly*

   A. 53.0 B. 107.8 C. 43.0 D. 97.8

57. A 45° offset in a stack is made by means of 2 1/2 lengths of X.H.C.I, drainage pipe. As a result, the horizontal centerline shift of the stack is *most nearly*

   A. 3'8" B. 5'0" C. 7'1" D. 8'10"

58. A roof tank is used to furnish the domestic water supply to a ten story building. This tank has a capacity of 5900 gallons. At 10:00 A.M. one morning, the tank is half full. If water is being used at the rate of 50 gals/ min., the pump which is used to fill the tank has a rated capacity of 90 gals/min., the time it would take to fill the tank under these conditions is *most nearly* _____ hours, _____ minutes.

   A. 2; 8 B. 1; 14 C. 2; 32 D. 1; 2

59. Various types of fittings can be used to connect a 4" stack to a house drain (base stack fittings). The fitting or combination of fittings which offers the LEAST resistance to discharge from the stack are *most likely*

   A. 90°-4" sweep with a radius of 4"
   B. two 1/8 bends with an 11" nipple between them (4" fittings)
   C. 90°-4" long radius sweep with a radius of 12"
   D. 4" Y and 1/8 bend combination with an 11" nipple between them

60. A particular house drain has a total developed length (without vertical drops) of 208 feet. The house drain starts at the furthest stack at a centerline elevation of -12.72'.
If the first half of the house drain is run at a pitch of 1/2" per foot and the remainder at a pitch of 1/4" per foot, then the center line elevation at the house trap is *most nearly*

   A. -19.22' B. -6.22' C. -6.32' D. -18.32'

10 (#2)

61. A circular roof tank is 10'6" in diameter and 12'0" high. The inlet pipe is 11'8" above the inside bottom. The lateral pressure in pounds per square inch on the sides at the bottom of the tank when it is full of water is *most nearly*

   A. 26.5 B. 50.0 C. 2.66 D. 5.0

62. In order to prevent back-siphonage in a flushometer valved water closet, the piping thereto shall be

   A. properly vented
   B. equipped with an approved vacuum breaker set not less than 4" above the flood rim level
   C. equipped with an approved vacuum breaker set not less than 2" above the flood rim level
   D. equipped with both a continuous vent and an approved vacuum breaker set not less than 2" above the flood rim level

63. On an alteration job, the plumbing specifications call for the installation of a bidet. With regard to the water connections, it can be said that a direct water supply

   A. can be made
   B. with an approved vacuum breaker and check valve, both properly set, can be made
   C. is prohibited
   D. with an approved vacuum breaker properly set can be made

64. Where hot water supply systems are installed, the hot water riser shall be covered with approved insulating material unless the hot and cold water risers are _____ inches or more apart.

   A. 4 B. 6 C. 5 D. 3

65. The type of water closet which may be used ONLY when the superintendent is convinced that there is exposure to frost is *most likely* the _____ closet.

   A. long hopper B. plunger
   C. offset washout D. washout

66. A particular plumbing installation is made of the following fixtures and groups of fixtures:
   12 bathroom groups (each one water closet, one lavatory, and one bathtub with shower)
   12 bathroom groups (each one water closet, one lavatory, one bathtub, and one shower stall)
   24 combination kitchen fixtures
   4 floor drains 6 slop sinks
   2 shower stalls (or shower/bath)
   The total number of fixture unit equivalents for this plumbing installation is *most nearly*

   A. 240 B. 250 C. 260 D. 360

67. A particular swimming pool has a water volume, when filled, to overflow rim level of 2500 cubic feet. The fixture unit equivalent of this pool is *most nearly*

   A. 21 B. 16 C. 9 D. 19

68. In accordance with C26-1296.0-a of the Plumbing Code, every oil separator shall have an individual three-inch vent extending from the top of such separator to the outer air

    A. by connecting it to the vent piping of the gravity drainage system
    B. by connecting it to the F.A.I. piping of the gravity drainage system
    C. at a point at least 12 inches above street level
    D. at a point at least 12 feet above street level

69. In a plumbing system, two 4" stacks and a 2" stack are grouped together at the top of the structure into one pipe which extends through the roof.
    The MINIMUM pipe size (C.I. pipe) of this one pipe shall be *most nearly*

    A. 5"   B. 6"   C. 8"   D. 10"

Questions 70-74.

DIRECTIONS: Questions 70 to 74 relate to the minimum size of individual soil and waste branches to individual fixtures. For each of the listed (and numbered) fixtures in the left-hand column, select the "lettered" minimum size of the individual soil or waste branch in the right-hand column.

70. Slop sink   A. 4"
71. Drinking fountain   B. 1 1/2"
72. Urinal   C. 2"
73. Sink (except slop sink)   D. 2 1/2"
74. Floor drain   E. 3"
                                 F. 1 1/4"

75. A sanitary and storm drainage system is made up of 18 F.U. and 1000 sq. ft. of drained area. In order to determine the size of the house drain for the combined storm and sanitary drainage system after the point of junction, one should allow _____ sq. ft. for the F.U. and a total of _____ sq. ft. for the combined system.

    A. 490; 1490   B. 372; 1372   C. 420; 1420   D. 108; 1108

76. In the installation of a plumbing system, which one of the following fixtures or traps MUST be installed with a vent?

    A. Floor drain set one floor above the house drain
    B. Drinking fountains connected to an indirect waste system
    C. Backwater valves set in the basement of a building
    D. Drinking fountains connected to a direct waste system

77. Relative to a plumbing installation, before air test on the roughing shall be accepted in lieu of a water test, one shall

    A. obtain the express permission from the borough superintendent
    B. set all fixtures, fill all trap seals, and run a peppermint test first

12 (#2)

    C. obtain the express permission from the Commissioner of Housing and Buildings
    D. obtain the express permission from the Commissioner of Water Supply, Gas and Electricity

78. The MINIMUM diameter of outlets for gas ranges within a building shall be *most nearly*   78.____

    A. 3/8"   B. 1/2"   C. 5/8"   D. 3/4"

79. When applying a test to gas piping, after all piping is installed and all outlets capped, the plumber shall apply an air pressure test equal, *most nearly,* to a column of   79.____

    A. water at least 6" in height
    B. mercury at least 6" in height
    C. water at least 12" in height
    D. mercury at least 12" in height

80. A particular plumbing specification states that the maximum velocity in the house main is not to exceed 5 feet per second. A study shows that the greatest demand will be 120 g.p.m. If double extra strong galvanized pipe is to be used, then the MINIMUM internal diameter of the pipe to be used should be *most nearly*   80.____

    A. 2.50"   B. 2.75"   C. 3.25"   D. 4.25"

KEY (CORRECT ANSWERS)

1.	C	21.	C	41.	C	61.	D
2.	D	22.	B	42.	C	62.	B
3.	A	23.	C	43.	B	63.	C
4.	A	24.	B	44.	B	64.	B
5.	B	25.	A	45.	D	65.	A
6.	D	26.	B	46.	A	66.	C
7.	B	27.	C	47.	C	67.	D
8.	A	28.	D	48.	D	68.	D
9.	D	29.	B	49.	A	69.	B
10.	A	30.	C	50.	E	70.	E
11.	C	31.	C	51.	A	71.	B
12.	D	32.	A	52.	D	72.	C
13.	B	33.	A	53.	C	73.	C
14.	D	34.	D	54.	B	74.	E
15.	A	35.	D	55.	B	75.	B
16.	A	36.	C	56.	A	76.	D
17.	C	37.	A	57.	D	77.	A
18.	B	38.	A	58.	B	78.	D
19.	D	39.	C	59.	C	79.	B
20.	B	40.	A	60.	A	80.	C

EXAMINATION SECTION
TEST 1

DIRECTIONS: Each question or incomplete statement is followed by several suggested answers or completions. Select the one that BEST answers the question or completes the statement. *PRINT THE LETTER OF THE CORRECT ANSWER IN THE SPACE AT THE RIGHT.*

1. It is usually necessary to insulate the hot water riser from the cold water riser when the distance between the two risers is

    A. 4" B. 7" C. 9" D. 11"

    1.____

2. The number of threads per inch of 3/4" pipe, as compared with the number of threads per inch of 1/4" pipe, is that the

    A. 3/4" pipe has less threads per inch than 1 1/4" pipe
    B. 3/4" pipe and 1 1/4" pipe have the same number of threads per inch
    C. 1 1/4" pipe has less threads per inch than the 3/4" pipe
    D. 1 1/4" pipe has more threads per inch than 3/4" pipe.

    2.____

3. In comparing the volume of water flowing through 1/2" I.D. tubing line and a 1" I.D. tubing line with the same pressure in each line, the volume through the

    A. 1/2" tubing and the 1" tubing will be the same
    B. 1" tubing will be double the volume of the 1/2" tubing
    C. 1" tubing will be three times the volume of the 1/2" tubing
    D. 1" tubing will be four times the volume of the 1/2" tubing

    3.____

4. Pressure relief valves must be installed on hot water heaters. The reason for this is

    A. to drain water from the tank for repair
    B. that when pressure becomes excessive, the relief valve will open and reduce the pressure
    C. that water will be released when tank is full
    D. to prevent air pockets from forming at the bottom of the tank

    4.____

5. The plumbing code requires that water service piping be buried at least four feet below outside ground level. The reason for this is to

    A. prevent the water in the pipe from freezing during the winter season
    B. permit gas service lines to be installed two feet below outside ground level
    C. permit the use of larger diameter pipes
    D. keep the water cool the year round

    5.____

6. A building drain which is buried under ground may NOT be made of

    A. extra heavy cast iron   B. brass
    C. galvanized steel   D. lead

    6.____

7. Brass is an alloy of

    A. lead and copper   B. tin and copper
    C. lead and tin   D. zinc and copper

    7.____

51

8. The MAIN reason for providing a trap for a plumbing fixture is to
   A. permit cleaning of the fixture when clogged
   B. equalize the pressure in the system
   C. prevent the passage of gases in a reverse direction
   D. catch foreign objects such as jewelry, hair pins, etc.

9. The pipe which delivers water under pressure from a street main to a building is called the _____ pipe.
   A. service
   B. interceptor
   C. distribution
   D. fixture

10. The MAIN reason that a trap must be properly ventilated is to
    A. vary the pressure in the waste line
    B. provide an overflow for the fixture
    C. drain the waste water when the trap is closed
    D. maintain the water seal in the trap

11. The valve which offers the LEAST resistance to water flow in a plumbing system is a(n) _____ valve.
    A. angle   B. gate   C. check   D. globe

12. Outlets for gas ranges must have a MINIMUM standard pipe size of
    A. 1/4"   B. 3/8"   C. 3/4"   D. 1"

13. The oakum for a caulked joint is packed into place by ramming it down with a
    A. yarning iron
    B. jointer
    C. caulking tool
    D. cold chisel

14. The ESSENTIAL difference in making up vertical and horizontal caulked joints in cast iron pipe is that horizontal caulked joints require the use of
    A. less lead
    B. less oakum
    C. a pouring rope
    D. a special caulking tool

15. Galvanized pipe has a coating of
    A. tin   B. zinc   C. lead   D. aluminum

16. A fixture unit has a discharge rate of one cubic foot of water per minute. This discharge rate, expressed in gallons per minute, is equal to
    A. 4.5   B. 5   C. 7.5   D. 9.5

17. Sweating or condensation of moisture on the outside of a pipe is MOST likely to occur on _____ pipe.
    A. live steam
    B. compressed air
    C. hot water
    D. cold water

18. Extra strong pipe, as compared to standard pipe of the same nominal size, has _____ diameter.

    A. *the same* outside diameter but a smaller inside
    B. *a larger* outside diameter and a smaller inside
    C. *the same* inside diameter but a larger outside
    D. *a larger* inside and outside diameter

19. You observe a plumber use a hammer to strike the hub and spigot ends of each piece of cast iron pipe before installing it in a soil line.
    This practice is

    A. *poor* because it may nick and weaken the pipe
    B. *poor* because it may break the brittle cast iron
    C. *good* because it loosens any rust which may have gathered
    D. *good* because it enables the plumber to tell if the pipe is sound

20. If a drain line pitches one foot in a length of 48 feet, the pitch of the line is MOST NEARLY _____ per foot.

    A. 1/4"   B. 3/8"   C. 1/2"   D. 3/4"

21. A plumbing sketch is drawn to a scale of eighth-size.
    A line measuring 3" on the sketch would be equivalent to _____ feet.

    A. 2   B. 6   C. 12   D. 24

22. Plumbing riser diagrams are GENERALLY drawn to _____ scale.

    A. no   B. 1/8" = 1'0"
    C. 1/4" = 1'0"   D. 1/2" = 1'0"

23. A building has a color marked dual water distribution system, one potable water and the other non-potable. The color used to identify the potable water system is

    A. yellow   B. orange   C. green   D. blue

24. Of the following potable water supply systems, the one which is NOT considered to be an auxiliary potable water supply system is a

    A. street main water supply system
    B. elevated gravity water supply system
    C. hydropneumatic pressure booster
    D. water pressure pump system

25. A pit and cover and/or manhole with cover is required for a building (house) trap when the distance from the center-line of the drain to the floor exceeds

    A. 12"   B. 16"   C. 18"   D. 24"

26. The MINIMUM rinse water temperature that can be used in a commercial type dishwasher is _____ °F.

    A. 140   B. 160   C. 180   D. 200

27. Assume that the flow rate through a grease interceptor is 60 g.p.m. Under this flow rate, the grease interceptor should have a minimum *grease retention capacity* of _____ pounds.

    A. 6   B. 30   C. 60   D. 120

28. The MAIN purpose for increasing the diameter of a vent stack from 2" to 4" when going through a roof is to

    A. provide sufficient area for proper flashing
    B. minimize clogging by hoarfrost
    C. increase the stability of the stack
    D. facilitate testing procedures

29. A pot of wiping solder is overheated.
    If this wiping soldier is used, the appearance of the wiped joint would MOST likely be

    A. flaky   B. spotted with bright specks
    C. frosty   D. coarse and grainy

30. Assume that the end of a piece of pipe has been threaded with a well-constructed threading pipe die.
    The number of imperfect threads that would be formed due to the chamfer on the die would be MOST NEARLY

    A. zero   B. 2 1/2   C. 3 1/2   D. 4 1/2

31. A pipe threading die with four chasers is used to thread the end of a length of pipe. The resultant threads are rough and torn.
    This condition is MOST probably caused by

    A. an improper lip angle
    B. too little clearance between the heel of the chaser and the work
    C. insufficient chip space
    D. not using a cutting oil

32. A deep seal trap has a minimum liquid seal of

    A. 2"   B. 3"   C. 4"   D. 5"

33. Of the following installations, the one which does NOT conform to the plumbing code (i.e., illegal) is the installation of a

    A. water closet with a 4" x 3" closet bend
    B. shower receptor with a 3" drain outlet
    C. washdown urinal with an integral strainer
    D. ball cock in a flush tank 1" above the floor rim of the bowl and provided with a vacuum breaker

34. A *dual vent* is commonly known as a _____ vent.

    A. crown   B. common   C. side   D. yoke

35. Of the following piping materials, the one which is NOT used for potable water service is

    A. copper pipe   B. type *L* tubing
    C. type *K* tubing   D. type *TP* tubing

36. The discharge rate for an ejector pump is 100 g.p.m. The *fixture unit value* for this pump is

    A. 10   B. 50   C. 75   D. 100

37. The flood level rim of a fixture is defined as

    A. the invert or bottom of the overflow
    B. the inside top of the overflow pipe
    C. 1" above the top of the overflow pipe
    D. the top edge or rim of the fixture

38. Of the following statements, the one which BEST defines the plumbing term *cross-connection* is the connection between

    A. the domestic hot water and potable cold water
    B. steam and a potable water supply
    C. potable water at 40 psig and potable water at 90 psig
    D. two different potable water distribution pipes

39. Of the following types of water closets, the one which shall be used for public use is the _____ type.

    A. elongated bowl   B. pan
    C. washout   D. offset

40. The MAXIMUM interval between hangers for supporting horizontal 1 1/2" diameter threaded pipe is _____ feet.

    A. 6   B. 8   C. 10   D. 12

KEY (CORRECT ANSWERS)

1. A	11. B	21. A	31. A
2. C	12. C	22. A	32. B
3. D	13. A	23. C	33. C
4. B	14. C	24. A	34. B
5. A	15. B	25. C	35. B
6. C	16. C	26. C	36. D
7. D	17. D	27. D	37. D
8. C	18. A	28. B	38. B
9. A	19. D	29. D	39. A
10. D	20. A	30. C	40. D

TEST 2

DIRECTIONS: Each question or incomplete statement is followed by several suggested answers or completions. Select the one that BEST answers the question or completes the statement. *PRINT THE LETTER OF THE CORRECT ANSWER IN THE SPACE AT THE RIGHT.*

1. The pipe fitting which should be used to connect a 1" pipe to a 1 1/2" valve is a

   A. reducing elbow
   B. bushing
   C. reducing coupling
   D. street ell

2. A 2 percent pitch in a pipe line is MOST NEARLY equal to a slope of _____ to the foot.

   A. 1/16"   B. 1/8"   C. 1/4"   D. 1/2"

3. The MAIN function of a standpipe system in a building is to

   A. supply water for the roof tank
   B. keep the hot water circulating in order to maintain a constant temperature
   C. provide water for use in case of fire
   D. increase the pressure in the water supply piping

4. The one of the following valves which offers the LEAST resistance to the flow of water is a(n) _____ valve.

   A. check   B. gate   C. globe   D. angle

5. The cast iron drainage fitting that is called a Tucker connection has

   A. male threads on one end and female threads on the other end
   B. one end in the form of a hub and female threads on the other end
   C. one end in the form of a hub and male threads on the other end
   D. each end in the form of a hub

6. When bending copper tubing in the field, special equipment is required _____ -temper tubing.

   A. only for hard
   B. only for soft
   C. for both soft-temper and hard
   D. for neither soft-temper nor hard.

7. If the diameter of the vertical stack in a building is smaller than the diameter of the house drain which connects to it, then the bend which joins them should be

   A. *at least* one size smaller than the stack
   B. *at least* one size larger than the stack
   C. *at least* one size larger than the drain
   D. *larger* than both the stack and the drain

8. If water is flowing into the top of a tank at the rate of 150 gallons per hour and flowing out at the rate of 3/4 of a gallon every 20 seconds, then the amount of water in the tank is _____ gallon per minute.

   A. *increasing* by 1/4   B. *increasing* by 3/4
   C. *decreasing* by 1/4   D. *decreasing* by 3/4

9. A flexible coupling between a pump shaft and a motor shaft is GENERALLY provided in order to

   A. reduce the load on the pump
   B. permit excess heat to escape
   C. permit minor misalignment between the shafts
   D. increase the power of the motor

10. The BEST way to prevent a water pocket from forming when two horizontal steam pipes of different diameter are joined is to

    A. use an eccentric fitting
    B. use a long fitting so that the slope between the pipes is very gradual
    C. provide a drain cock
    D. slope the pipe so that the smaller pipe is lower

11. The BEST way to make a temporary repair in a water line with a small leak is by

    A. wrapping a rag around it
    B. welding or brazing
    C. using a clamped patch
    D. drilling, tapping, and inserting a plug

12. Brass is an alloy of

    A. lead and copper
    B. lead and tin
    C. tin and copper
    D. zinc and copper

13. The information that a plumber would NOT normally expect to find on each section of cast iron pipe delivered from the factory is the

    A. manufacturer's name
    B. weight category
    C. diameter
    D. length

14. Steel pipe is GENERALLY connected to copper tubing by

    A. brazing
    B. soldering
    C. wiping
    D. special fittings

15. Pipe is galvanized by coating it with

    A. chrome   B. tin   C. aluminum   D. zinc

16. A return bend in a pipe line changes the direction of flow by

    A. 45°   B. 90°   C. 135°   D. 180°

17. When lagging is used on steam pipes, its MAIN function is to

    A. compensate for expansion
    B. prevent corrosion
    C. reduce radiation heat loss
    D. reduce steam leaks

18. If the drawing of a piping layout is made to a scale of 1/4" equals one foot, then a 7'9" length of piping would be represented by a scaled length on the drawing of APPROXIMATELY _____ inches.

    A. 2 B. 7 3/4 C. 23 1/4 D. 31

19. A pipe reducing coupling normally has _____ thread(s).

    A. two female
    B. two male
    C. one continuous female
    D. one male and one female

20. All bullhead tees have run openings which are

    A. smaller than the outlet
    B. larger than the outlet
    C. of the same size
    D. of different sizes

21. A close nipple

    A. has a short section with no threads
    B. is always less than 3/4" long
    C. has ends of different diameters
    D. has threads over its entire length

22. A reducing tee ALWAYS has

    A. one opening which is larger than the other two
    B. openings of three different sizes
    C. a branch opening which is smaller than the run
    D. a branch which is at an angle of 45 degrees to the run

23. In addition to acting as a filler between threads, pipe joint compound ALSO acts as a

    A. lubricant
    B. hardener
    C. coolant
    D. permanent bond

24. The valve which is used to permit flow of water in one direction only is called a _____ valve.

    A. check B. globe C. gate D. angle

25. A method which should be used to free a pipe die from chips while threading a pipe is to

    A. use as little lubricating oil as possible
    B. set the die loosely on the pipe stock
    C. clean the chips off the pipe after each thread is cut
    D. partially back off the die at intervals during the turning process

26. The MAIN difference between making up horizontal and vertical caulked joints in cast iron pipe is that, when making up a vertical caulked joint, you should NOT use a

    A. smaller amount of lead
    B. smaller amount of oakum
    C. pouring rope
    D. special caulking tool

27. Assume that a 2" pipe is connected to a 3" pipe by means of a coupling. If the velocity of flow in the 2" pipe is 36 feet per second, then the velocity of flow in the 3" pipe is APPROXIMATELY _____ feet per second.

    A. 16 B. 24 C. 54 D. 81

28. When ordering a cross which is to have two outlet openings which are 1" in diameter and two run openings which are 1 1/2" in diameter, a plumber should specify a _____ cross.

   A. 1" x 1 1/2" x 1" x 1 1/2"
   B. 1 1/2" x 1" x 1 1/2" x 1"
   C. 1" x 1 1/2"
   D. 1 1/2" x 1"

29. The LEAST likely cause of a leak in a threaded pipe joint is that

   A. not enough pipe joint compound was used
   B. the threads are not smooth
   C. the number of threads is not sufficient
   D. too much pipe joint compound has been used

30. The BEST way to assemble a line of piping between a waste stack and a trapped fixture is to

   A. start at the fixture and work toward the waste stack
   B. start at the waste stack and work toward the fixture
   C. let the order of assembly be determined by the details of the proposed installation
   D. work from the most accessible location

31. When referring to a building drainage system, the term *waste pipe* should NORMALLY be applied to

   A. piping which does not receive human waste
   B. piping which drains water closets
   C. any pipe which carries water-borne wastes
   D. any pipe which connects to the building drain

32. The one of the following which has the SMALLEST *fixture unit rating* is a

   A. drinking fountain
   B. wash basin
   C. slop sink
   D. shower head

33. Pipe joint compound should be applied on

   A. the threads of male fittings only
   B. the threads of female fittings only
   C. the threads of both male and female fittings
   D. either male or female threads, depending on the type of fitting

34. If a pipe with an outside diameter of 7" is to be fastened against the ceiling with a U-strap, the distance from the ceiling around the pipe and back to the ceiling should be APPROXIMATELY _____ inches.

   A. 14   B. 16   C. 18   D. 20

35. The MAIN reason cast iron pipe is particularly suitable for underground service is that it

   A. resists corrosion very well
   B. has a low initial cost
   C. is easy to handle and join
   D. can withstand high pressures

36. The BEST procedure to follow in most cases when a pipe does not screw into a fitting easily is to

    A. use a heavier pipe wrench
    B. cut the threads off the end of the pipe and rethread
    C. attempt to true up defective threads with a die or a tap
    D. heat the fitting with a torch

37. If the hand-operated shut-off valve in a water line is turned to the fully closed position, and water continues to flow through the valve, the MOST likely defect a plumber would expect to find is

    A. a loose gland
    B. excessive packing
    C. improper seating of the valve disc
    D. a loose stuffing nut

38. The MAIN function of a trap in a drainage system is to

    A. prevent freezing of the pipes
    B. block off sewer gases
    C. prevent loss of water pressure
    D. catch rings and other objects

39. A combustible gas which may be present in sewer air and which is explosive in the presence of oxygen is

    A. carbon dioxide   B. freon
    C. hydrogen sulfide   D. nitrogen

40. The MAIN function of a back-pressure valve which is sometimes found in the connection between a water drain pipe and the sewer system is to

    A. equalize the pressure between the drain pipe and the sewer
    B. prevent sewer water from flowing into the drain pipe
    C. provide pressure to enable waste to reach the sewer
    D. make sure that there is not too much water pressure in the sewer line

KEY (CORRECT ANSWERS)

1.	B	11.	C	21.	D	31.	A
2.	C	12.	D	22.	C	32.	A
3.	C	13.	D	23.	A	33.	A
4.	B	14.	D	24.	A	34.	C
5.	B	15.	D	25.	D	35.	A
6.	A	16.	D	26.	C	36.	C
7.	B	17.	C	27.	A	37.	C
8.	A	18.	A	28.	D	38.	B
9.	C	19.	A	29.	D	39.	C
10.	A	20.	A	30.	B	40.	B

TEST 3

DIRECTIONS: Each question or incomplete statement is followed by several suggested answers or completions. Select the one that BEST answers the question or completes the statement. *PRINT THE LETTER OF THE CORRECT ANSWER IN THE SPACE AT THE RIGHT.*

1. The piping of a newly installed drainage system shall be tested upon completion of the rough plumbing with a head of water of NOT LESS THAN _____ feet.

    A. 10   B. 15   C. 20   D. 25

2. The one of the following which should NOT be considered as a *water conserving device* is a(n)

    A. evaporative condenser
    B. water cooling tower
    C. spray pond
    D. water closet

3. In high pressure steam heating systems, the steam pressure is GREATER than _____ psig.

    A. 15   B. 20   C. 25   D. 30

4. Type *K* water service pipe is made of

    A. cast iron
    B. copper
    C. lead
    D. galvanized steel

5. All water services shall be installed below the finished ground surface at a distance of AT LEAST _____ feet.

    A. 2   B. 4   C. 6   D. 8

6. The piping in all buildings having dual water distribution systems shall be identified by a color coding of _____ for potable water lines and _____ for non-potable water lines.

    A. green; red
    B. green; yellow
    C. yellow; green
    D. yellow; red

7. In buildings over four stories high, approved plastic pipe may be used for

    A. water service pipe only
    B. all water distribution system piping
    C. all drainage system piping
    D. chemical waste drainage systems only

8. The minimum required diameter of any soil stack extension which passes through the roof is _____ inches.

    A. 3   B. 4   C. 5   D. 6

9. A device used to prevent backflow by siphonic action is called a

    A. relief valve
    B. sewage ejector
    C. foot valve
    D. vacuum breaker

10. The MAXIMUM distance permitted between cleanouts in horizontal drainage lines is _____ feet.

    A. 10 B. 30 C. 50 D. 70

11. A horizontal drainage pipe must have a minimum slope of 1/4" per foot if the pipe diameter measures _____ inches.

    A. 2 B. 4 C. 6 D. 8

12. Curb valves should be installed on all domestic service pipes with a diameter larger than _____ inch(es).

    A. 1 B. 1 1/2 C. 2 D. 2 1/2

13. A public water supply system shall be deemed available to a two-family dwelling if a property line of such dwelling is within a distance from the public water supply which is NO GREATER THAN _____ feet.

    A. 50 B. 100 C. 150 D. 200

14. The minimum pressure available near a faucet or water outlet with the water outlet wide open shall be _____ psi.

    A. 2 B. 4 C. 6 D. 8

15. When it is necessary to open a sidewalk in order to do plumbing work, a permit shall be obtained from the department of

    A. water resources
    B. public works
    C. buildings
    D. highways

16. The MINIMUM number of fixture units allowed for a bathroom group containing one lavatory, one bathtub, and one water closet (flush tank) is

    A. 4 B. 6 C. 8 D. 10

17. The MINIMUM number of plumbing fixtures required for a particular type of building occupancy depends MAINLY on

    A. the number of persons expected to use the building
    B. whether the building is publicly or privately owned
    C. the load factor numbers
    D. the age group of the occupants

18. The waste water which would be MOST likely to corrode a cast iron pipe would have a pH value of

    A. 3.0 B. 5.0 C. 7.0 D. 9.0

19. The MAIN factor to consider in determining whether permission from a city department is required before connecting automatic power pumps directly to the street main is the

    A. total water storage capacity in the building
    B. total automatic pump capacity
    C. number of persons expected to occupy the building
    D. number of fixture units in the building

20. In locations where tags are used to designate certain water lines, non-potable water lines should be identified by _____ tags which say _____.

    A. round; WATER UNSAFE
    B. triangular; WATER UNSAFE
    C. round; UNSAFE FOR DRINKING
    D. triangular; UNSAFE FOR DRINKING

21. Trap seals should be vented so that they are at no time subjected to a pressure differential of MORE THAN

    A. 1 inch of water
    B. 2 inches of water
    C. .1 pound per square inch
    D. .2 pound per square inch

22. One trap may serve more than one drain if none of the drains are at a greater distance from the trap than _____ feet.

    A. 5   B. 10   C. 15   D. 20

23. With the exception of commercial dishwashers or laundries, hot water may NOT be discharged into any part of a drainage system at a temperature above

    A. 150°   B. 160°   C. 170°   D. 180°

24. A type of hospital equipment which does NOT require an air gap on the water supply is a(n)

    A. operating table   B. aspirator
    C. toilet   D. sterilizer

25. The percentage of the total connected fixture unit flow rate is likely to occur at any point in the drainage system is called the

    A. discharge coefficient   B. velocity coefficient
    C. load factor   D. hydraulic factor

26. The top edge over which water in a receptacle can overflow is called the

    A. inlet rim   B. air-gap level
    C. drain level   D. flood-level rim

27. A device designed to separate and retain undesirable matter from normal wastes and permit normal sewage to discharge into the disposal terminal is called a(n)

    A. catch basin   B. dead end
    C. seepage pit   D. interceptor

28. Paint is NOT permitted on the jointing material at a joint in cast iron pipe

    A. at any time
    B. until two days after construction of the joint
    C. until the entire plumbing installation is complete
    D. until after the joint has been tested and accepted

29. Wall-hung trough urinals are permitted in   29._____
    A. public bath houses
    B. only in temporary locations
    C. where a limited number of people are expected to use them
    D. under no circumstances

30. Drainage pipe cleanouts are required   30._____
    A. to be not more than 80 feet apart in a horizontal direction
    B. to extend horizontally from an underground drain
    C. at each change of direction greater than 45°
    D. to be 3/4 of the nominal size of pipe for diameters up to 4 inches

31. All water used in the construction of a building shall be metered if the building is higher than _____ stories.   31._____
    A. 3   B. 4   C. 5   D. 6

32. Gas piping should be tested under a pressure of NO LESS THAN _____ psig.   32._____
    A. 3   B. 5   C. 7   D. 9

33. When installing gas lines in a building, it is permissible to   33._____
    A. reuse gas pipe which has been removed from an existing installation
    B. use gas piping for an electrical ground
    C. use malleable iron fittings
    D. use gasket unions.

34. If the water pressure in the street main is 100 psi,   34._____
    A. a gravity tank shall be installed on the roof
    B. the pressure at the closed fixtures shall be reduced to 85 psi
    C. a stop-and-waste valve shall be installed underground
    D. a booster pump shall be connected to the main

35. When modernizing a multiple dwelling, a plumbing permit is required if   35._____
    A. several broken toilets are to be replaced by new fixtures
    B. an additional washing machine and standpipe are to be installed in the laundry room
    C. gas stoves in all apartments are to be replaced by a newer model
    D. the hot water storage tank is to be replaced

36. When an adjoining building is erected next to an existing building which is higher, all waste stacks of the new building shall be located a distance from the common lot line of AT LEAST _____ feet.   36._____
    A. 5   B. 10   C. 15   D. 20

37. A type of trap which is prohibited is the _____ trap.   37._____
    A. S   B. 1/2S   C. bottle   D. running

38. Air chambers installed at individual fixtures   38.____

    A. need not be accessible
    B. shall be accessible
    C. are required for loads of less than 5 fixture units
    D. are required for loads of more than 5 fixture units

39. In the installation of a hot water storage tank, it is PROHIBITED to install a   39.____

    A. combination pressure and temperature relief valve
    B. separate pressure relief valve and separate temperature relief valve
    C. pressure relief valve whose opening pressure is greater than 25 lbs. above normal system working pressure
    D. check valve between the relief valve and the storage tank

40. Sanitary drainage piping must be sloped so that the minimum velocity of flow is _____   40.____
    ft. per second.

KEY (CORRECT ANSWERS)

1.	A	11.	A	21.	A	31.	D
2.	D	12.	C	22.	C	32.	A
3.	A	13.	B	23.	A	33.	C
4.	B	14.	D	24.	C	34.	B
5.	B	15.	D	25.	C	35.	B
6.	B	16.	B	26.	D	36.	B
7.	D	17.	A	27.	D	37.	C
8.	B	18.	A	28.	D	38.	A
9.	D	19.	B	29.	B	39.	D
10.	C	20.	B	30.	C	40.	C

EXAMINATION SECTION
TEST 1

DIRECTIONS: Each question or incomplete statement is followed by several suggested answers or completions. Select the one that BEST answers the question or completes the statement. *PRINT THE LETTER OF THE CORRECT ANSWER IN THE SPACE AT THE RIGHT.*

1. A fitting with a 1/8th bend would be used to make an offset of about _____ degrees.

    A. 11 1/4   B. 22 1/2   C. 45   D. 67 1/2

2. To dig a trench 3'0" wide, 50'0" long, and 5'6" deep, the total number of cubic yards of earth to be removed is MOST NEARLY

    A. 30   B. 90   C. 140   D. 825

3. The percentage of copper in *Red Brass Pipe* which conforms to standard specifications is about

    A. 25   B. 50   C. 60   D. 85

4. A fixture unit is equal to a water discharge rate of one

    A. cubic foot per minute
    B. cubic foot per second
    C. gallon per minute
    D. gallon per second

5. The total length of four pieces of 2" pipe, whose lengths are 7'3 1/2", 4'2 3/16", 5'7 5/16", and 8'5 7/8", respectively, is

    A. 24'6 3/4"   B. 24'7 15/16"
    C. 25'5 13/16"   D. 25'6 7/8"

6. Under the same conditions, the group of pipes that gives the same flow as one 6" pipe is (neglecting friction) _____ pipes.

    A. 3 3"   B. 4 3"   C. 2 4"   D. 3 4"

7. The PRIMARY difference between a schedule 40 pipe and a schedule 80 pipe, of the same material and size, is that schedule 80 pipe

    A. weighs more per foot
    B. has fewer threads per inch
    C. has a larger inside diameter
    D. has a thinner wall thickness

8. The purpose of a vacuum breaker used with an automatic flush valve is to

    A. limit the flow of water to the fixture
    B. control the water pressure to the fixture
    C. equalize the water pressure
    D. prevent pollution of the water supply

9. Wiping solder for lead pipe usually has a melting range of _____ to _____ °F.

    A. 150; 250   B. 251; 350   C. 360; 470   D. 475; 60

10. The fixture with the LARGEST fixture unit rating would be a

    A. water closet   B. urinal
    C. slop sink   D. lavatory

11. Vents to the outer air are required to be installed at plumbing fixtures for the purpose of

    A. removing room odors
    B. preventing the sewer from backing up into the fixtures
    C. preventing the siphoning of traps
    D. obtaining rapid removal of wastes

12. Where it is required to keep friction resistance to a minimum in a piping layout, the type of valve to be used is a _____ valve.

    A. gate   B. globe   C. angle   D. needle

13. A CORRECT statement is that the number of threads cut per inch on standard pipe

    A. *increases* as the diameter of pipe increases
    B. *decreases* as the diameter of pipe increases
    C. *remains constant* for all diameters of pipe
    D. *depends* on the length of thread to be cut on the pipe

14. The plan for a plumbing installation which is to be renovated by your crew shows the use of certain types of fittings which you believe to be wrong.
    Your PROPER procedure would be to

    A. immediately report the error to your superior
    B. use the fittings according to the plan
    C. hold up the job until you have checked with the man who delivered the material
    D. use the type of fitting you believe to be correct and revise the plan

15. A water pipe is to run under a structural beam and be suspended from the beam. The pipe should be suspended by a hanger _____ the beam.

    A. passing through a hole in the web of
    B. passing through a hole in the flange of
    C. welded to
    D. clamped to

16. It is INCORRECT to say that

    A. a gasoline torch must be fully filled with gasoline
    B. there is a difference between fittings for threaded drainage pipe and fittings for ordinary threaded pipe
    C. for pipe designated as 200 WOG, the letters stand for water, oil, gas
    D. loose parts in a faucet may cause noisy operation

17. If the drain of a sink frequently emits a gurgling sound, it is MOST probable that the

    A. drain plug of the sink trap leaks
    B. sink trap is partially blocked by some solids
    C. drain line is pitched in the wrong direction
    D. venting for the sink trap is imperfect

18. If a set of plumbing plans are drawn to a scale of 1 1/2" to the foot, the plans are said to be one _____ size.

    A. half
    B. quarter
    C. eighth
    D. sixteenth

19. The length of 3/4" pipe which should be allowed for screwing into a 3/4" elbow when laying out a job is MOST NEARLY

    A. 1"   B. 7/8"   C. 1/2"   D. 1/4"

20. The type of valve which is generally used for controlling the water flow in a plumbing system is a

    A. gate valve
    B. globe valve
    C. needle valve
    D. plug cock

KEY (CORRECT ANSWERS)

1.	C	11.	C
2.	A	12.	A
3.	D	13.	B
4.	A	14.	A
5.	D	15.	D
6.	B	16.	A
7.	A	17.	B
8.	D	18.	C
9.	C	19.	C
10.	A	20.	B

TEST 2

DIRECTIONS: Each question or incomplete statement is followed by several suggested answers or completions. Select the one that BEST answers the question or completes the statement. *PRINT THE LETTER OF THE CORRECT ANSWER IN THE SPACE AT THE RIGHT.*

Questions 1-6.

DIRECTIONS: Questions 1 through 6, inclusive, are to be answered in accordance with plumbing code requirements.

1. The MINIMUM distance that a vacuum breaker must be set above the flood level rim of a fixture is

    A. 2" B. 4" C. 6" D. 8"

2. The MINIMUM weight of a 5-foot length of a 4-inch single hub *extra heavy* cast iron soil pipe should be, in pounds,

    A. 40 B. 50 C. 60 D. 70

3. Horizontal drainage piping shall be run in practical alignment and at uniform grade per foot of AT LEAST

    A. 1/8" B. 1/4" C. 1/2" D. 1"

4. A pressure relief valve shall be provided in a hot water supply system and, between this relief valve and the water heating boiler, there shall be installed _____ valve.

    A. a gate
    B. a check
    C. a globe
    D. no other

5. When soil waste and vent pipes are extended through a roof, they must have a diameter of AT LEAST

    A. 3" B. 4" C. 5" D. 6"

6. The type of pipe NOT permitted for underground use is that made of

    A. cast iron
    B. lead
    C. brass
    D. galvanized steel

7. The MAXIMUM theoretical suction lift of water pumps, expressed in feet of water at sea level elevation, is MOST NEARLY _____ feet.

    A. 36 B. 32 C. 28 D. 24

8. The type of pipe that should NOT be used for drainage within a building is

    A. vitrified clay
    B. cast iron
    C. bronze
    D. copper

9. A 5" drain 25' long is to be installed with a pitch of 1/4" per foot, the difference in elevation of the two ends of the drain is

    A. 1 1/4" B. 5" C. 6 1/4" D. 7 1/4"

10. When threading pipe with properly adjusted and correctly made pipe dies, the PROPER thread is obtained when

   A. three threads protrude the die
   B. five non-taper threads are made
   C. the pipe end is flush with the face of the dies
   D. the thread length is approximately twice the diameter of the pipe

11. A hot water line made of copper has a straight horizontal run of 150 feet and when installed is at a temperature of 45° F. In use its temperature rises to 190° F.
    If the coefficient of expansion for copper is 0.0000095" per foot per degree F., the total expansion, in inches, in the run of pipe is given by the product of 150 multiplied by 0.0000095 by

   A. 145
   B. 145 x 12
   C. 145 divided by 12
   D. 145 x 12 x 12

12. The use of hard water in piping systems is *undesirable* MAINLY because it causes

   A. leaky joints
   B. corrosion
   C. high friction losses
   D. scaling

13. A water storage tank measures 5' long, 4' wide, and 6' deep and is filled to the 5 1/2' mark with water.
    If one cubic foot of water weighs 62 pounds, the number of pounds of water required to COMPLETELY fill the tank is

   A. 7440   B. 6200   C. 1240   D. 620

14. The BASIC function of a trap on a drainage system is to prevent

   A. sewer gases from entering the house
   B. waterborne diseases
   C. blocking the drainage
   D. insects from entering the house through the drain pipe

15. The INCORRECTLY matched pair is

   A. wiped joint - lead pipe
   B. swedge and solder joint - copper pipe
   C. caulked joint - wiped joint
   D. screw thread joint - wrought pipe

16. For BEST results, the coil of an indirect water heater should be connected so that the top of the coil is connected to the _____ of the tank.

   A. lower opening on the side
   B. opening in the bottom
   C. hot water outlet on top
   D. top opening in the side

17. The one fitting NOT used in a plumbing installation is

   A. street ell
   B. Y branch
   C. angle folds
   D. reducing tee

18. The CORRECTLY matched pair is:

    A. Hot water heating system - quick vent air valve
    B. Hot radiators - convection air currents
    C. Expansion tank - steam-heating system
    D. Altitude gauge - steam-heating system

    18.____

19. A pipe reamer is used to

    A. thread pipe
    B. enlarge the size of a pipe
    C. remove burrs from the inside of a pipe
    D. join pipes of different sizes

    19.____

20. A 5-inch length of pipe with male threads at each end is called a

    A. stud   B. coupling   C. sleeve   D. nipple

    20.____

KEY (CORRECT ANSWERS)

1.	B	11.	A
2.	C	12.	D
3.	A	13.	D
4.	D	14.	A
5.	B	15.	C
6.	D	16.	D
7.	B	17.	C
8.	A	18.	B
9.	C	19.	C
10.	C	20.	D

READING COMPREHENSION
UNDERSTANDING AND INTERPRETING WRITTEN MATERIAL
EXAMINATION SECTION
TEST 1

DIRECTIONS: Each question or incomplete statement is followed by several suggested answers or completions. Select the one that BEST answers the question or completes the statement. *PRINT THE LETTER OF THE CORRECT ANSWER IN THE SPACE AT THE RIGHT.*

Questions 1-5.

DIRECTIONS: Questions 1 through 5 are to be answered SOLELY on the basis of the following paragraph.

The strength of the seal of a trap is closely proportional to the depth of the seal, regardless of the size of the trap. Unfortunately, an increase in the depth of the seal also increases the probability of solids being retained in the trap, and a limit of about a 4" depth of seal for traps that must pass solids has been imposed by some plumbing codes. The depth of seal most commonly found in simple traps is between $1\frac{1}{2}$" and 2". The Hoover Report recommends a minimum depth of 2" as a safeguard against seal rupture and a maximum depth of 4" to avoid clogging, fungus growths, and similar difficulties. Traps in rain-water leaders and other pipes carrying clear-water wastes only, and which are infrequently used, should have seal depths equal to or greater than 4". The increase in the volume of water retained in the trap helps very little in increasing the strength of the seal, but it does materially reduce the velocity of flow through the trap so as to increase the probability of the sedimentation of solids therein.

1. In accordance with the above, it may be said that traps carrying rain-water should have a seal of

    A. 5"   B. $3\frac{1}{2}$"   C. 2"   D. $1\frac{1}{2}$"

1.____

2. In accordance with the preceding paragraph, which one of the following statements is MOST NEARLY correct?

    A. Simple traps have a depth of seal between $1\frac{1}{2}$" to 4".
    B. A minimum depth of 4" is recommended to avoid seal rupture.
    C. The strength of the seal is proportional to the size of the trap.
    D. The higher the depth of seal, the more chance of collecting solids.

2.____

3. In accordance with the above, it may be said that increasing the volume of water retained in a trap may

   A. *greatly* increase the velocity of flow
   B. *slightly* increase the velocity of flow
   C. *greatly* increase the trap seal
   D. *slightly* increase the trap seal

4. Of the following, the title which BEST explains the main idea of this paragraph is

   A. TRAP SEAL DEPTHS
   B. THE EFFECTS OF SEDIMENTATION ON TRAP SEALS
   C. COMMON TRAP SIZES
   D. TRAP SIZES AND VELOCITY OF FLOW

5. Assume that the strength of a trap seal is indicated by 8 units when the trap depth is 2". In accordance with the above paragraph, increasing the depth of seal to 4" will cause the strength of the trap seal to be MOST NEARLY _____ units.

   A. 2   B. 4   C. 8   D. 16

Questions 6-10.

DIRECTIONS: Questions 6 through 10 are to be answered SOLELY on the basis of the following paragraph.

The thickness of insulation necessary for the most economical results varies with the steam temperature. The standard covering consists of 85 percent magnesia with 10 percent of long-fibre asbestos as a binder. Both magnesia and laminated asbestos—felt and other forms of mineral wool including glass wool—are also used for heat insulation. The magnesia and laminated asbestos coverings may be safely used at temperatures up to 600° F. Pipe insulation is applied in molded sections 3 feet long. The sections are attached to the pipe by means of galvanized iron wire or netting. Flanges and fittings can be insulated by direct application of magnesia cement to the metal without reinforcement. Insulation should always be maintained in good condition because it saves fuel. Routine maintenance of warm-pipe insulation should include prompt repair of damaged surfaces. Steam and hot water leaks concealed by insulation will be difficult to detect. Underground steam or hotwater pipes are best insulated using a concrete trench with removable cover.

6. The word *reinforcement*, as used above, means MOST NEARLY

   A. resistance   B. strengthening
   C. regulation   D. removal

7. According to the above paragraph, magnesia and laminated-asbestos coverings may be safely used at temperatures up to

   A. 800° F   B. 720° F   C. 675° F   D. 600° F

8. According to the above paragraph, insulation should ALWAYS be maintained in good condition because it

   A. is laminated   B. saves fuel
   C. is attached to the pipe   D. prevents leaks

9. According to the above paragraph, pipe insulation sections are attached to the pipe by means of

   A. binders
   B. mineral wool
   C. netting
   D. staples

10. According to the above paragraph, a leak in a hot-water pipe may be difficult to detect because when insulation is used, the leak is

    A. underground
    B. hidden
    C. routine
    D. cemented

Questions 11-15.

DIRECTIONS: Questions 11 through 15 are to be answered SOLELY on the basis of the following paragraph.

Reductions in pipe size of a building heating system are made with eccentric fittings and are pitched downward. The ends of mains with gravity return shall be at least 18" above the water line of the boiler. As condensate flows opposite to the stream, runouts are one size larger than the vertical pipe and are pitched upward. In a one-pipe system, an automatic air vent must be provided at each main to relieve air pressure and to let steam enter the radiator. As steam enters the radiator, a thermal device causes the vent to close, thereby holding the steam. Steam mains should not be less than two inches in diameter. The end of the steam main should have a minimum size of one-half of its greatest diameter. Small steam systems should be sized for a 2 oz. pressure drop. Large steam systems should be sized for a 4 oz. pressure drop.

11. The word *thermal,* as used in the above paragraph, means MOST NEARLY

    A. convector   B. heat   C. instrument   D. current

12. According to the above paragraph, the one of the following that is one size larger than the vertical pipe is the

    A. steam main
    B. valve
    C. water line
    D. runout

13. According to the above paragraph, small steam systems should be sized for a pressure drop of _____ ounces.

    A. 2   B. 3   C. 4   D. 5

14. According to the above paragraph, ends of mains with gravity return shall be AT LEAST

    A. 18" above the water line of the boiler
    B. one-quarter of the greatest diameter of the main
    C. twice the size of the vertical pipe in the main
    D. 18" above the steam line of the boiler

15. According to the above paragraph, the one of the following that is provided at each main to relieve air pressure is a(n)

    A. gravity return
    B. convector
    C. eccentric
    D. vent

Questions 16-17.

DIRECTIONS: Questions 16 and 17 are to be answered SOLELY on the basis of the following paragraph.

In determining the size of a storm drain, a number of factors must be taken into consideration. One factor which makes sizing the storm drain difficult is the matter of predicting rainfall over a given period. Using a maximum estimate of about 1 inch of rain in a 10-minute interval, the approximate volume of water that will fall on a roof or surface in one minute's time can be determined readily. Another factor is the pitch and material of a roof or surface upon which the rain falls. A surface that has a pitch and smooth surface would increase the flow of water into a drain pipe.

16. According to the above paragraph, the statement which includes all factors needed to determine the size of a drain pipe is the

   A. maximum rainfall on a surface
   B. pitch and surface of the area
   C. amount of water to be piped in a definite time interval
   D. area of the surface

17. A roof that has a 45° pitch would PROBABLY have a drain pipe size

   A. smaller than a roof with no pitch
   B. larger than a roof with no pitch
   C. equal to that of a flat roof
   D. equal to the amount of water falling in ten minutes

Questions 18-19.

DIRECTIONS: Questions 18 and 19 are to be answered SOLELY on the basis of the following paragraph.

Because of the large capacity of unit heaters, care should be taken to see that the steam piping leading to them is of sufficient size. Unit heaters should not be used on one-pipe systems. If the heating system contains direct radiators operated with steam under vacuum, it is best to have the unit heaters served by a separate main so that steam above atmospheric pressure can be supplied to the units, if desired, without interfering with the operation of the direct radiators.

18. According to the above paragraph, unit heaters are supplied with

   A. steam under vacuum
   B. steam from direct radiators
   C. separate steam lines
   D. steam preferably from a one-pipe system

19. According to the above paragraph, it may be said that unit heaters work BEST with

   A. steam above atmospheric pressure   B. direct radiators
   C. one-pipe system   D. vacuum systems

Questions 20-21.

DIRECTIONS: Questions 20 and 21 are to be answered SOLELY on the basis of the following paragraph.

Most heating units emit heat by radiation and convection. An exposed radiator emits approximately half of its heat by radiation, the amount depending upon the size and number of sections. In general, a thin radiator, such as a wall radiator, emits a larger proportion of its heat by radiation than does a thick radiator. When a radiator is enclosed or shielded, the proportion of heat emitted by radiation is reduced. The balance of the emission occurs by conduction to the air in contact with the heating surface, and this heated air rises by circulation due to convection and transmits this warm air to the space which is to be heated.

20. According to the above paragraph, when a radiator is enclosed, a GREATER portion of the heat is emitted to the room by

    A. convection
    B. radiation
    C. conduction
    D. transmission

21. According to the above paragraph, the amount of heat that a radiator emits is

    A. approximately half of its heat by radiation
    B. determined by the thickness of the radiator
    C. dependent upon whether it is exposed or enclosed
    D. dependent upon the size and number of sections of the radiator

Questions 22-25.

DIRECTIONS: Questions 22 through 25 are to be answered SOLELY on the basis of the following paragraph.

Safety valves are required to operate without chattering and to be set to close after blowing down not more than 4% of the set pressure, but not less than 2 lbs. in any case. For pressure between 100 and 300 lbs., inclusive, the blow down is required to be not less than 2% of the set pressure. The blow down adjustment is made and sealed by the manufacturer. The popping-point tolerance plus or minus is required not to exceed 2 lbs. for pressure up to and including 70 lbs., 3 lbs. for pressure 71 to 300 lbs., and 10 lbs. for pressure over 300 lbs.

22. A boiler is being installed to operate at a maximum allowable pressure of 10 lb., and the safety valve has been set to blow at this pressure.
    This valve should close after the boiler blows down to NOT MORE THAN _____ lb.

    A. 9.6   B. 4.0   C. 9.8   D. 8.0

23. A boiler is being installed to operate at a maximum allowable working pressure of 300 lb., and the safety valve is set to blow at this pressure. This valve should close after the boiler blows down to NOT MORE THAN _____ lb.

    A. 204   B. 298   C. 12   D. 6

24. A sealed safety valve is to be installed on a superheater header in a power steam generating plant. The marking on this valve shows that it is set to pop at 425 lb.
This valve would operate satisfactorily if it popped at EITHER _____ or _____ lb.

   A. 425; 445
   B. 415; 435
   C. 372.5; 467.5
   D. 412.25; 437.75

25. A sealed safety valve is to be installed on a boiler in a high pressure steam generating station. The marking on the valve shows that it is set to pop at 300 lb.
This valve would operate satisfactorily if it popped at EITHER _____ or _____ lb.

   A. 290; 310
   B. 297; 303
   C. 291; 309
   D. 288; 312

KEY (CORRECT ANSWERS)

1.	A		11.	B
2.	D		12.	D
3.	D		13.	A
4.	A		14.	A
5.	D		15.	D
6.	B		16.	C
7.	D		17.	B
8.	B		18.	C
9.	C		19.	A
10.	B		20.	A

21. D
22. D
23. A
24. B
25. B

TEST 2

DIRECTIONS: Each question or incomplete statement is followed by several suggested answers or completions. Select the one that BEST answers the question or completes the statement. *PRINT THE LETTER OF THE CORRECT ANSWER IN THE SPACE AT THE RIGHT.*

Questions 1-6.

DIRECTIONS: Questions 1 through 6 are to be answered SOLELY on the basis of the following paragraph.

FIRST AID INSTRUCTIONS

The main purpose of first aid is to put the injured person in the best possible position until medical help arrives. This includes the performance of emergency treatment for the purpose of saving a life if a doctor is not present. When a person is hurt, a crowd usually gathers around the victim. If nobody uses his head, the injured person fails to get the care he needs. You must stay calm and, most important, it is your duty to take charge at an accident. The first thing for you to do is to see, as best you can, what is wrong with the injured person. Leave the victim where he is until the nature and extent of his injury are determined. If he is unconscious, he should not be moved, except to lay him flat on his back if he is in some other position. Loosen the clothing of any seriously hurt person, and make him as comfortable as possible. Medical help should be called as soon as possible. You should remain with the injured person and send someone else to call the doctor. You should try to make sure that the one who calls for a doctor is able to give correct information as to the location of the injured person. In order to help the physician to know what equipment may be needed in each particular case, the person making the call should give the doctor as much information about the injury as possible.

1. If nobody uses his head at the scene of an accident, there is danger that

    A. no one will get the names of all the witnesses
    B. a large crowd will gather
    C. the victim will not get the care he needs
    D. the victim will blame the city for negligence

2. When an accident occurs, the FIRST thing you should do is

    A. call a doctor
    B. loosen the clothing of the injured person
    C. notify the victim's family
    D. try to find out what is wrong with the injured person

3. If you do NOT know the extent and nature of the victim's injuries, you should

    A. let the injured person lie where he is
    B. immediately take the victim to a hospital yourself
    C. help the injured person to his feet to see if he can walk
    D. have the injured person sit up on the ground while you examine him

4. If the injured person is breathing and unconscious, you should

   A. get some hot liquid such as coffee or tea into him
   B. give him artificial respiration
   C. lift up his head to try to stimulate blood circulation
   D. see that he lies flat on his back

5. If it is necessary to call a doctor, you should

   A. go and make the call yourself since you have all the information
   B. find out who the victim's family doctor is before making the call
   C. have someone else make the call who know the location of the victim
   D. find out which doctor the victim can afford

6. It is important for the caller to give the doctor as much information as is available regarding the injury so that the doctor

   A. can bring the necessary equipment
   B. can make out an accident report
   C. will be responsible for any malpractice resulting from the first aid treatment
   D. can inform his nurse on how long he will be in the field

Questions 7-8.

DIRECTIONS: Questions 7 and 8 are to be answered SOLELY on the basis of the following paragraph.

PRECIPITATION AND RUNOFF

In the United States, the average annual precipitation is about 30 inches, of which about 21 inches is lost to the atmosphere by evaporation and transpiration. The remaining 9 inches becomes runoff into rivers and lakes. Both the precipitation and runoff vary greatly with geography and season. Annual precipitation varies from more than 100 inches in parts of the northwest to only 2 or 3 inches in parts of the southwest. In the northeastern part of the country, including New York State, the annual average precipitation is about 45 inches, of which about 22 inches becomes runoff. Even in New York State, there is some variation from place to place and considerable variation from time to time. During extremely dry years, the precipitation may be as low as 30 inches and the runoff below 10 inches. In general, there are greater variations in runoff rates from smaller watersheds. A critical water supply situation occurs when there are three or four abnormally dry years in succession.

Precipitation over the state is measured and recorded by a network of stations operated by the U.S. Weather Bureau. All of the precipitation records and other data such as temperature, humidity, and evaporation rates are published monthly by the Weather Bureau in *Climatological Data*. Runoff rates at more than 200 stream-gauging stations in the state are measured and recorded by the U.S. Geological Survey in cooperation with various state agencies. Records of the daily average flows are published annually by the U.S. Geological Survey in *Surface Water Records of New York*. Copies may be obtained by writing to the Water Resources Division, United States Geological Survey, Albany, New York 23301.

7. From the above paragraphs, it is APPROPRIATE to conclude that 7.____

   A. critical supply situations do not occur
   B. the greater the rainfall, the greater the runoff
   C. there are greater variations in runoff from larger watersheds
   D. the rainfall in the southwest is greater than the average in the country

8. From the above paragraphs, it is APPROPRIATE to conclude that 8.____

   A. an annual rainfall of about 50 inches does not occur in New York State
   B. the U.S. Weather Bureau is only interested in rainfall
   C. runoff is equal to rainfall less losses to the atmosphere
   D. information about rainfall and runoff in New York State is unavailable to the public

Questions 9-10.

DIRECTIONS: Questions 9 through 10 are to be answered SOLELY on the basis of the following paragraph.

NATURAL LAKES

Large lakes may yield water of exceptionally fine quality except near the shore line and in the vicinity of sewer outlets or near outlets of large streams. Therefore, minimum treatment is required. The availability of practically unlimited quantities of water is also a decided advantage. Unfortunately, however, the sewage from a city is often discharged into the same lake from which the water supply is taken. Great care must be taken in locating both the water intake and the sewer outlet so that the pollution handled by the water treatment plant is a minimum.

Sometimes the distance from the shore where dependable, satisfactory water can be found is so great that the cost of water intake facilities is prohibitive for a small municipality. In such cases, another supply must be found, or water must be obtained from a neigh-boring large city. Lake water is usually uniform in quality from day to day and does not vary in temperature as much as water from a river or small impounding reservoir.

9. A DISADVANTAGE of drawing a water supply from a large lake is that 9.____

   A. expensive treatment is required
   B. a limited quantity of water is available
   C. nearby cities may dump sewage into the lake
   D. the water is too cold

10. An ADVANTAGE of drawing a water supply from a large lake is that the 10.____

    A. water is uniform in quality
    B. water varies in temperature
    C. intake is distant from the shore
    D. intake may be near a sewer outlet

Questions 11-13.

DIRECTIONS: Questions 11 through 13 are to be answered SOLELY on the basis of the following paragraph.

Excavation of trench—The trench shall be excavated as directed; one side of the street or avenue shall be left open for traffic at all times. In paved streets, the length of trench that may be opened between the point where the backfilling has been completed and the point where the pavement is being removed shall not exceed fifteen hundred feet for pipes 24 inches or less in diameter. For pipes larger than 24-inch, the length of open trenches shall not exceed one thousand feet. The completion of the backfilling shall be interpreted to mean the backfilling of the trench and the consolidation of the backfill so that vehicular traffic can be resumed over the backfill, and also the placing of any temporary pavement that may be required.

11. According to the above paragraph, the street

    A. can be closed to traffic in emergencies
    B. can be closed to traffic only when laying more than 1500 feet of pipe
    C. is closed to traffic as directed
    D. shall be left open for traffic at all times

12. According to the above paragraph, the MAXIMUM length of open trench permitted in paved streets depends on the

    A. traffic on the street
    B. type of ground that is being excavated
    C. water conditions met with in excavation
    D. diameter of the pipe being laid

13. According to the above paragraph, the one of the following items that is included in the *completion of the backfilling* is

    A. sheeting and bracing   B. cradle
    C. temporary pavement   D. bridging

Questions 14-16.

DIRECTIONS: Questions 14 through 16 are to be answered SOLELY on the basis of the following paragraph.

The Contractor shall notify the Engineer by noon of the day immediately preceding the date when he wishes to shut down any main; and if the time set be approved, the Contractor shall provide the men necessary to shut down the main at the time stipulated, and to previously notify all consumers whose supply may be affected. These men shall be under the direction of the Department employees, who will superintend all operations of valves and hydrants. Shut-downs for making connections will not be made unless and until the Contractor has everything on the ground in readiness for the work.

14. According to the above paragraph, before a contractor can make a shut-down, he MUST notify the

    A. police department   B. District Foreman
    C. Engineer   D. Highway Department

15. According to the above paragraph, the operation of the valves will be supervised by the   15.____

    A. Department employees
    B. Contractor's men
    C. Contractor's superintendent
    D. Engineer

16. According to the above paragraph, shut-downs for connections are made   16.____

    A. the day before the connection is to be made
    B. first and then consumers are notified
    C. at any time convenient to the Contractor
    D. when the Contractor has everything on the ground in readiness for the work

Questions 17-22.

DIRECTIONS: Questions 17 through 22 are to be answered SOLELY on the basis of the following paragraphs.

HOT WATER GENERATION

The hot water that comes from a faucet is called Domestic Hot Water. It is heated by a steam coil that runs through a storage tank full of water in the basement of each building.

As the tenants take the hot water, fresh cold water enters the tank and is heated. The temperature of this water is automatically kept at approximately 140° F.

The device which controls the temperature is called a temperature regulator valve. It is operated by a bellows, capillary tube, and thermo bulb which connects between the valve and the hot water being stored in the tank. This bulb, tube, and bellows contains a liquid which expands and contracts with changes in temperatures.

As the water in the tank reaches 140° F, the liquid in the thermo bulb expands and causes pressure to travel along the capillary tube and into the bellows. The expanded liquid forces the bellows to push the Temperature Regulator Valve Stem down, closing the valve. No more steam can enter the coil in the tank, and the water will get no hotter.

As the hot water is used by the tenants, cold water enters the tank and pulls the temperature down. This causes the liquid in the thermo bulb to cool and contract (shrink). The pressure is no longer in the bellows, and a spring pushes it up, allowing the valve to open and allowing steam to again enter the heating coil in the storage tank, raising the temperature of the Domestic Hot Water to 140° F.

17. Domestic hot water is heated by   17.____

    A. coal   B. electricity
    C. hot water   D. steam

18. The temperature of domestic hot water is MOST NEARLY   18.____

    A. 75° F   B. 100° F   C. 140° F   D. 212° F

19. The temperature of the hot water is controlled by a

    A. thermometer
    B. temperature regulator valve
    C. pressuretrol
    D. pressure gauge

20. The temperature regulator valve is operated by a combination of a

    A. thermometer and a thermo bulb
    B. thermometer and a pyrometer
    C. bellows, capillary tube, and a thermometer
    D. bellows, capillary tube, and a thermo bulb

21. Closing of the temperature regulator valve prevents _____ from entering the heating coil in the tank.

    A. water   B. steam
    C. electricity   D. air

22. As hot water is used by the tenants, the temperature of the water in the tank

    A. increases   B. decreases
    C. remains the same   D. approaches 212° F

Question 23.

DIRECTIONS: Question 23 is to be answered SOLELY on the basis of the following paragraph.

Lack of service meters has a definite effect on water consumption. Metering of all services of a city should reduce consumption to about 50 percent of the consumption without meters. Although metering reduces water consumption, there is a tendency for consumption to increase gradually after all services are metered.

23. According to the above paragraph, the one of the following statements that is CORRECT is:

    A. Consumption of water is cut approximately in half by metering, but once all services are metered, the consumption then increases gradually
    B. After all services are metered, water consumption continues to decrease steadily
    C. Metering of all services reduces the consumption of water by much more than half
    D. Water consumption is not affected by metering of all services

Question 24.

DIRECTIONS: Questions 24 is to be answered SOLELY on the basis of the following paragraph.

A venturi meter operates without moving parts and hence is the simplest type of meter in use so far as its construction is concerned. It is a velocity meter, and it is suitable for measuring only high rates of flow. Rates of flow below its capacity limit are not accurately measured. It is, therefore, not suitable for use in measuring the low intermittent demand of most consumers.

24. According to the above paragraph, the flow in a pipe which would MOST accurately be measured by a venturi meter is   24._____

    A. an intermittent flow below the meter's capacity
    B. a steady flow below the meter's capacity
    C. a steady flow at the meter's capacity
    D. intermittent flows above or below capacity of the meter

Question 25.

DIRECTIONS: Question 25 is to be answered SOLELY on the basis of the following paragraph.

A house service water supply connection may be taken from the sprinkler water supply connection to the public main if the diameter of the house service water supply connection is not greater than onehalf the diameter of the sprinkler water supply connection. No shutoff valve shall be placed on the sprinkler supply line other than the main shut-off valve for the building on the street side of the house service water supply connection. If such a connection is made and if a tap also exists for the house service water supply, the tap shall be plugged.

25. According to the above paragraph, the one of the following statements that is CORRECT is: 25._____

    A. A sprinkler water supply connection should be at least twice the diameter of any house service water supply connection taken from it
    B. A shut-off valve, in addition to the main shut-off valve, is required on sprinkler supply lines on the street side of the house service water supply connection
    C. Where a house service water supply is connected to the sprinkler water supply and there is a tap for the house service water supply, the tap may remain in service
    D. A house service water supply connection may be taken off each side of the main shut-off valve of the sprinkler water supply

KEY (CORRECT ANSWERS)

1. C
2. D
3. A
4. D
5. C

6. A
7. B
8. C
9. C
10. A

11. D
12. D
13. C
14. C
15. A

16. D
17. D
18. C
19. B
20. D

21. B
22. B
23. A
24. C
25. A

TEST 3

DIRECTIONS: Each question or incomplete statement is followed by several suggested answers or completions. Select the one that BEST answers the question or completes the statement. *PRINT THE LETTER OF THE CORRECT ANSWER IN THE SPACE AT THE RIGHT.*

Questions 1-4.

DIRECTIONS: Questions 1 through 4 are to be answered SOLELY on the basis of the following paragraph.

Welds in sheet metal up to 1/16 inch in thickness can be made satisfactorily by flanging the edges of the joint. The edges are prepared by turning up a very thin lip or flange along the line of the joint. The height of this flange should be equal to the thickness of the sheet being welded. The edges should be aligned so that the flanges stand up, and the joint should be tack-welded every 5 or 6 inches. Heavy angles or bars should be clamped on each side of the joint to prevent distortion or buckling. No filler metal is required for making this joint. The raised edges are quickly melted by the heat of the welding flame so as to produce an even weld bead which is nearly flush with the original sheet metal surface. By controlling the speed of welding and the motion of the flame, good fusion to the under side of the sheets can be obtained without burning through.

1. According to the above paragraph, satisfactory welds may be made in sheet metal by flanging the edges.
   The MAXIMUM thickness of metal recommended is

   A. 20 gauge　　　　　　　　　B. 18 gauge
   C. 1/16"　　　　　　　　　　　D. 5/64"

2. According to the above paragraph, good fusion may be obtained without burning through of the metal by controlling the motion of the flame and the

   A. size of tip　　　　　　　　　B. speed of welding
   C. oxygen flow　　　　　　　　D. acetylene flow

3. According to the above paragraph, if the thickness of the metal is 1/32", then the flange height should be

   A. 1/64"　　　B. 1/32"　　　C. 1/16"　　　D. 1/8"

4. According to the above paragraph, distortion in the welding of sheet metal may be prevented by

   A. controlling the speed of welding
   B. use of a flange of correct height
   C. use of proper filler metal
   D. clamping angles on each side of the joint

Questions 5-12.

DIRECTIONS: Questions 5 through 12 are to be answered SOLELY on the basis of the Edison storage battery maintenance procedure below.

EDISON STORAGE BATTERY MAINTENANCE PROCEDURE

Take a voltage reading of each cell in the battery with a voltmeter. Any battery with two or more dead or reverse cells is to be removed and sent to the shop. All cell caps are to be opened, and the water level brought up to 2 3/4" above the plates. Any battery requiring a considerable amount of water must be called to the foreman's attention. All cell caps must be brushed clean and Edison battery oil applied to them. No batteries are to remain in service with cell caps broken or missing. The normal specific gravity reading of the solution must not be above 1.230 nor below 1.160. This reading is to be taken only on batteries which are found to be weak. Batteries with specific gravity lower than 1.160 must be sent to the shop. Be careful when disconnecting leads from the battery since a slight, turn of the connecting post will result in a dead cell due to the cell plates becoming short-circuited. When disconnecting leads, use a standard Edison terminal puller. When recording defective cells, give the battery number, the car number, and the position of the cell in the battery. No. 1 cell is the cell to which the positive battery lead is connected and so on up to the last cell, No. 26, to which the negative lead is connected.

5. A normal specific gravity reading would be

   A. 1.450 B. 1.294 C. 1.200 D. 1.180

6. Batteries with below normal specific gravity reading MUST

   A. always have water added
   B. be called to the foreman's attention
   C. not be given a voltmeter test
   D. be sent to the shop

7. The battery leads are disconnected by using

   A. gas pliers
   B. Edison battery oil to free them
   C. a screwdriver to pry them off
   D. a standard Edison terminal puller

8. To completely record a defective cell, _____ required.

   A. only one identifying number is
   B. two identifying numbers are
   C. three identifying numbers are
   D. four identifying numbers are

9. A battery MUST be taken out of service if it has

   A. one dead cell   B. broken cell caps
   C. one reversed cell   D. a low water level

10. The battery water level should be brought up above the plates by _____ inches.

    A. 2.75 B. 1.370 C. 1.264 D. 0.600

11. Specific gravity readings are to be taken only on batteries which

 A. are removed from service
 B. have missing cell caps
 C. are weak
 D. have a high water level

12. Dead cells are sometimes caused by

 A. a slight turn of the connecting post
 B. taking unnecessary gravity readings
 C. adding too little battery oil
 D. adding too much water

Questions 13-14.

DIRECTIONS: Questions 13 and 14 are to be answered SOLELY on the basis of the following paragraph.

It cannot be stressed too strongly that the greatest care should be taken in handling tools. If they are handled carelessly, serious accidents may result. Many accidents can be avoided if the back of the trowel is kept clean and if the trowel is not allowed to contain too much mortar. Where there is an *excess* of mortar, some might drop or splash into the plasterer's eyes. Any mortar which is dropped onto the hands, wrists, ankles, or underclothing should be removed immediately.

13. The MAIN point of the above paragraph is that

 A. all accidents will be avoided if tools are kept clean
 B. most accidents can be avoided by the use of protective gloves
 C. many accidents are caused by careless handling of tools
 D. trowels should be kept free of mortar at all times

14. In the above paragraph, the word *excess* means MOST NEARLY

 A. surplus   B. minor   C. scant   D. short

Questions 15-18.

DIRECTIONS: Questions 15 through 18 are to be answered SOLELY on the basis of the following paragraph.

There are two unfounded ideas that must be discarded before tackling the lube-simplification job. *Oil is oil* was a common expression from the middle of the nineteenth century up to the early 1900s. Then, as the century got well underway, *the pendulum swung in a wide arc*. At present, we find many oils being used, each with supposedly special properties. The large number of lube oils used at present results from the rapid growth at the same time of machine development and oil refining. The refiner acts to market new oils for each machine developed, and the machine manufacturer feels that each new mechanical unit is different from the others and needs a special lube oil. These feelings may be well-founded, but in many cases they are based on misinformation or blind faith in certain lube oil qualities. At the present time, operators and even lube engineers are finding it tough to keep track of all the claimed properties of all the lube oils.

15. It follows from the sense of this paragraph that the idea that *oil is oil* is unfounded because 15.____

    A. it was conceived in the middle of the nineteenth century
    B. the basic and varying properties of lube oils have now been shown to exist
    C. lube oil properties, though fully known, were kept secret for economic reasons
    D. there was no need for but one basic lube oil in the latter part of the nineteenth century

16. In the above paragraph, the phrase *the pendulum swung in a wide arc* means MOST NEARLY 16.____

    A. oil refining was unable to keep up with machinery development
    B. before 1900, lube oil engineers found it difficult to keep track of lube oil characteristics
    C. the simplification of lube oils and their application was developed about 1900
    D. many different lube oils with varying characteristics were marketed

17. As indicated in this paragraph, the simplification of the characteristics and the uses of lube oils is needed because the 17.____

    A. manufacturers develop new machines to overcome competition
    B. change in process at the refineries for a new lube oil is costly
    C. present market is flooded with many so-called *special purpose* lube oils
    D. *blind faith* of the operators in lube oil qualities should be rewarded

18. A reason given for the claimed need for special lube oil, as indicated in this paragraph, is that 18.____

    A. development of new lube oils created the need for new machine units
    B. lube oil engineers developed new tests and standards
    C. basic crudes, from which lube oil is obtained, allow different refining methods
    D. newly developed machines are so very different from each other

Questions 19-22.

DIRECTIONS: Questions 19 through 22 are to be answered SOLELY on the basis of the following paragraph.

ACCIDENT PREVENTION

Many accidents and injuries can be prevented if employees learn to be more careful. The wearing of shoes with thin or badly worn soles or open toes can easily lead to foot injuries from tacks, nails, and chair and desk legs. Loose or torn clothing should not be worn near moving machinery. This is especially true of neckties, which can very easily become caught in the machine. You should not place objects so that they block or partly block hallways, corridors, or other passageways. Even when they are stored in the proper place, tools, supplies, and equipment should be carefully placed or piled so as not to fall, nor have anything stick out from a pile. Before cabinets, lockers, or ladders are moved, the tops should be cleared of anything which might injure someone or fall off. If necessary, use a dolly to move these or other bulky objects.

Despite all efforts to avoid accidents and injuries, however, some will happen. If an employee is injured, no matter how small the injury, he should report it to his supervisor and have the injury treated. A small cut that is not attended to can easily become infected and can cause more trouble than some injuries which at first seem more serious. It never pays to take chances.

19. According to the above passage, the one statement that is NOT true is that   19.___

    A. by being more careful, employees can reduce the number of accidents that happen
    B. women should wear shoes with open toes for comfort when working
    C. supplies should be piled so that nothing is sticking out from the pile
    D. if an employee sprains his wrist at work, he should tell his supervisor about it

20. According to the above passage, you should NOT wear loose clothing when you are   20.___

    A. in a corridor   B. storing tools
    C. opening cabinets   D. near moving machinery

21. According to the above passage, before moving a ladder, you should   21.___

    A. test all rungs
    B. get a dolly to carry the ladder at all times
    C. remove everything from the top of the ladder which might fall off
    D. remove your necktie

22. According to the above passage, an employee who gets a slight cut should   22.___

    A. have it treated to help prevent infection
    B. know that a slight cut becomes more easily infected than a big cut
    C. pay no attention to it as it can't become serious
    D. realize that it is more serious than any other type of injury

Questions 23-25.

DIRECTIONS: Questions 23 through 25 are to be answered SOLELY on the basis of the following paragraph.

Keeping the city operating day and night requires the services of more than 400,000 civil service workers – roughly the number of people who live in Syracuse. This huge army of specialists works at more than 2,000 different jobs. The city's civil service workers are able to do everything that needs doing to keep our city running. Their only purpose is the well-being, comfort, and safety of the citizens of the city.

23. Of the following titles, the one that MOST nearly gives the meaning of the above paragraph is   23.___

    A. CIVIL SERVICE IN SYRACUSE
    B. EVERYONE WORKS
    C. JOB VARIETY
    D. SERVING THE CITY

24. According to the above paragraph, in order to keep the city operating 24 hours a day, 24._____
    A. half of the civil service workers work days and half work nights
    B. more than 400,000 civil service workers are needed on the day shift
    C. the city needs about as many civil service workers as there are people in Syracuse
    D. the services of some people who live in Syracuse is required

25. According to the above paragraph, it is MOST reasonable to assume that in the city's civil 25._____
    service,
    A. a worker can do any job that needs doing
    B. each worker works at a different job
    C. some workers work at more than one job
    D. some workers work at the same jobs

KEY (CORRECT ANSWERS)

1. C	11. C
2. B	12. A
3. B	13. C
4. D	14. A
5. C	15. B
6. D	16. D
7. D	17. C
8. C	18. D
9. B	19. B
10. A	20. D

21. C
22. A
23. D
24. C
25. D

ARITHMETICAL REASONING
EXAMINATION SECTION
TEST 1

DIRECTIONS: Each question or incomplete statement is followed by several suggested answers or completions. Select the one that BEST answers the question or completes the statement. *PRINT THE LETTER OF THE CORRECT ANSWER IN THE SPACE AT THE RIGHT.*

1.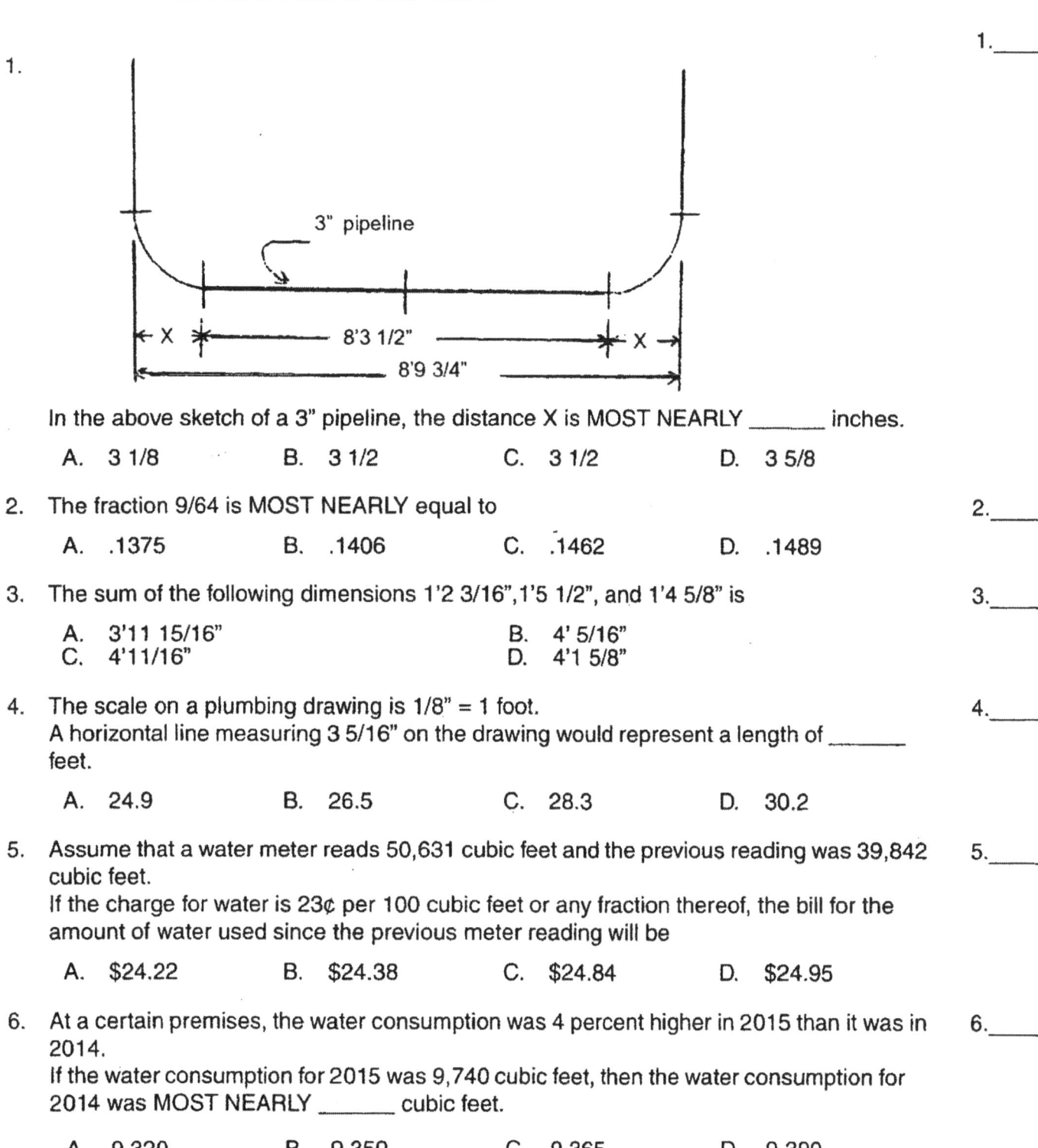

   In the above sketch of a 3" pipeline, the distance X is MOST NEARLY _____ inches.

   A. 3 1/8   B. 3 1/2   C. 3 1/2   D. 3 5/8

2. The fraction 9/64 is MOST NEARLY equal to

   A. .1375   B. .1406   C. .1462   D. .1489

3. The sum of the following dimensions 1'2 3/16", 1'5 1/2", and 1'4 5/8" is

   A. 3'11 15/16"   B. 4' 5/16"
   C. 4'11/16"   D. 4'1 5/8"

4. The scale on a plumbing drawing is 1/8" = 1 foot.
   A horizontal line measuring 3 5/16" on the drawing would represent a length of _____ feet.

   A. 24.9   B. 26.5   C. 28.3   D. 30.2

5. Assume that a water meter reads 50,631 cubic feet and the previous reading was 39,842 cubic feet.
   If the charge for water is 23¢ per 100 cubic feet or any fraction thereof, the bill for the amount of water used since the previous meter reading will be

   A. $24.22   B. $24.38   C. $24.84   D. $24.95

6. At a certain premises, the water consumption was 4 percent higher in 2015 than it was in 2014.
   If the water consumption for 2015 was 9,740 cubic feet, then the water consumption for 2014 was MOST NEARLY _____ cubic feet.

   A. 9,320   B. 9,350   C. 9,365   D. 9,390

7. A pump delivers water at a constant rate of 40 gallons per minute.
   If there are 7.5 gallons to a cubic foot of water, the time it will take to fill a tank 6 feet x 5 feet x 4 feet is MOST NEARLY _____ minutes.

   A. 15   B. 22.5   C. 28.5   D. 30

8. The total weight, in pounds, of three lengths of 3" cast-iron pipe 7'6" long, weighing 14.5 pounds per foot, and four lengths of 4" cast-iron pipe each 5'0" long, weighing 13.0 pounds per foot, is MOST NEARLY

   A. 540   B. 585   C. 600   D. 665

9. The water pressure at the bottom of a column of water 34 feet high is 14.7 lbs./sq.in. The water pressure in lbs./sq.in. at the bottom of the column of water 12 feet high is MOST NEARLY

   A. 3   B. 5   C. 7   D. 9

10. The number of cubic yards of earth that would be removed when digging a trench 8 feet wide x 9 feet deep x 63 feet long is

    A. 56   B. 168   C. 314   D. 504

11. On test, a meter registered one cubic foot for each 1 1/3 cubic feet of water that passed through it.
    If the meter had a reading of 1,200 cubic feet, we may conclude that the CORRECT amount should be _____ cubic feet.

    A. 800   B. 900   C. 1,500   D. 1,600

12. A water use meter reads 87,463 cubic feet.
    If the previous reading was 17,377 cubic feet and the rate charged is 15 cents per 100 cubic feet, the bill for water use during this period is about

    A. $45.00   B. $65.00   C. $85.00   D. $105.00

13. Under proper conditions, the one of the following groups of pipes that gives the same flow in gals/min as one 6" diameter pipe is (neglect friction) _____ pipes of _____ diameter each.

    A. 3; 3"   B. 4; 3"   C. 2; 4"   D. 3; 4"

14. A roof tank is used to furnish the domestic water supply to a ten story building. This tank has a capacity of 5,900 gallons. At 10:00 A.M. one morning, the tank is half full.
    If water is being used at the rate of 50 gals/min, the pump which is used to fill the tank has a rated capacity of 90 gals/min, the time it would take to fill the tank under these conditions is MOST NEARLY _____ hour(s), _____ minutes.

    A. 2; 8   B. 1; 14   C. 2; 32   D. 1; 2

15. The number of gallons of water contained in a cylindrical swimming pool 8 feet in diameter and filled to a depth of 3 feet 6 inches is MOST NEARLY (assume 7.5 gallons = 1 cubic foot)

    A. 30   B. 225   C. 1,320   D. 3,000

16. The charge for metered water is 52 1/2 cents per hundred cubic feet, with a minimum charge of $21 per annum. Of the following, the SMALLEST water usage in hundred cubic feet that would result in a charge GREATER than the minimum is

   A. 39 B. 40 C. 41 D. 42

17. The annual frontage rent on a one-story building 40 ft. in length is $735.00. For each additional story, $52.50 per annum is added to the frontage rent. For demolition, the charge for wetting down is 3/8 of the annual frontage charge.
   The charge for wetting down a building six stories in height, with a 40 ft. frontage, is MOST NEARLY

   A. $369 B. $371 C. $372 D. $374

18. If the drawing of a piping layout is made to a scale of 1/4" equals one foot, then a 7'9" length of piping would be represented by a scaled length on the drawing of APPROXIMATELY _____ inches.

   A. 2 B. 7 3/4 C. 23 1/4 D. 31

19. A plumbing sketch is drawn to a scale of eighth-size. A line measuring 3" on the sketch would be equivalent to _____ feet.

   A. 2 B. 6 C. 12 D. 24

20. If 500 feet of pipe weighs 800 lbs., the number of pounds that 120 feet will weigh is MOST NEARLY

   A. 190 B. 210 C. 230 D. 240

21. If a trench is excavated 3'0" wide by 5'6" deep and 50 feet long, the total number of cubic yards of earth removed is MOST NEARLY

   A. 30 B. 90 C. 150 D. 825

22. Assume that a plumber earns $86,500 per year.
   If eighteen percent of his pay is deducted for taxes and social security, his net weekly pay will be APPROXIMATELY

   A. $1,326 B. $1,365 C. $1,436 D. $1,457.50

23. Assume that a plumbing installation is made up of the following fixtures and groups of fixtures: 12 bathroom groups each containing one W.C., one lavatory, and one bathtub with shower; 12 bathroom groups each containing one W.C., one lavatory, one bathtub, and one shower stall; 24 combination kitchen fixtures; 4 floor drains; 6 slop sinks without flushing rim; and 2 shower stalls (or shower bath).
   The total number of fixtures for the above plumbing installation is MOST NEARLY

   A. 60 B. 95 C. 120 D. 210

24. A triangular opening in a wall forms a 30-60 degree right triangle.
   If the longest side measures 12'0", then the shortest side will measure

   A. 3'0" B. 4'0" C. 6'0" D. 8'0"

25. You are directed to cut 4 pieces of pipe, one each of the following length: 2'6 1/4", 3'9 3/8", 4'7 5/8", and 5'8 7/8".
The total length of these 4 pieces is

   A. 15'7 1/4"   B. 15'9 3/8"   C. 16'5 7/8"   D. 16'8 1/8"

25.___

KEY (CORRECT ANSWERS)

1. A
2. B
3. B
4. B
5. C

6. C
7. B
8. B
9. B
10. B

11. D
12. D
13. B
14. B
15. C

16. C
17. D
18. A
19. A
20. A

21. A
22. B
23. C
24. C
25. D

5 (#1)

SOLUTIONS TO PROBLEMS

1. 8'3 1/2" + x + x = 8'9 3/4" Then, 2x = 6 1/4", so x = 3 1/8"

2. 9/64 = .140625 = .1406

3. 1'2 3/16" + 1'5 1/2" + 1'4 5/8" = 3'11 21/16" = 4'5/16"

4. 3 5/16" ÷ 1/8" = 53/16 x 8/1 = 26.5. Then, (26.5)(1 ft.) = 26.5 feet

5. 50,631 - 39,842 = 10,789; 10,789 ÷ 100 = 107.89
   Since the cost is .23 per 100 cubic feet or any fraction thereof, the cost will be
   (.23)(107) + .23 = $24.84

6. 9740 ÷ 1.04 = 9365 cu.ft.

7. 40 ÷ 7.5 = 5 1/3 cu.ft. of water per minute. The volume = (6)(5)(4) = 120 cu.ft. Thus, the number of minutes needed to fill the tank is 120 ÷ 5 1/3 = 22.5

8. 3" pipe: 3 x 7'6" = 22 1/2' x 14.5 lbs. = 326.25
   4" pipe: 4 x 5' = 20' x 13 lbs. = 260
   326.25 + 260 = 586.25 (most nearly 585)

9. Let x = pressure. Then, 34/12 = 14.7/x. So, 34x = 176.4
   Solving, x ≈ 5 lbs./sq.in.

10. (8)(9)(63) = 4536 cu.ft. Since 1 cu.yd. = 27 cu.ft., 4536 cu.ft. is equivalent to 168 cu.yds.

11. Let x = correct amount. Then, $\dfrac{1}{1200} = \dfrac{1\frac{1}{3}}{x}$. Solving, x = 1600

12. 87,463 - 17,377 = 70,086; and 70,086 ÷ 100 = 700.86 ≈ 700 Then, (700)(.15) = $105.00

13. Cross-sectional area of a 6" diameter pipe = $(\pi)(3")^2 = 9\pi$ sq. in. Note that the combined cross-sectional areas of four 3" diameter pipes = $(4)(\pi)(1.5")^2 = 9\pi$ sq. in.

14. 90 - 50 = 40 gals/min. Then, 2950 ÷ 40 = 73.75 min. ≈ 1 hr. 14 min.

15. Volume = $(\pi)(4)^2(3\ 1/2) = 56\pi$ cu.ft. Then, $(56\pi)(7.5) = 1320$ gals.

16. For 4100 cu.ft., the charge of (.525)(41) = $21,525 > $21

17. Rent = $73,500 + (5)($52.50) = $997,50. For demolition, the charge = (3/8)($997.50)
    $374

18. (1/4")(7.75) = 2"

19. (3")(8) = 24" = 2 ft.

6 (#1)

20. Let x = weight. Then, 500/800 = 120/x . Solving, x = 192 190 lbs.

21. (3')(5 1/2')(50') = 825 cu.ft. Then, 825 ÷ 27 ≈ 30 cu.yds.

22. Net pay = (.82)($86,500) = $70,930/yr. Weekly pay = $70,930 ÷ 52 ≈ $1365

23. (12x3) + (12x4) +24+4+6+2= 120

24. The shortest side = (1/2)(hypotenuse) = (1/2)(12') = 6'

25. 2'6 1/4" + 3'9 3/8" + 4'7 5/8" + 5'8 7/8 " = 14'30 17/8" = 16'8 1/8"

TEST 2

DIRECTIONS: Each question or incomplete statement is followed by several suggested answers or completions. Select the one that BEST answers the question or completes the statement. *PRINT THE LETTER OF THE CORRECT ANSWER IN THE SPACE AT THE RIGHT.*

1. The sum of the following pipe lengths, 15 5/8", 8 3/4", 30 5/16" and 20 1/2", is   1._____

    A. 77 1/8"   B. 76 3/16"   C. 75 3/16"   D. 74 5/16"

2. If the outside diameter of a pipe is 6 inches and the wall thickness is 1/2 inch, the inside area of this pipe, in square inches, is MOST NEARLY   2._____

    A. 15.7   B. 17.3   C. 19.6   D. 23.8

3. Three lengths of pipe 1'10", 3'2 1/2", and 5'7 1/2", respectively, are to be cut from a pipe 14'0" long.
Allowing 1/8" for each pipe cut, the length of pipe remaining is   3._____

    A. 3'1 1/8"   B. 3'2 1/2"   C. 3'3 1/4"   D. 3'3 5/8"

4. According to the building code, the MAXIMUM permitted surface temperature of combustible construction materials located near heating equipment is 76.5°C. (°F=(°Cx9/5)+32) Maximum temperature Fahrenheit is MOST NEARLY   4._____

    A. 170° F   B. 195° F   C. 210° F   D. 220° F

5. A pump discharges 7.5 gals/minutes.
In 2.5 hours the pump will discharge _____ gallons.   5._____

    A. 1125   B. 1875   C. 1950   D. 2200

6. A pipe with an outside diameter of 4" has a circumference of MOST NEARLY _____ inches.   6._____

    A. 8.05   B. 9.81   C. 12.57   D. 14.92

7. A piping sketch is drawn to a scale of 1/8" = 1 foot.
A vertical steam line measuring 3 1/2" on the sketch would have an ACTUAL length of _____ feet.   7._____

    A. 16   B. 22   C. 24   D. 28

8. A pipe having an inside diameter of 3.48 inches and a wall thickness of .18 inches will have an outside diameter of _____ inches.   8._____

    A. 3.84   B. 3.64   C. 3.57   D. 3.51

9. A rectangular steel bar having a volume of 30 cubic inches, a width of 2 inches, and a height of 3 inches will have a length of _____ inches.   9._____

    A. 12   B. 10   C. 8   D. 5

10. A pipe weighs 20.4 pounds per foot of length.
The total weight of eight pieces of this pipe with each piece 20 feet in length is MOST NEARLY _____ pounds.   10._____

    A. 460   B. 1,680   C. 2,420   D. 3,260

11. Assume that four pieces of pipe measuring 2'1 1/4", 4'2 3/4", 5'1 9/16", and 6'3 5/8", respectively, are cut with a saw from a pipe 20"0" long.
Allowing 1/16" waste for each cut, the length of the remaining pipe is

    A. 2'1 9/16" B. 2'2 9/16" C. 2'4 13/16" D. 2'8 9/16"

12. If one cubic inch of steel weighs 0.28 pounds, the weight, in pounds, of a steel bar 1/2" x 6" x 2'0" long is MOST NEARLY

    A. 11 B. 16 C. 20 D. 24

13. If the circumference of a circle is equal to 31.416 inches, then its diameter, in inches, is equal to MOST NEARLY

    A. 8 B. 9 C. 10 D. 13

14. Assume that a steam fitter's helper receives a salary of $171.36 a day for 250 days is considered a full work year. If taxes, social security, hospitalization, and pension deducted from his salary amounts to 16 percent of his gross pay, then his net yearly salary will be MOST NEARLY

    A. $31,788 B. $35,982 C. $41,982 D. $42,840

15. If the outside diameter of a pipe is 14 inches and the wall thickness is 1/2 inch, then the inside area of the pipe, in square inches, is MOST NEARLY

    A. 125 B. 133 C. 143 D. 154

16. A steam leak in a pipe line allows steam to escape at a rate of 50,000 pounds each month.
Assuming that the cost of steam is $2.50 per 1,000 pounds, the TOTAL cost of wasted steam from this leak for a 12-month period would amount to

    A. $125 B. $300 C. $1,500 D. $3,000

17. If 250 feet of 4" pipe weighs 400 pounds, the weight of this pipe per linear foot is _____ pounds.

    A. 1.25 B. 1.50 C. 1.60 D. 1.75

18. A set of heating plan drawings is drawn to a scale of 1/4" = 1 foot.
If a length of pipe measures 4 5/8" on the drawing, the ACTUAL length of the pipe, in feet, is

    A. 16.3 B. 16.8 C. 17.5 D. 18.5

19. The TOTAL length of four pieces of pipe whose lengths are 3'4 1/2", 2'1 5/16", 4'9 3/8", and 2'3 1/4", respectively, is

    A. 11'5 7/16" B. 11'6 7/16"
    C. 12'5 7/16" D. 12'6 7/16"

20. Assume that a pipe trench is 3 feet wide, 3 feet deep, and 300 feet long.
If the unit cost of excavating the trench is $120 per cubic yard, the TOTAL cost of excavating the trench is

    A. $1,200 B. $12,000 C. $27,000 D. $36,000

21. The TOTAL length of four pieces of 1 1/2" galvanized steel pipe whose lengths are 7 ft. + 3 1/2 inches, 4 ft. + 2 1/4 inches, 6 ft. + 7 inches, and 8 ft. +5 1/8 inches is

   A. 26 feet + 5 7/8 inches
   B. 25 ft. + 6 7/8 inches
   C. 25 feet + 4 1/4 inches
   D. 25 ft. + 3 3/8 inches

21._____

22. A swimming pool is 25' wide by 75' long and has an average depth of 5'. 1 cubic foot contains 7.5 gallons of water. The capacity, when filled to the overflow, is _____ gallons.

   A. 9,375   B. 65,625   C. 69,005   D. 70,312

22._____

23. The sum of 3 1/4, 5 1/8, 2 1/2 , and 3 3/8 is

   A. 14   B. 14 1/8   C. 14 1/4   D. 14 3/8

23._____

24. Assume that it takes 6 men 8 days to do a particular job. If you have only 4 men available to do this job and they all work at the same speed, then the number of days it would take to complete the job would be

   A. 11   B. 12   C. 13   D. 14

24._____

25. The total length of four pieces of 2" O.D. pipe, whose lengths are 7'3 1/2", 4'2 3/16", 5'7 5/16", and 8'5 7/8", respectively, is MOST NEARLY

   A. 24'6 3/4"
   B. 24'7 15/16"
   C. 25'5 13/16"
   D. 25'6 7/8"

25._____

KEY (CORRECT ANSWERS)

1. C	11. B
2. C	12. C
3. D	13. C
4. A	14. B
5. A	15. B
6. C	16. C
7. D	17. C
8. A	18. D
9. D	19. D
10. D	20. B

21. A
22. D
23. C
24. B
25. D

SOLUTIONS TO PROBLEMS

1. 15 5/8" + 8 3/4" + 30 5/16" + 20 1/2" = 73 35/16" = 75 3/16"

2. Inside diameter = 6" - 1/2" - 1/2" = 5". Area = (π)(5/2")$^2 \approx$ 19.6 sq. in.

3. Pipe remaining = 14' - 1'10" - 3'2 1/2" - 5'7 1/2" - (3)(1/8") = 3'3 5/8"

4. 76.5 x 9/5 = 137.7 + 32 = 169.7

5. 7.5 x 150 = 1125

6. Radius = 2" Circumference = (2π)(2") $\approx$ 12.57"

7. 3 1/2" 1/8" = (7/2)(8/1) = 28 Then, (28)(1 ft.) = 28 feet

8. Outside diameter = 3.48" + .18" + .18" = 3.84"

9. 30 = (2)(3)(length). So, length = 5"

10. Total weight = (20.4)(8)(20) $\approx$ 3260 lbs.

11. 20' - 2'1 1/4" - 4'2 3/4" - 5'1 9/16" - 6'3 5/8" - (4)(1/16") = 2'2 9/16"

12. Weight = (.28)(1/2")(6")(24") = 20.16 $\approx$ 20 lbs.

13. Diameter = 31.416" $\div \pi \approx$ 10"

14. His net pay for 250 days = (.84)($171.36)(250) = $35,985.60 $\approx$ $35,928 (from answer key)

15. Inside diameter = 14" - 1/2" - 1/2" = 13". Area = (π)(13/2")$^2 \approx$ 133 sq.in

16. (50,000 lbs.)(12) = 600,000 lbs. per year. The cost would be ($2.50)(600) = $1500

17. 400 $\div$ 250 = 1.60 pounds per linear foot

18. 4 5/8" $\div$ 1/4" = 37/8 . 4/1 = 18.5 Then, (18.5)(1 ft.) = 18.5 feet

19. 3'4 1/2" + 2'1 5/16" + 4'9 3/8" + 2'3 1/4" = 11'17 23/16" = 12'6 7/16"

20. (3')(3')(300') = 2700 cu.ft., which is 2700 $\div$ 27 = 100 cu.yds. Total cost = ($120)(100) = $12,000

21. 7'3 1/2" + 4'2 1/4" + 6'7" + 8'5 1/8" = 25'17 7/8" = 26'5 7/8"

22. (25)(75)(5) = 9375 cu.ft. Then, (9375)(7.5) $\approx$ 70,312 gals.

23. 3 1/4 + 5 1/8 + 2 1/2 + 3 3/8 = 13 10/8 = 14 1/4

24. (6) (8) = 48 man-days. Then, 48 $\div$ 4 = 12 days

25. 7'3 1/2" + 4'2 3/16" + 5'7 5/16" + 8'5 7/8"= 24'17 30/16" = 25'6 7/8"

TEST 3

DIRECTIONS: Each question or incomplete statement is followed by several suggested answers or completions. Select the one that BEST answers the question or completes the statement. *PRINT THE LETTER OF THE CORRECT ANSWER IN THE SPACE AT THE RIGHT.*

1. The time required to pump 2,500 gallons of water out of a sump at the rate of 12 1/2 gallons per minutes would be _____ hour(s) _____ minutes. 1._____

    A. 1; 40   B. 2; 30   C. 3; 20   D. 6; 40

2. Copper tubing which has an inside diameter of 1 1/16" and a wall thickness of .095" has an outside diameter which is MOST NEARLY _____ inches. 2._____

    A. 1 5/32   B. 1 3/16   C. 1 7/32   D. 1 1/4

3. Assume that 90 gallons per minute flow through a certain 3-inch pipe which is tapped into a street main.
   The amount of water which would flow through a 1-inch pipe tapped into the same street main is MOST NEARLY _____ gpm. 3._____

    A. 90   B. 45   C. 30   D. 10

4. The weight of a 6 foot length of 8-inch pipe which weighs 24.70 pounds per foot is _____ lbs. 4._____

    A. 148.2   B. 176.8   C. 197.6   D. 212.4

5. If a 4-inch pipe is directly coupled to a 2-inch pipe and 16 gallons per minute are flowing through the 4-inch pipe, then the flow through the 2-inch pipe will be _____ gallons per minute. 5._____

    A. 4   B. 8   C. 16   D. 32

6. If the water pressure at the bottom of a column of water 34 feet high is 14.7 pounds per square inch, the water pressure at the bottom of a column of water 18 feet high is MOST NEARLY _____ pounds per square inch. 6._____

    A. 8.0   B. 7.8   C. 7.6   D. 7.4

7. If there are 7 1/2 gallons in a cubic foot of water and if water flows from a hose at a constant rate of 4 gallons per minute, the time it should take to COMPLETELY fill a tank of 1,600 cubic feet capacity with water from that hose is _____ hours. 7._____

    A. 300   B. 150   C. 100   D. 50

8. Each of a group of fifteen water meter readers read an average of 62 water meters a day in a certain 5-day work week. A total of 5,115 meters are read by this group the following week.
   The TOTAL number of meters read in the second week as compared to the first week shows a 8._____

    A. 10% increase   B. 15% increase
    C. 20% increase   D. 5% decrease

2 (#3)

9. A certain water consumer used 5% more water in 1994 than he did in 1993. If his water consumption for 1994 was 8,375 cubic feet, the amount of water he consumed in 1993 was MOST NEARLY _____ cubic feet.

   A. 9,014   B. 8,816   C. 7,976   D. 6,776

10. Assume that a water meter reads 40,175 cubic feet and that the previous reading was 29,186 cubic feet.
    If the charge for water is 92 cents per 100 cubic feet or any fraction thereof, the bill for the amount of water used since the previous meter reading should be

    A. $100.28   B. $101.04   C. $101.08   D. $101.20

11. A leaking faucet caused a loss of 216 cubic feet of water in a 30-day month. If there are 7.5 gallons in a cubic foot of water, then the AVERAGE loss of water per hour for that month was _____ gallons.

    A. 2 1/4   B. 2 1/8   C. 2   D. 1 3/4

12. The fraction which is equal to .375 is

    A. 3/16   B. 5/32   C. 3/8   D. 5/12

13. A square backyard swimming pool, each side of which is 10 feet long, is filled to a depth of 3 1/2 feet.
    If there are 7 1/2 gallons in a cubic foot of water, the number of gallons of water in the pool is MOST NEARLY _____ gallons.

    A. 46.7   B. 100   C. 2,625   D. 3,500

14. When 1 5/8, 3 3/4, 6 1/3, and 9 1/2 are added, the resulting sum is

    A. 21 1/8   B. 21 1/6   C. 21 5/24   D. 21 1/4

15. When 946 1/2 is subtracted from 1,035 1/4, the result is

    A. 87 1/4   B. 87 3/4   C. 88 1/4   D. 88 3/4

16. When 39 is multiplied by 697, the result is

    A. 8,364   B. 26,283   C. 27,183   D. 28,003

17. When 16.074 is divided by .045, the result is

    A. 3.6   B. 35.7   C. 357.2   D. 3,572

18. To dig a trench 3'0" wide, 50'0" long, and 5'6" deep, the total number of cubic yards of earth to be removed is MOST NEARLY

    A. 30   B. 90   C. 140   D. 825

19. The TOTAL length of four pieces of 2" pipe, whose lengths are 7'3 1/2", 4'2 3/16", 5'7 5/16", and 8'5 7/8", respectively, is

    A. 24'6 3/4"   B. 24'7 15/16"
    C. 25'5 13/16"   D. 25'6 7/8"

20. A hot water line made of copper has a straight horizontal run of 150 feet and, when installed, is at a temperature of 45° F. In use, its temperature rises to 190° F. If the coefficient of expansion for copper is 0.0000095" per foot per degree F, the TOTAL expansion, in inches, in the run of pipe is given by the product of 150 multiplied by 0.0000095 by

    A. 145
    B. 145 x 12
    C. 145 divided by 12
    D. 145 x 12 x 12

21. A water storage tank measures 5' long, 4' wide, and 6' deep and is filled to the 5 1/2' mark with water.
    If one cubic foot of water weighs 62 pounds, the number of pounds of water required to COMPLETELY fill the tank is

    A. 7,440   B. 6,200   C. 1,240   D. 620

22. Assume that a pipe worker earns $83,125.00 per year.
    If seventeen percent of his pay is deducted for taxes, social security, and pension, his net weekly pay will be APPROXIMATELY

    A. $1598.50   B. $1504.00   C. $1453.00   D. $1325.00

23. If eighteen feet of 4" cast iron pipe weighs approximately 390 pounds, the weight of this pipe per lineal foot will be MOST NEARLY _____ lbs.

    A. 19   B. 22   C. 23   D. 25

24. If it takes 3 men 11 days to dig a trench, the number of days it will take 5 men to dig the same trench, assuming all work is done at the same rate of speed, is MOST NEARLY

    A. 6 1/2   B. 7 3/4   C. 8 1/4   D. 8 3/4

25. If a trench is dug 6'0" deep, 2'6" wide, and 8'0" long, the area of the opening, in square feet, is MOST NEARLY

    A. 48   B. 32   C. 20   D. 15

KEY (CORRECT ANSWERS)

1. C
2. D
3. D
4. A
5. B

6. B
7. D
8. A
9. C
10. D

11. A
12. C
13. C
14. C
15. D

16. C
17. C
18. A
19. D
20. A

21. D
22. D
23. B
24. A
25. C

5 (#3)

SOLUTIONS TO PROBLEMS

1. 2500 ÷ 12 1/2 = 200 min. = 3 hrs. 20 min.

2. 1 1/16" + .095" + .095" = 1.0625 + .095 + .095 = 1.2525" ≈ 1 1/4"

3. Cross-sectional areas for a 3-inch pipe and a 1-inch pipe are $(\pi)(1.5)^2$ and $(\pi)(.5)^2$ = 2.25 π and .25 π, respectively. Let x = amount of water flowing through the 1-inch pipe. Then, $\frac{90}{x} = \frac{2.25\pi}{.25\pi}$. Solving, x = 10 gals/min

4. (24.70)(6) = 148.2 lbs.

5. $\frac{4" \text{ pipe}}{16 \text{ gallons}} = \frac{2" \text{ pipe}}{x \text{ gallons}}$, 4x = 32, x = 8

6. Let x = pressure. Then, 34/18 = 14.7/x . Solving, x ≈ 7.8

7. (1600)(7.5) = 12,000 gallons. Then, 12,000 ÷ 4 = 3000 min. = 50 hours

8. (15)(62)(5) = 4650. Then, (5115-4650)/4650 = 10% increase

9. 8375 ÷ 1.05 ≈ 7976 cu.ft.

10. 40,175 - 29,186 = 10,989 cu.ft. Then, 10,989 100 = 109.89. Since .92 is charged for each 100 cu.ft. or fraction thereof, total cost = (.92)(110) = $101.20

11. (216)(7.5) = 1620 gallons. In 30 days, there are 720 hours. Thus, the average water loss per hour = 1620 ÷ 720 = 2 1/4 gallons.

12. .375 = 375/1000 = 3/8

13. Volume = (10)(10)(3 1/2) = 350 cu.ft. Then, (350)(7 1/2) = 2625 gallons

14. 1 5/8 + 3 3/4 + 6 1/3 + 9 1/2 = 19 53/24 = 21 5/24

15. 1035 1/4 - 946 1/2 = 88 3/4

16. (39)(697) = 27,183

17. 16.074 .045 = 357.2

18. (3')(50')(5 1/2') = 825 cu.ft. ≈ 30 cu.yds., since 1 cu.yd. = 27 cu.ft.

19. 7'3 1/2" + 4'2 3/16" + 5'7 5/16" + 8'5 7/8" = 24'17 30/16" = 25'6 7/8"

20. Total expansion = (150)(.0000095)(145)

21. Number of pounds needed = (5) (4)(6-5 1/2)(62) = 620

22. Net annual pay = ($83,125)(.83) ≈ $69000. Then, the net weekly pay = $69000 ÷ 52 ≈ $1325 (actually about $1327)

23. 390 lbs. ÷ 18 = 21.6 lbs. per linear foot

24. (3)(11) = 33 man-days. Then, 33 ÷ 5 = 6.6 ≈ 6 1/2 days

25. Area = (8')(2 1/2') = 20 sq.ft.

BASIC PLUMBING

TABLE OF CONTENTS

	Page
PLANNING	1
ROUGHING-IN	3
WATER-SUPPLY PIPING	4
Materials	4
Size	4
DRAINAGE PIPING	4
Materials	5
Size and Slope	6
Traps and Venting	6
Floor Drains	8
PIPE FITTINGS AND CLEANOUTS	9
Fittings	9
Cleanouts	10
FIXTURES	11
WATER HEATERS	13
PROTECTING WATER PIPES FROM FREEZING	14
CONDENSATION	15
SERVICE BUILDING PLUMBING	15
Water-Supply Piping	15
Drainage Piping	16

BASIC PLUMBING

Careful planning and proper installation are essential for a safe and adequate plumbing system in the home or other farmstead buildings.

Installation of plumbing requires special knowledge and tools and should be done by, or under the guidance of, an experienced person. It must be done in accordance with applicable State, county, or local plumbing codes. Code requirements take precedence over recommendations given in this bulletin.

Planning the plumbing system should be done by the family, who know most about their own living habits and needs. A knowledge of the kinds of piping, fixtures, and other equipment required and available will aid in planning. Also, advice should be obtained from qualified persons.

PLANNING

In planning a plumbing system, consider your future needs as well as your present. It costs less to install a few extra tees with plugs for future connections than it does to cut into a plumbing system to make connections later on.

Adding or remodeling plumbing in existing buildings involves the additional expense and labor of opening up walls or floors. It may be more economical to run piping along the exposed face of a wall or floor and then box it in for appearance.

In the home, there are at least three areas where water is needed the kitchen, the bathroom, and the laundry. Around the farmstead, water is needed in the dairy barn and milkhouse. in other buildings where stock are kept or watered, in the shop, and in the yard or family garden. The location of appliances, fixtures, and faucets in each of these areas must be planned in advance.

Planning a plumbing system also includes providing for proper drainage of wastes. Improper handling of wastes can lead to contamination of the water supply and consequent spread of diseases. Poor planning or workmanship can also mean hours of unpleasant work in repairing or clearing clogged drains.

Plumbing costs can often be kept down by good planning in locating fixtures. Fixtures located back to back on opposite sides of a wall, as shown in figure 1 on page 2, save on piping. Locating all bathroom fixtures on one wall, as shown in the illustration, also saves piping. In the arrangement shown in figure 1, one vent stack serves all fixtures.

Figure 2, on page 2, shows a vertical arrangement of fixtures to reduce the amount of piping needed in multi-storied houses. Locating fixtures in a continuous line, as shown in figures 3 and 4, saves piping in single-story houses.

A water heater should be located as close as practical to the fixture where hot water will be used most frequently. Long runs of hot water pipe result in unnecessary use of water and heat.

Precautions

Every precaution must be taken to insure a safe water supply and otherwise protect the health of the family. When installing plumbing, be sure that

• There are no leaks in the drainage system through which sewage or sewer gases can escape.

• There are no cross connections between the water-supply system and any other piping carrying water or other materials.

• All fixtures are designed and installed so that there can be no back siphonage from the fixture into the water-supply system. This precaution also applies to fixtures, such as water bowls, installed in service buildings for use by animals.

2

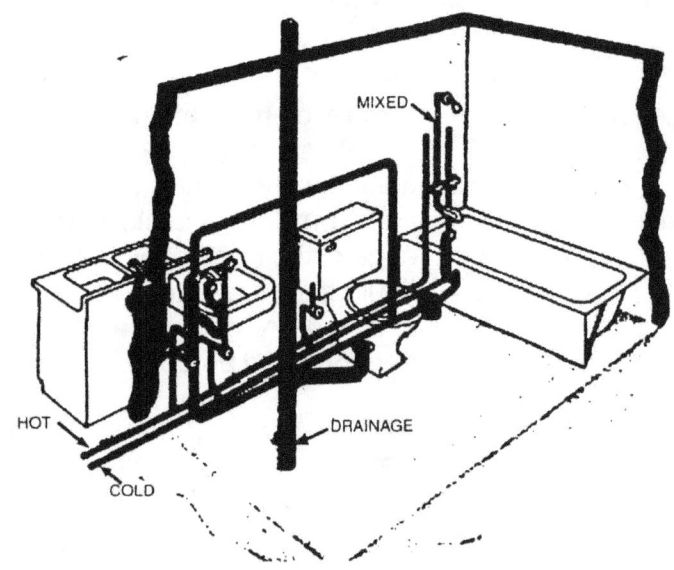

Figure 1 – Plumbing fixtures located back to back on opposite sides of a wall.

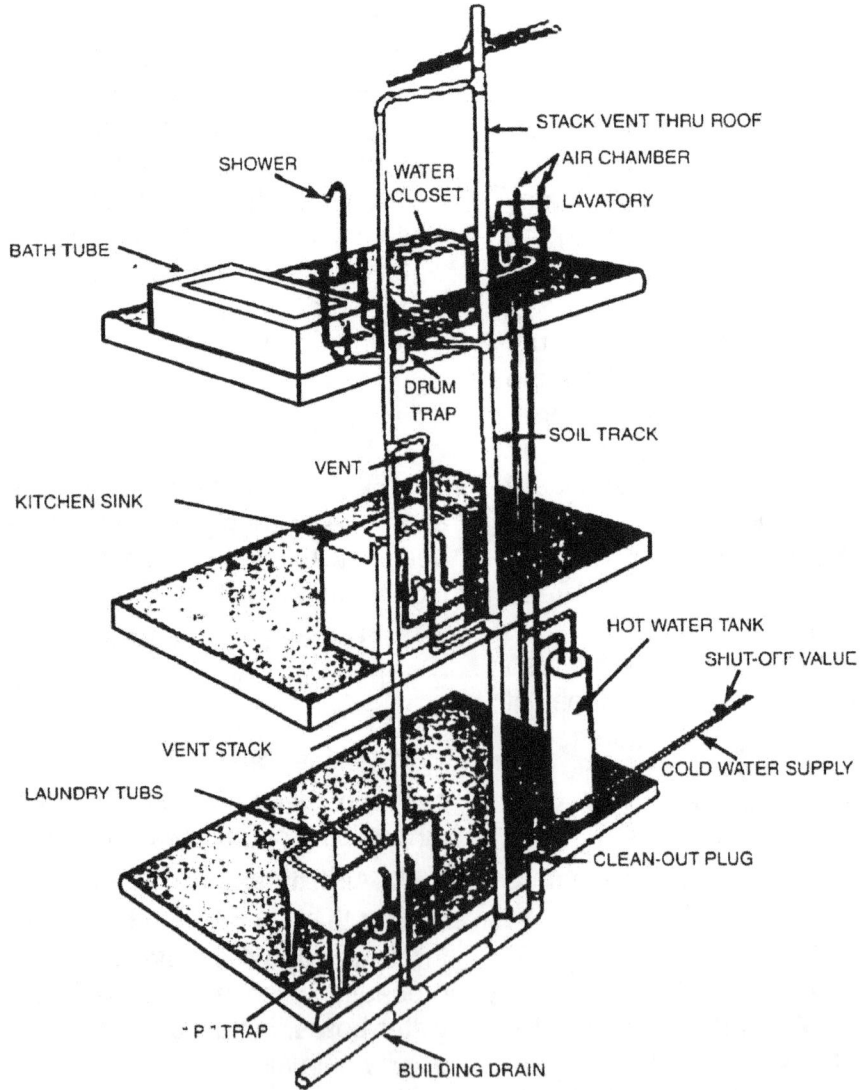

Figure 2 - Plumbing arrangement in a two-story house with basement.

ROUGHING-IN

The term "roughing-in" refers to placing the piping that will be concealed in the walls or under the floors of a building during construction or remodeling. The fixtures are normally connected to this piping after construction work is completed. Future fixtures may also be provided for in this manner. Building drains may be laid under concrete floors before the superstructure framing is started.

Roughing-in includes installation and testing of the water-supply and drainage piping and the fixture supports. The location and height of sinks, lavatories, and other fixtures must be precisely indicated on the

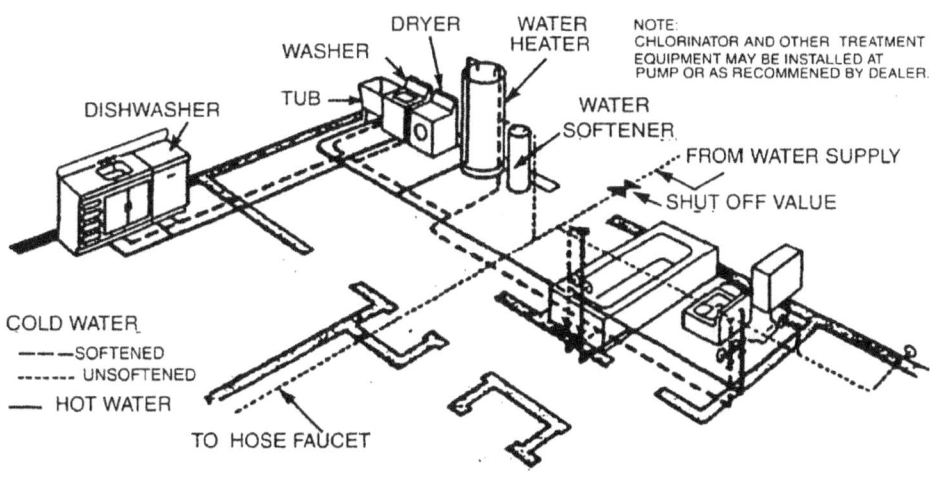

Figure 3 - A fixture and water-supply-piping layout for a one-story house.

building plans to insure correct installation of the piping and supports. For sinks a height of 36 inches and for lavatories a height of 33 to 35 inches, measured from the floor to the top of the rim, should suit most adults. Some families may find it more convenient to have the fixtures slightly higher or lower.

After the roughed-in work is completed, and before it is concealed, the plumbing system should be tested for leaks. Local plumbing codes usually include a standard testing procedure. Where no code is in effect, the drainage and water-supply systems may be tested as follows:

Drainage system—Tightly plug all openings, except the highest one. Fill the system with water, and let the water stand for about 15 minutes. Then check the entire system for leaks.

The system can be checked by sections. If done that way, test each section under a head (depth, measured vertically) of water of at least 10 feet to be sure that each section and joint will withstand at least that much pressure.

Water-supply system—This system can be tested in the same way as the drainage system, but only potable (drinkable) water should be used, and it should be under pressure at least equal to the working pressure of the system, but not less than 60 pounds per square inch. A pump and pressure gage will be needed to make the test.

4
WATER-SUPPLY PIPING

Materials

Galvanized pipe or copper tubing is normally used for water-supply, or distribution piping. However, these two materials should not be joined directly to each other (see p. 12).

Copper tubing may cost a little more than galvanized pipe, but it is easier to install and has a smoother inside surface.

Both hard-drawn (rigid) and soft-drawn (flexible) copper tubing are available. The soft-drawn tubing can be installed with long sweeping bends. Less pressure is lost when water runs through sweeping bends than when it makes abrupt changes in direction.

Characteristics of the water should be considered when selecting piping. Some waters corrode some piping materials. Check with neighbors who use water from the same water-bearing stratum; their experience can guide you in selecting the piping material. Or, have a chemical analysis made of a sample of the water. Your State college or university may be equipped to make an analysis. If not, it can direct you to a private laboratory. Firms in the water treatment equipment business make analyses for prospective customers.

Size

Water-distribution piping should be as short and as straight as possible. The longer the pipe and the smaller its diameter, the greater the loss of pressure. Some pressurew is lost whenever water passes around bends and through elbows and other fittings.

To improve service by providing higher residual pressures, quieter operation, and reduced water hammer, the following water-velocity limits or specific pipe sizes are recommended:

Service mains

Buried lines to buildings: 1¼ inch minimum size pipe; 4 feet per second velocity.

Service branches

Lines serving one or more fixture supply lines: 6 feet per second velocity.

Fixture supply lines

Lines serving individual fixtures, as follows:

Automatic washer, hose bibbs, and wall hydrants: ¾-inch minimum pipe size.

Bathtub, dishwasher, kitchen sink, laundry trays, and shower stall: ½-inch minimum pipe size.

Lavatory and water closet: Check local plumbing code for specific requirements.

DRAINAGE PIPING

The building drainage system includes all piping that carries sewage or other liquid waste to the building sewer, which, in turn, carries it to the disposal facility. Since the escape of sewage or sewer gases can be a serious health hazard, this system must be as carefully designed and installed as the water-distribution system.

A house or building drainage system generally includes these basic parts:

Fixture drain–The piping through which a fixture drains. Each fixture must be trapped and vented.

Fixture branch–A pipe connecting several fixture drains.

Soil stack–The vertical soil pipe into which the water closet or other fixture having a similar function drains, with or without the discharge from other fixtures. It connects to the building drain and is vented up through the roof to the outside air. The vent portion is called the stack vent.

Building drain–The main horizontal drain that receives the discharge from soil, waste, or other drainage pipes inside the building and carries it outside the building to the building sewer, which carries it to the disposal facility.

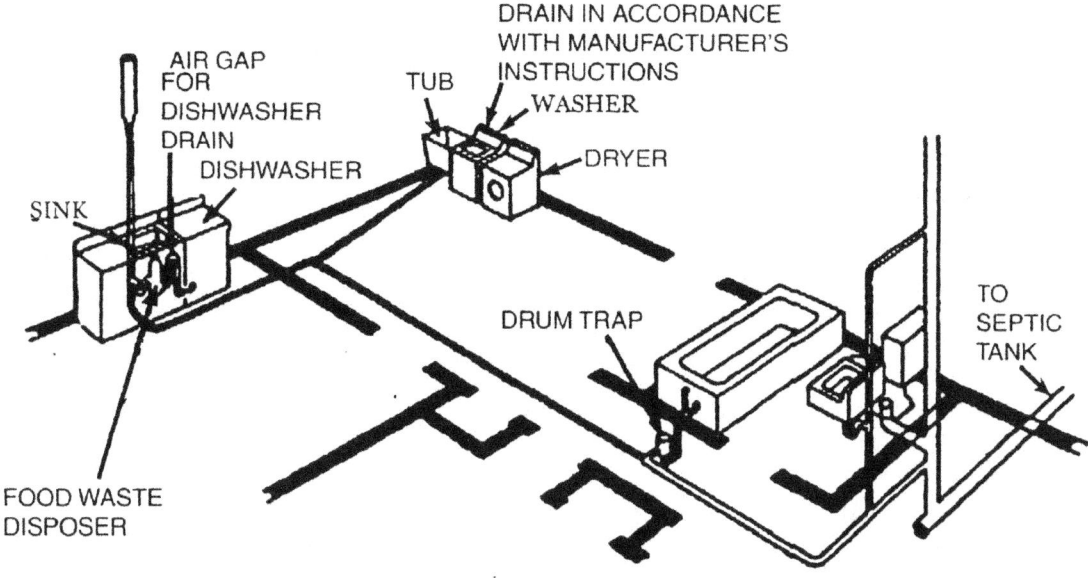

Figure 4 - Drainage system layout for the arrangement in figure 3.

Plastic Piping

Carefully selected and properly installed plastic pipe offers several advantages over conventional piping materials such as galvanized steel and copper pipe or tube. There are no perfect plumbing materials and all must be installed with knowledge of their physical properties and limitations.

Today's plastic pipe and fittings are often the most economical and are nearly immune to the attack of aggressive waters. At this time PE (polyethylene) pipe is used most commonly for underground service. Since it is furnished in long coils, it requires a minimum of fittings for long piping runs. For short runs, the friction loss in the insert fittings is a disadvantage. PVC (polyvinyl-chloride) pipe is available in nearly twice the pressure rating for the same cost as PE. PVC pipe is most often assembled with solvent-welded fittings. Heavy-wall PVC Schedule 80 pipe may be threaded. CPVC (chlorinated-polyvinyl-chloride) pipe is available for hot water service.

ABS (acrilonitrile-butadienestyrene) pipe was once primarily used in potable water distribution in a size known as SWP (solvent-welded pipe). Today ABS is used in DWV (drainage-waste-vent) systems. PVC is also used in DWV systems.

To be sure of getting quality plastic pipe and fittings, make sure that the material is marked with the manufacturer's name or trademark, pipe size, the plastic material type or class code, pressure rating, standard to which the pipe is manufactured (usually an ASTM standard), and the seal of approval of an accredited testing laboratory (usually N.S.F. the National Sanitation Foundation).

Materials

Drainage piping may be made of cast iron, galvanized wrought iron or steel, copper, brass, or plastic. Cast iron is commonly used for building drains that are buried under concrete floors or underground. Steel pipe should not be laid under-ground or under concrete.

Size and Slope

Wastes normally flow through the drainage system by gravity. (Sometimes wastes flow by gravity to a sump, then are lifted by a pump.) The drainage piping must be of the proper size and slope to insure good flow.

Local plumbing codes should be checked for the sizes of drain pipe required. Minimum sizes recommended are:

	Minimum size in inches
Piping for-	
Fixture drains:	
Bathtub, dishwasher, kitchen sink, and laundry trays	1½
Lavatory	1¼
Floor drain and shower stall	2
Water closet	3
Fixture branch	1½
Soil stack	3
Building drain:	
Beyond soil stack connection	3
Above soil stack connection	(¹)

¹ Not less than connecting branch.

Horizontal drainpipes—pipes that slope less than 45° from the horizontal—3 inches or less in diameter should slope at least one-fourth of an inch per foot. Larger pipes should slope not less than one-eighth of an men per foot.

Traps and Venting

Gases develop in sewers and septic tanks and flow back through the drainage piping system. To prevent these gases from backing up through open fixture drains or over-flows and escaping into the house, a trap is required at each fixture (figs. 5 and 6). The trap should be the same size as the drainpipe and as close as possible to the fixture outlet. The water seal in the trap should be at least 2 inches, but not more than 4 inches. Water closets usually have built-in traps and no additional one is required. Never double-trap a fixture.

Grease Traps

A grease trap is different from a fixture trap and serves an entirely different purpose. It is designed to prevent greases and fats from entering a sewerage system. It should be used only where large amounts of grease may be discharged into the waste disposal system for example, in a restaurant or boarding house. It is not needed in the average dwelling.

If used, a grease trap should not receive the discharge from a food waste disposer. Grease accumulations must be removed from the trap at frequent intervals.

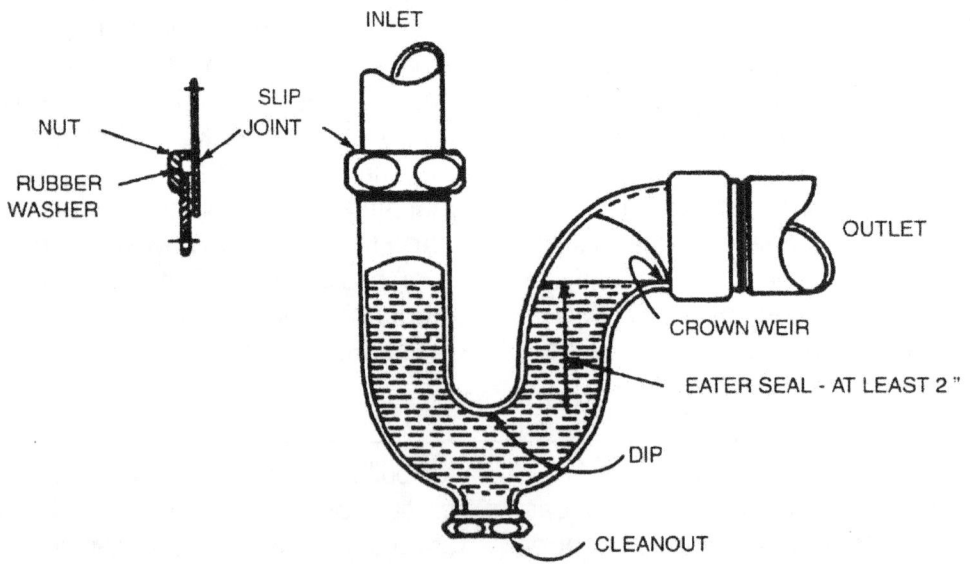

Figure 5 - P trap assembly.

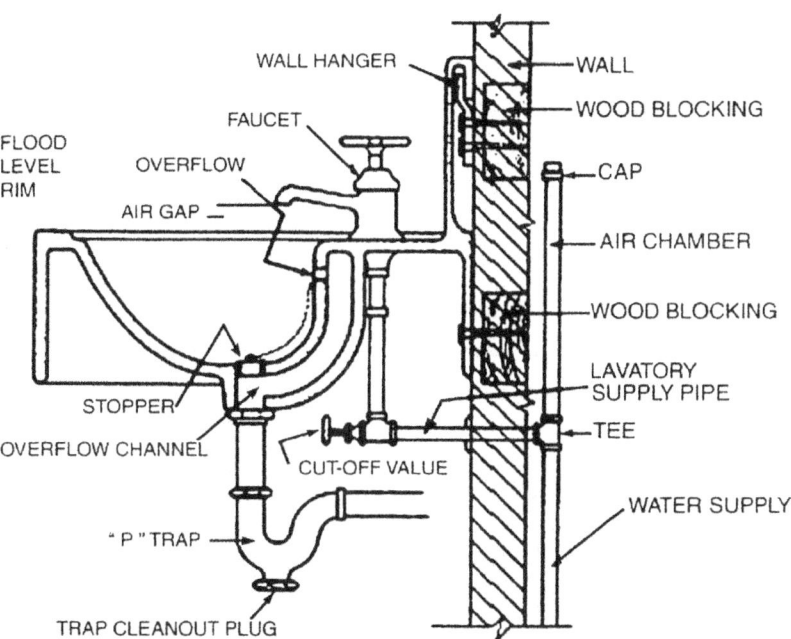

Figure 6 - Lavatory, showing water-supply and drainage piping. Note air gap at faucet and air chamber. An air chamber prevents water hammer.

Drum traps (see fig. 7) are commonly used in bathtub drain lines. A trap should be 3 or 4 inches in diameter, and the bottom or top should be removable to permit cleaning of the trap and drainpipe.

Sewer gases that are confined can develop pressure and bubble through the water seal in fixture traps. Therefore, at least one vent must be provided through which these gases can escape to the outside air and thus prevent any build up of pressure or vacuum on the trap seal.

The soil stack should always be vented to the outside, above the roof and undiminished in size. Additional vents directly to the outside may be needed or required for individual fixtures. Plumbing codes specify the venting required. Where there is no code, the recommendations given herein may be followed.

A vent pipe (or stack, as the vertical portion is called) should extend far enough above the roof to prevent it from being blocked by snow, but at least 6 inches. The opening in the roof through which the pipe passes must be flashed (tightly sealed) to make it watertight (fig. 8).

In very cold climates, the part of a vent above the roof should be at least 3 inches in diameter to prevent frost closure in cold weather. Where individual vents are used for fixtures, 1½-inch pipe is recommended. Vent increasers (see fig. 8) may be used to increase the diameter of the vent stacks above the roof.

Each fixture drain must be vented to prevent the siphoning of the water from the fixture trap. Figures 1, 2, 4, and 7 show the methods of venting fixture drains. Vent piping for each fixture should be installed between the trap and the sewerline, and should be the same size as the drain piping. If connected to the soil stack, the vent piping should be connected above the highest fixture drain. Otherwise, it should extend separately to above the roof. The distance from the fixture trap to the vent is governed by the size of the fixture drain. Maximum distances recommended are:

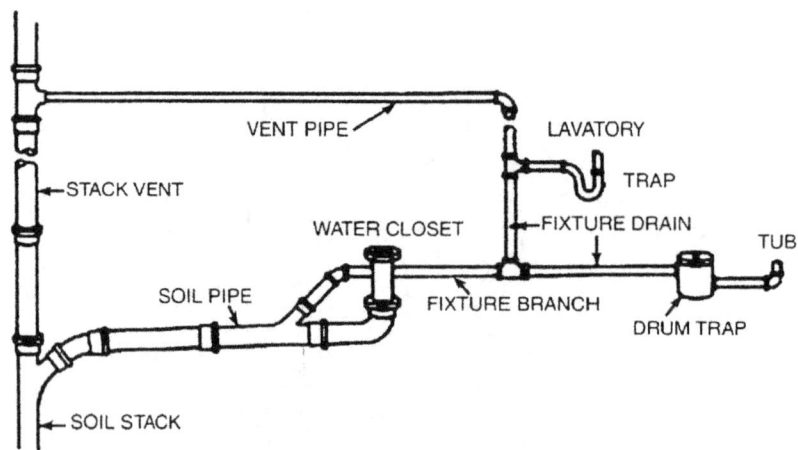

Figure 7 - Method of venting a group of bathroom fixtures.

Size of fixture drain (inches)	Maximum distance from trap to vent (feet)
1¼	2½
1½	3½
2	5
3	6
4	10

It is a good idea to plan the locations of fixtures so that most, if not all, can be vented through one stack. For example, figure 1 shows that by locating the bathroom next to the kitchen, it is practical to vent all fixtures in both rooms through the one stack. This consideration should not necessarily dictate overall room arrangement.

Floor Drains

Floor drains are required in shower stalls, milkrooms, and milking parlors. They are often installed in laundry rooms, basements, and utility rooms.

Floor drains should be trapped. If the building drain is laid under the floor, it must be at a sufficient depth to permit installation of the trap. Floor drains are usually set close enough to the building drain to make separate venting unnecessary.

A floor drain should be flush with the floor, and the floor should slope toward the drain from all directions. The grating of the drain should be removable so the drain can be cleaned.

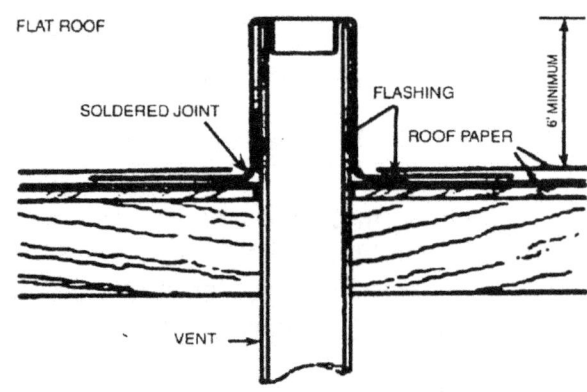
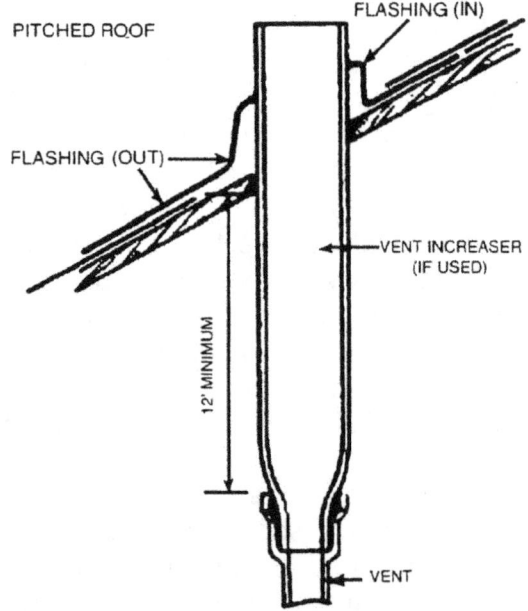

Figure 8 - Installation of roof flashing arround vent stacks.

PIPE FITTINGS AND CLEANOUTS

Fittings

If copper tubing is joined directly to galvanized-iron or steel piping, electrolysis will take place under certain conditions and the joint will eventually corrode. Special non-electrical-conducting fittings are available for joining copper tubing to iron or steel piping.

Pipe fittings, such as elbows, tees, nipples, reducers, and couplings, when used with iron or steel pipes, are usually made of the same material as the pipe. Brass fittings are used with brass pipes and copper tubing.

Valves and faucets are usually made of brass or wrought copper. Brass valves made for use with wrought iron, steel, and rigid copper tubing are threaded; those for use with flexible copper tubing are designed for soldering.

Sections of copper tubing and their fittings are joined by soldering. The soldering should be done as follows:

1. Clean the tube end and the cup (inside) of the fitting with steel wool or emery cloth. Remove all loose particles after cleaning. Clean surfaces are essential for good solder connections.
2. Apply a thin coat of flux to the cleaned surfaces of both the tube and the fitting.
3. Assemble the tube and fitting.
4. Apply heat and solder. Heat by directing the flame onto the fitting toward the tube until the solder melts. The solder will flow and fill the joint.
5. Remove excess flux and solder with a small brush or soft cloth while the metal is still hot.
6. Allow the joint to cool, with-out moving it.

Cast-iron drainage pipe sections and fittings are usually of the hub-and-spigot type and are joined by packing with hemp tow or oakum and sealing with lead (fig. 9). The joint must be fitted and packed so that the sections are concentric, leaving no obstructions to the flow of liquid or projections against which solids can lodge. The direction of waste flow must always be as shown in figure 9.

A recently developed system for joining cast-iron drainage, waste, and vent piping requires only a wrench to assemble. The pipe sections are manufactured without the usual hub and spigot ends and are joined by a neoprene sleeve gasket held in place oy a wraparound stainless steel shield fastened by stainless steel bands with worm-drive clamps (fig. 10). The absence of hubs enables 2- and 3-inch piping to be installed inside standard 2 x 4's. This method of connection may be used both above and below grade.

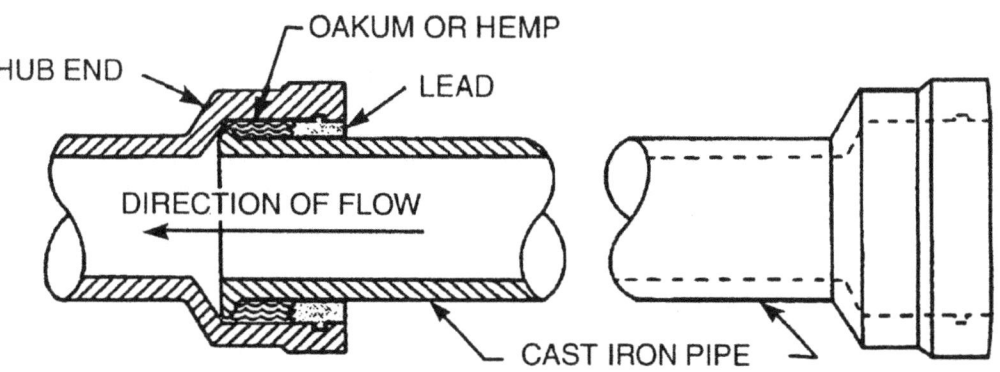

Figure 9 - Bell-and-spigot joint in cast-iron pipe.

Branch drainpipes should be connected to larger drainpipes so that the direction of flow in the system is maintained (see fig. 7).

Where a change in the direction of drainage piping is necessary, sweep bends (fig. 11) should be used whenever possible, because angled turns tend to reduce the rate of flow.

Cleanouts

Wastes that will cling to the inside of pipe walls are sometimes discharged into drainage sytems.

Also, when cool, greases congeal and may stick to pipe walls. To permit cleaning of pipes, cleanouts should be provided through which such matter can be removed or dislodged. Cleanouts usually consist of 45-degree Y-fittings with removable plugs (figs. 11 and 12). They should be the same size as the pipe in which they are installed.

Cleanouts should be installed where they are readily accessible and where cleanout tools can be easily inserted into the drainpipe. Place one cleanout at or near the foot of the soil stack (fig. 13). Install others at intervals of not more than 50 feet along horizontal drainage lines that are 4 inches or less in diameter.

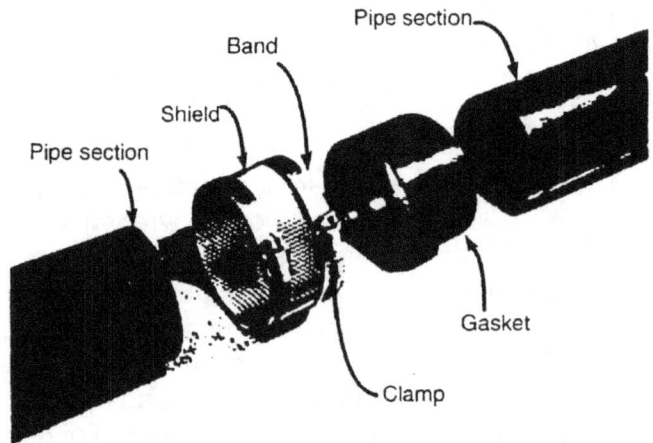

Figure 10 - The newest method of joining pipe is with neoprene gasket shield, and clamps.

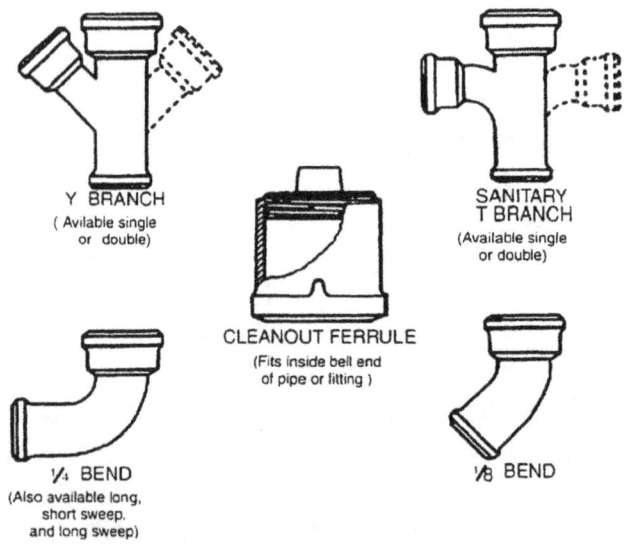

Figure 11 - Common cast-iron soil-pipe fittings.

FIXTURES

Many styles of each type of plumbing fixture are available. Selection is mostly a matter of personal preference. The style and size of a fixture should harmonize with the room in which it is installed.

When designing a new house or building, allow enough space for the desired fixtures. When selecting new fixtures for existing buildings, be sure they will fit into the space available. Draw to scale floor plans of the rooms in which fixtures will be installed (for example, 1/4 or 1/2 inch can equal 1 foot). Arrange cardboard cutouts of the fixtures, drawn to the same scale, on the floor plans.

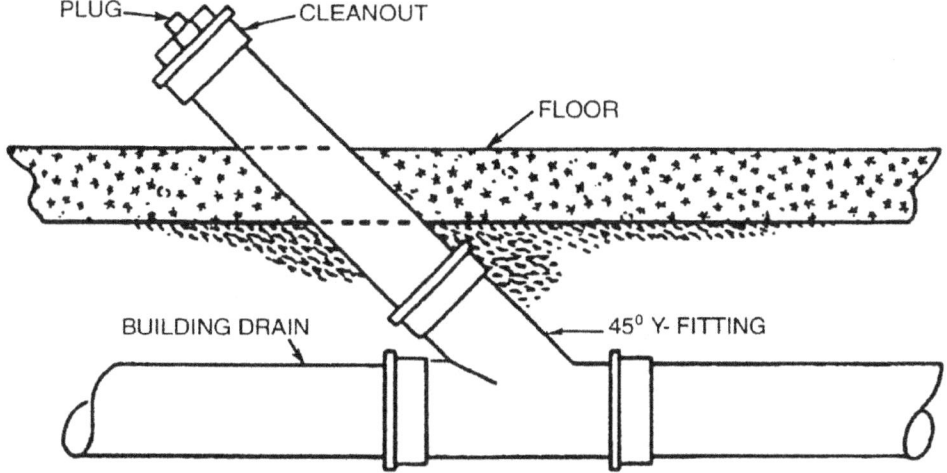

Figure 12 - A 45° Y-fitting and cleanout in building drain.

Manufacturers of plumbing fixtures sometimes have cutouts of their equipment available for planning purposes.

Some plumbing fixtures are supported on the floor alone, some on the wall alone, and some partly on each. Support must be substantial; otherwise a fixture may pull away from the wall and leave a crack. Appropriate carriers or brackets are available for supporting wall-hung fixtures. Guidance on necessary support framing and attachment may be had from fixture manufacturers or dealers.

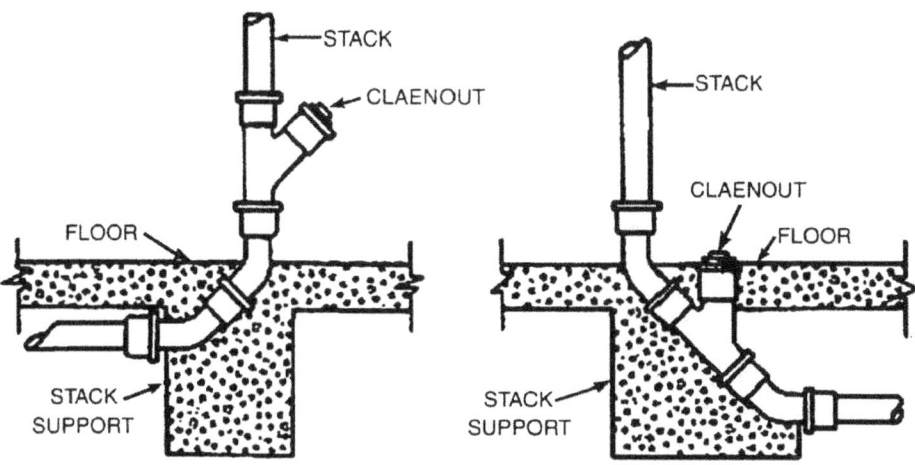

Figure 13 - Soil and waste pipe cleanouts and supports.

12

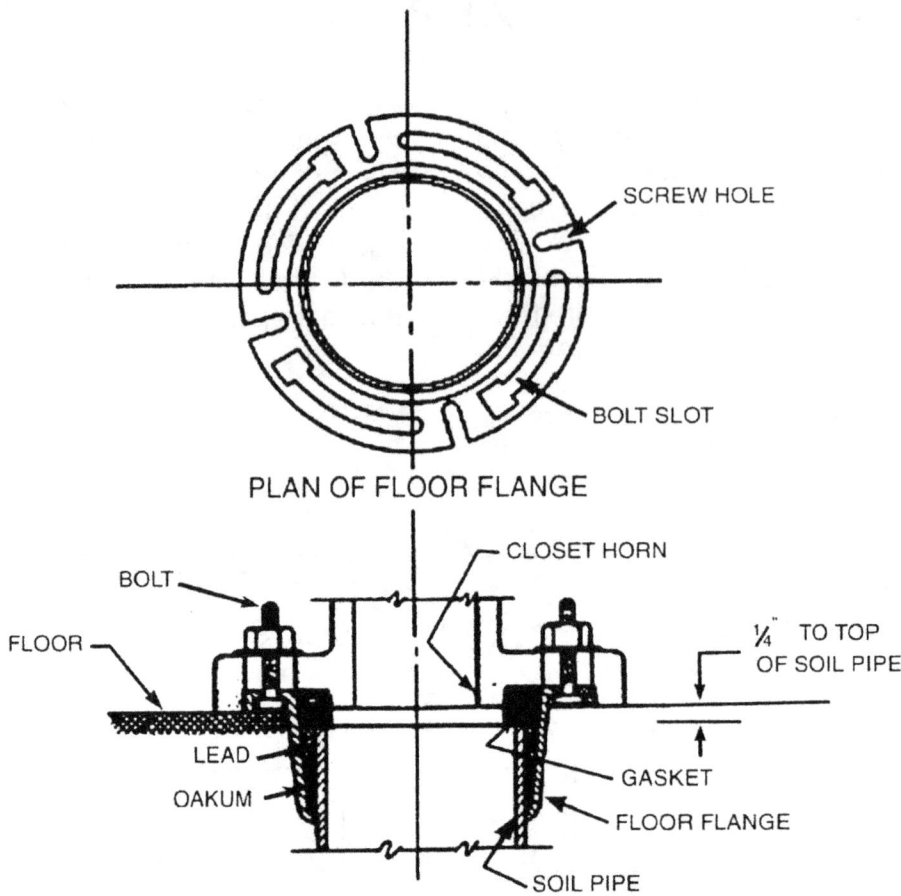

Figure 14 - One method of connecting water closet to the soil pipe.

Water closets are available for either floor or wall mounting. The floor-mounted type bolts to a floor flange, which in turn attaches to the floor (fig. 14) or to the closet bend below. The wall-mounted type is supported by carriers attached to the wall studding or to both the wall and the floor (chair carriers). Six-inch wall studding is recommended if wall-type carriers are used. Tubs are available either for floor support alone or for floor and wall support combined, and may require additional framing in the wall or floor, or in both.

Faucet spouts must be high enough above a lavatory or sink rim to prevent water in the fixture from being drawn back into the faucet if a vacuum should be created in the plumbing system. The height, which is known as "air gap," should be at least twice the diameter of the faucet opening (see fig. 6). Normally it should not be less than 1 inch for lavatories; 1 1/2 inches for sinks, laundry trays, and 3/4-inch bath faucets; and 2 inches for 1-inch bath faucets.

Water Treatment

Water for domestic use may require treatment to make it suitable. An analysis will determine the treatment required. Dealers can advise on the selection and use of water-treatment equipment.

Plumbing Check for House Buyers

If you are considering buying a previously occupied house, you should examine and evaluate the condition of the plumbing. The following questions will suggest features that should not be overlooked:

Are there water stains in the building, indicating leaks in the water-supply or drainage piping? If so, have the leaks been corrected satisfactorily?

Is the flow of water from the faucets good and strong, indicating absence of corrosion or scaling in the supply piping? If not, can the deficiency be corrected economically?

Do the fixtures drain quickly and quietly and maintain the water seals in the traps, indicating an adequate vented drainage system? If not, can the deficiency be corrected economically?

Are all fixtures and piping firmly anchored or supported!

Does the water closet flush completely and shut off completely? Does the tank refill quietly? If not, can the deficiency be corrected economically?

Do faucets and valves operate freely and close completely? If not, can the deficiency be corrected economically?

Are the fixtures chipped and stained? Do they need to be replaced?

Do the stoppers hold? If not, can they be readily and cheaply replaced or repaired?

WATER HEATERS

A house plumbing system usually includes a water heater or a hot-water storage tank if the water is heated in the central heating plant. (Water heaters are also required in milkhouses, see p. 16.)

Electric, gas, and oil-fueled water heaters are available. Each type comes in a wide variety of sizes. Instructions for connecting water heaters to plumbing systems come with the units. The tanks have the necessary internal piping already installed and the only connections required are the hot- and cold-water and fuel lines. Gas- or oil-fired water heaters require flues to vent the products of combustion.

Pressure and temperature relief valves are essential and should be on all water heaters and hot-water storage tanks. Their purpose is to relieve pressure in the tank and pipes if other control equipment fails and the water temperature goes high enough to generate dangerous pressure. As water heats it expands, and the expansion may be enough to rupture the tank or pipes if the water cannot be forced back into the cold-water line or discharged through a relief outlet.

The size of hot-water storage tank needed in the house depends upon the number of persons in the family, the volume of hot water that may be required during peak use periods (for example, during bathing or laundering periods), and the "recovery rate" of the heating unit. Household water heaters are generally available with tanks in a range of sizes from about 30 to 80 gallons.

The "recovery rate" of water heaters varies with the type and capacity of the heating element. In standard conventional models, oil and gas heaters usually have higher recovery rates than electric heaters of similar size. However, a relatively new "quick recovery" type of electric water heater is available. Its two high-wattage heating elements provide hot water at a rapid rate.

For a family of 4 or 5 persons, tank sizes should be about 30 to 40 gallons for oil or gas heaters, 40 gallons for quick-recovery electric heaters, and 40 to 52 gallons for standard electric heaters. For larger families, or where unusually heavy use will be made of hot water, correspondingly larger capacity heaters should be installed. Advice on the size needed may be obtained from Extension home demonstration agents, equipment dealers, and power company representatives. Power suppliers may offer special reduced rates for electric water heating. If "off peak" electric heating will be used, be sure that the tank will hold enough hot water to last from one heating period to the next.

PROTECTING WATER PIPES FROM FREEZING

If water freezes in a pipe, the pipe may be ruptured or otherwise damaged.

Freezing will not occur if a pipe is well insulated (fig. 15) and the water is allowed to flow continuously. However, insulation does not stop the loss of heat it merely reduces the rate of loss and the water may freeze if it stands in a pipe, even a well-insulated one, for some time in cold weather.

Pipes laid in the ground are usually difficult to insulate effectively because of moisture; insulation must stay dry to be effective. But a pipe laid below the frostline is not likely to freeze even if not insulated.

In areas subject to freezing temperatures, it is advisable not to install water pipes in outside walls of buildings. Should it be necessary to do so, they should be protected from freezing.

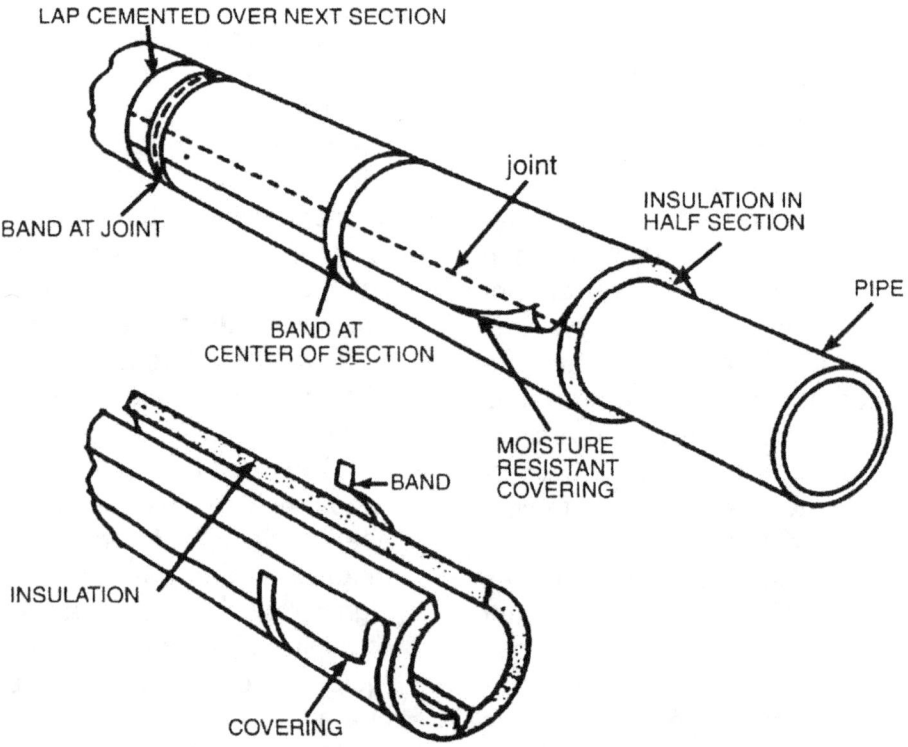

Figure 15 - One method of applying insulation to pipe

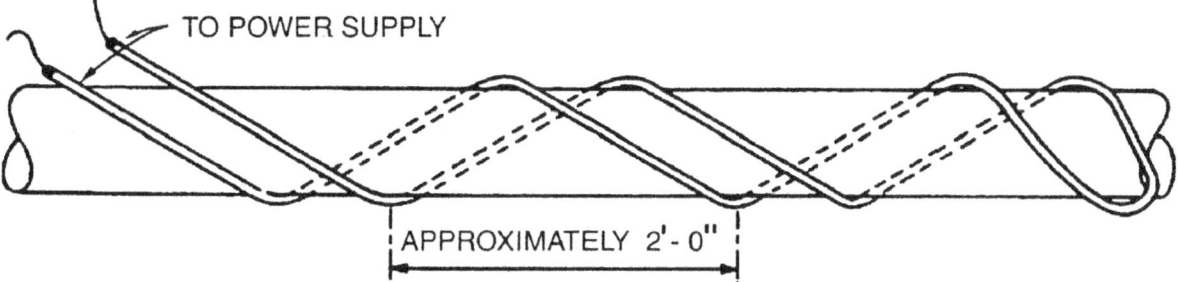

Figure 16 - Application of heating cable to pipe to prevent freezing

Electric heating cable can be used to prevent pipes from freezing. Each unit of cable should be folded at the midpoint and wrapped around the pipe as shown in figure 16. Electric heating cable may also be used to thaw frozen pipe.

CONDENSATION

In areas where the air gets hot and humid, condensation (sweating) is very likely to occur on pipes carrying cold water. This can be prevented by insulating the pipes. The insulation will also help to keep the water cool. To prevent condensation from collecting in the insulation, it should be covered with a good vapor barrier. Vapor barriers are ordinarily available from the same sources as the insulation.

Condensation may also occur on a water-closet tank in hot, humid weather. This may be prevented by insulating the tank. Insulating jackets, or liners, that fit inside water-closet tanks are available. When installed, they prevent the water from cooling the outer surface of the tank.

SERVICE-BUILDING PLUMBING

Water-Supply Piping

Water is needed in all buildings and yards where livestock are kept.

In stall-type dairy barns, water is usually provided by means of water bowls. The bowls must be designed to prevent back siphoning of water into the water-supply piping. This may be done by using valves with outlets above the overflow rim of the bowl (fig. 17).

The supply piping for water bowls is often mounted on the stall frame where it may be subject to freezing. Freezing can be prevented by wrapping heating cable around the pipe, and covering the cable and pipe with insulation (figs. 15 and 16). If the pipe is laid underground, the riser to the bowl must be protected against freezing.

Precautions against back siphoning of water into the supply piping and against freezing must also be taken with troughs and other types of stock waterers. Heating devices are available to prevent freezing.

Where there is danger of the pipes freezing in service buildings, a stop-and-waste valve should be installed between the building service pipe and the distribution piping. The valve, which may be buried in the ground where the service pipe enters the building, will permit draining the piping in the building during cold weather. When the valve handle, which extends above the ground, is closed, the water in the service pipe drains through an opening in the valve

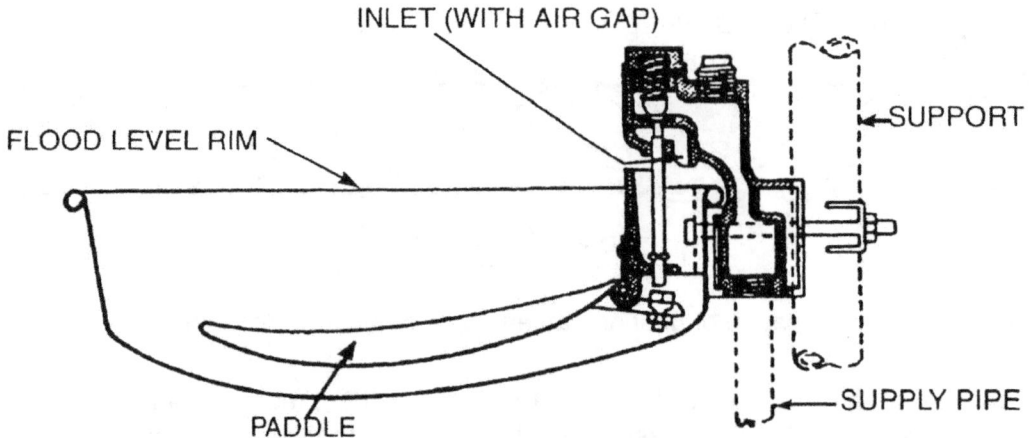

Figure 17 - Livestock watering bowl.

into the ground. If the ground around the valve is not sufficiently porous to absorb the drainage, it should be made so by packing with gravel or broken stone.

In cold climates, outdoor faucets should be the frostproof type. Frostproof hydrants are designed to drain the water left in them when they are turned off. This prevents freezing.

Water is needed for washing down stall barns and milking parlors. Both hot and cold water should be provided in the operator area of milking parlors for washing udders, rinsing pails, and other cleaning.

Hot and cold water are required in the milkhouse or milk room.

Note: Consult your dairy inspector regarding regulations before installing milkhouse plumbing. A water heater should be included in the milkhouse plumbing system. Water heaters for the dairy are usually larger than those used for household water heating and may operate at a higher temperature. On large dairy farms where a considerable amount of equipment must be washed and sterilized, a steam boiler may be advisable.

Hose connections or other outlets should be provided for flushing paved livestock feeding and resting areas.

Drainage Piping

Proper handling and disposal of dairy building wastes—especially from the gutters in stall barns, in milking parlors, and in milk rooms-is essential to prevent contamination of dairy products. Local health authorities should be consulted when planning a dairy waste-disposal system. All requirements in the milk code must be followed.

Milkhouse drainage systems must be adequate to carry away the waste water from washing utensils, the milk-cooling equipment, and the milkhouse. In small milkhouses, one 4-inch drain may be adequate; in larger ones, two drains may be needed-one under the washing vat and one in the center of the floor. The milkhouse wastes should not drain into the household sewage-disposal system, but into a separate system. Milkhouse drains should be trapped and vented; the method is the same as for house drains.

Your milk code may require a washroom with a lavatory and water closet for use by the dairy help. Wastes from this washroom are sewage and should not drain into the milkhouse or barn waste-disposal systems. Either provide a separate disposal system or, if practical, use the household sewage-disposal system.

BASIC FUNDAMENTALS OF PLUMBING

CONTENTS

CHAPTERS		Page
I.	DEFINITIONS	1
II.	GENERAL REGULATIONS	4
III.	QUALITY, WEIGHT, AND THICKNESS OF MATERIALS	5
IV.	JOINTS AND CONNECTIONS	6
V.	TRAPS AND CLEAN-OUTS	7
VI.	WATER SUPPLY AND DISTRIBUTION	8
VII.	PLUMBING FIXTURES	9
VIII.	SOIL AND WASTE PIPES FOR SANITARY SYSTEMS	9
IX.	STORM DRAINS	10
X.	VENTS AND VENTING	11
XI.	INDIRECT CONNECTIONS TO WASTE PIPES	13
XII.	MAINTENANCE	13
XIII.	INSPECTION AND TESTS	13

FIGURES		
1.	STANDARD PLUMBING SYMBOLS	15
2.	ILLUSTRATION OF DEFINITIONS	16

BASIC FUNDAMENTALS OF PLUMBING

CHAPTER I. DEFINITIONS

Sec. 101.—Definitions.

Accepted standards.—Accepted standards are the standards cited in this manual, or other standards approved by the authority having jurisdiction over plumbing.

Air gap.—The air gap in a water-supply system for plumbing fixtures is the vertical distance between the supply-fitting outlet (spout) and the highest possible water level in the receptor when flooded.

If the plane of the end of the spout is at an angle to the surface of the water, the mean gap is the basis for measurement.

Approved.—Approved means accepted as satisfactory to the authority having jurisdiction over plumbing.

Area drain.—An area drain is a drain installed to collect surface or rain water from an open area.

Backflow.—Backflow means the flow of water into a water-supply system from any source except its regular one. Back siphonage is one type of backflow.

Backflow connection.—A backflow connection is any arrangement whereby backflow can occur.

Back vent.—A back vent is a branch vent installed primarily for the purpose of protecting fixture traps from self-siphonage.

Branch.—A branch is any part of a piping system other than a main. (See *Main*.)

Branch interval.—A branch interval is a length of soil or waste stack corresponding in general to a story height, but in no case less than 8 feet, within which the horizontal branches from one floor or story of the building are connected to the stack.

Branch vent.—A branch vent is any vent pipe connecting from a branch of the drainage system to the vent stack.

Building drain.—The building (house) drain is that part of the lowest horizontal piping of a building-drainage system which receives the discharge from soil, waste, and other drainage pipes inside the walls of the building and conveys it to the building (house) sewer beginning 5 feet outside the inner face of the building wall.

Building-drainage system.—The building-drainage system consists of all piping provided for carrying waste water, sewage, or other drainage from the building to the street sewer or place of disposal.

Building main.—The building main is the water-supply pipe, including fittings and accessories, from the water (street) main or other source of supply to the first branch of the water-distributing system.

Building sewer.—The building (house) sewer is that part of the horizontal piping of a building-drainage system extending from the building drain 5 feet outside of the inner face of the building wall to the street sewer or other place of disposal (a cesspool, septic tank, or other type of sewage-treatment device or devices) and conveying the drainage of but one building site.

Building subdrain.—A building (house) subdrain is that portion of a drainage system which cannot drain by gravity into the building sewer.

Circuit vent.—A circuit vent is a group vent extending from in front of the last fixture connection of a horizontal branch to the vent stack.

Combination fixture.—Combination fixture is a trade term designating an integral combination of one sink and one or two laundry trays in one fixture.

Continuous-waste-and-vent.—A continuous-waste-and-vent is a vent that is a continuation of and in a straight line with the drain to which it connects. A continuous-waste-and-vent is further defined by the angle the drain and vent at the point of connection make with the horizontal; for example, vertical continuous-waste-and-vent, 45° continuous-waste-and-vent, and flat (small-angle) continuous-waste-and-vent.

Continuous waste.—A waste from two or more fixtures connected to a single trap.

Cross-connection.—See *Interconnection.*

Developed length.—The developed length of a pipe is its length along the center line of the pipe and fittings.

Diameter.—Unless specifically stated, the term diameter means the nominal diameter as designated commercially.

Distance.—The distance or difference in elevation between two sloping pipes is the distance between the intersection of their center lines with the center line of the pipe to which both are connected.

Double offset.—A double offset is two offsets installed in succession or series in the same line.

Drain.—A drain or drain pipe is any pipe which carries water or water-borne wastes in a building-drainage system.

Drainage piping.—Drainage piping is all or any part of the drain pipes of a plumbing system.

Dry vent.—A dry vent is any vent that does not carry water or water-borne wastes.

Dual vent.—A dual vent (sometimes called a unit vent) is a group vent connecting at the junction of two fixture branches and serving as a back vent for both branches.

Effective opening.—The effective opening is the minimum cross-sectional area between the end of the supply-fitting outlet (spout) and the inlet to the controlling valve or faucet. The basis of measurement is the diameter of a circle of equal cross-sectional area.

If two or more lines supply one outlet, the effective opening is the sum of the effective openings of the individual lines or the area of the combined outlet, whichever is the smaller.

Fixture branch.—A fixture branch is the supply pipe between the fixture and the water-distributing pipe.

Fixture drain.—A fixture drain is the drain from the trap of a fixture to the junction of the drain with any other drain pipe.

Fixture unit.—A fixture unit is a factor so chosen that the load-producing values of the different plumbing fixtures can be expressed approximately as multiples of that factor.

Flood level.—Flood level in reference to a plumbing fixture is the level at which water begins to overflow the top or rim of the fixture.

Grade.—The grade of a line of pipe is its slope in reference to a horizontal plane. In plumbing it is usually expressed as the fall in inches per foot length of pipe.

Group vent.—A group vent is a branch vent that performs its functions for two or more traps.

Horizontal branch.—A horizontal branch is a branch drain extending laterally from a soil or waste stack or building drain, with or without vertical sections or branches, which receives the discharge from one or more fixture drains and conducts it to the soil or waste stack or to the building (house) drain.

Indirect waste pipe.—An indirect waste pipe is a waste pipe which does not connect directly with the building-drainage system, but discharges into it through a properly trapped fixture or receptacle.

Interconnection.—An interconnection, as the term is used in this manual, is any physical connection or arrangement of pipes between two otherwise separate building water-supply systems whereby water may flow from one system to the other, the direction of flow depending upon the pressure differential between the two systems.

Where such connection occurs between the sources of two such systems and the first branch from either, whether inside or outside the building, the term cross-connection (American Water Works terminology) applies and is generally used.

Jumpover.—See *Return offset.*

Leader.—A leader or downspout is the water conductor from the roof to the storm drain or other means of disposal.

Loop vent.—A loop vent is the same as a circuit vent except that it loops back and connects with a soil- or waste-stack-vent instead of the vent stack.

Main.—The main of any system of continuous piping is the principal artery of the system to which branches may be connected.

Main vent.—See *Vent stack.*

Nonpressure drainage.—Nonpressure drainage refers to a condition in which a static pressure cannot be imposed safely on the building drain. This condition is sometimes referred to as gravity flow and implies that the sloping pipes are not completely filled.

Offset.—An offset in a line of piping is a combination of elbows or bends which brings one section of the pipe out of line with but into a line parallel with another section.

Plumbing.—Plumbing is the work or business of installing in buildings the pipes, fixtures, and other apparatus for bringing in the water supply and removing liquid and water-borne wastes. The term is also used to denote the installed fixtures and piping of a building.

Plumbing fixtures.—Plumbing fixtures are receptacles which receive and discharge water, liquid, or water-borne wastes into a drainage system with which they are connected.

Plumbing system.—The plumbing system of a building includes the water-supply distributing pipes; the fixtures and fixture traps; the soil, waste, and vent pipes; the building (house) drain and building (house) sewer; and the storm-drainage pipes; with their devices, appurtenances, and connections all within or adjacent to the building.

Pool.—A pool is a water receptacle used for swimming or as a plunge or other bath, designed to accommodate more than one bather at a time.

Pressure drainage.—Pressure drainage, as used in this manual, refers to a condition in which a static pressure may be imposed safely on the entrances of sloping building drains through soil and waste stacks connected thereto.

Primary branch.—A primary branch of the building (house) drain is the single sloping drain from the base of a soil or waste stack to its junction with the main building drain or with another branch thereof.

Relief vent.—A relief vent is a branch from the vent stack, connected to a horizontal branch between the first fixture branch and the soil or waste stack, whose primary function is to provide for circulation of air between the vent stack and the soil or waste stack.

Return offset.—A return offset or jumpover is a double offset installed so as to return the pipe to its original line.

Riser.—A riser is a water-supply pipe which extends vertically one full story or more to convey water to branches or fixtures.

Sand interceptor (Sand trap).—A sand interceptor (sand trap) is a watertight receptacle designed and constructed to intercept and prevent the passage of sand or other solids into the drainage system to which it is directly or indirectly connected.

Sanitary sewer.—A sanitary sewer is a sewer designed or used only for conveying liquid or water-borne waste from plumbing fixtures.

Secondary branch.—A secondary branch of the building drain is any branch of the building drain other than a primary branch.

Sewage-treatment plant.—A sewage-treatment plant consists of structures and appurtenances which receive the discharge of a sanitary drainage system, designed to bring about a reduction in the organic and bacterial content of the waste so as to render it less offensive or dangerous, including septic tanks and cesspools.

Side vent.—A side vent is a vent connecting to the drain pipe through a 45° wye.

Size of pipe and tubing.—The size of pipe or tubing, unless otherwise stated, is the nominal size by which the pipe or tubing is commercially designated. Actual dimensions of the different kinds of pipe and tubing are given in the specifications applying.

Soil pipe.—A soil pipe is any pipe which conveys the discharge of water closets or fixtures having similar functions, with or without the discharges from other fixtures.

Stack.—Stack is a general term for the vertical main of a system of soil, waste, or vent piping.

Stack-vent.—A stack-vent is the extension of a soil or waste stack above the highest horizontal or fixture branch connected to the stack.

Storm drain.—A storm drain is a drain used for conveying rain water, subsurface water, condensate, cooling water, or other similar discharges.

Storm sewer.—A storm sewer is a sewer used for conveying rain water, subsurface water, condensate, cooling water, or other similar discharges.

Subsoil drain.—A subsoil drain is a drain installed for collecting subsurface or seepage water and conveying it to a place of disposal.

Trap.—A trap is a fitting or device so designed and constructed as to provide a liquid trap seal which will prevent the passage of air through it.

Trap seal.—The trap seal is the vertical distance between the crown weir and the dip of the trap.

Vent.—A vent is a pipe installed to provide a flow of air to or from a drainage system or to provide a circulation of air within such system to protect trap seals from siphonage and back pressure.

Vent stack.—A vent stack, sometimes called a main vent, is a vertical vent pipe installed primarily for the purpose of providing circulation of air to or from any part of the building-drainage system.

Waste pipe.—A waste pipe is a drain pipe which receives the discharge of any fixture other than water closets or other fixtures receiving human excreta.

Water main.—The water (street) main is a water-supply pipe for public or community use.

Water-service pipe.—The water-service pipe is that part of a building main installed by or under the jurisdiction of a water department or company.

Water-supply system.—The water-supply system of a building consists of the water-service pipe, the water-distributing pipes, and the necessary connecting pipes, fittings, and control valves.

Wet vent.—A wet vent is a soil or waste pipe that serves also as a vent.

Yoke vent.—A yoke vent is a vertical or 45° relief vent of the continuous-waste-and-vent type formed by the extension of an upright wye-branch or 45° wye-branch inlet of the horizontal branch to the stack. It becomes a dual yoke vent when two horizontal branches are thus vented by the same relief vent. (See fig. 2, pt. III.)

CHAPTER II. GENERAL REGULATIONS

Sec. 201. INSTALLATION OF PIPING.—Horizontal drainage piping shall be run in practical alinement and shall be supported at intervals not exceeding 10 feet. The minimum slopes shall be as follows: Not less than ¼-inch fall per foot for 1¼- to 2-inch diameters, inclusive; not less than ⅛-inch fall per foot for 2½- to 4-inch diameters, inclusive; not less than 1/16-inch fall per foot for 5- to 8-inch diameters, inclusive; and a slope that will maintain a velocity of at least 2.0 fps in a pipe of 10-inch diameter or larger as computed by the pipe formula given in paragraph 201, part III. Stacks shall be supported at their bases, and shall be rigidly secured. Piping shall be installed without undue stresses or strains, and provision made for expansion, contraction, and structural settlement. No structural member shall be weakened or impaired beyond a safe limit by cutting, notching, or otherwise, unless provision is made for carrying the structural load.

Sec. 202. CHANGES IN DIRECTION.—Changes in direction in drainage piping shall be made by the appropriate use of cast-iron 45° wyes, half wyes, long-sweep quarter bends, sixth, eighth, or sixteenth bends, or by combinations of these fittings, or by use of equivalent fittings or their combinations; except that sanitary tees may be used in vertical sections of drains or stacks, and short quarter bends may be used in drainage lines where the change in direction of flow is from the horizontal to the vertical. Tees and crosses may be used in vent pipes and in water-distributing pipes. No change in direction greater than 90° in a single turn shall be made in drainage pipes.

Sec. 203. PROHIBITED FITTINGS.—No double hub, or double-tee branch, shall be used on soil or waste lines. The drilling and tapping of building drains, soil, waste, or vent pipes, and the use of saddle hubs or bands, are prohibited. Any fitting or connection which has an enlargement, chamber, or recess with a ledge, shoulder, or reduction of the pipe area, that offers an obstruction to flow through the drain, is prohibited.

Sec. 204. PROHIBITED CONNECTIONS.—(a) No fixture, device, or construction shall be installed which will provide a backflow connection between a distributing system of water for drinking and domestic purposes and a drainage system, soil, or waste pipe so as to permit or make possible the backflow of sewage or waste into the water-supply system.

(b) No interconnection or cross-connection shall be made between a water-supply system carrying water meeting accepted standards of purity and any other water-supply system.

Sec. 205. PROTECTION OF PIPES.—Pipes passing under or through walls shall be protected from breakage. Pipes passing through or under cinder concrete or other corrosive material shall be protected against external corrosion.

No soil or waste stack shall be installed or permitted outside a building or in an exterior wall unless adequate provision is made to protect it from freezing.

Sec. 206. PROTECTION OF ELECTRICAL MACHINERY.—No water or drainage piping shall be located over electrical machinery or equipment unless adequate protection is provided against drip caused by condensation on the piping.

Sec. 207. PROTECTION OF WATER TANKS.—Drainage piping shall not pass directly over water-supply tanks or reservoirs unless such tanks or reservoirs are tightly closed.

Sec. 208. WORKMANSHIP.—Workmanship shall be of such character as fully to secure the results sought in all sections of this manual.

CHAPTER III. QUALITY, WEIGHT, AND THICKNESS OF MATERIALS

Sec. 301. QUALITY OF MATERIALS.—Materials used in any plumbing system, or part thereof, shall meet accepted standards and shall be free from defects.

Refere ces made in the following sections to standards and specifications shall be taken to mean the latest issues thereof. (See par. 301, pt. III, for information about such issues and for similar and equivalent specifications.)

Sec. 302. IDENTIFICATION OF MATERIALS.—Each length of pipe, and each fitting, trap, fixture, and device used in a plumbing system shall be cast, stamped, or indelibly marked with the maker's mark or name; and also with the weight and quality thereof, when this is required in the specification that applies.

Sec. 303. VITRIFIED-CLAY PIPE.—Vitrified-clay pipe shall conform to Federal Specification for Pipe; Clay, Sewer.

Sec. 304. CONCRETE PIPE.—Concrete pipe shall conform to Federal Specification for Pipe; Concrete, Non-Pressure, Non-Reinforced and Reinforced.

Sec. 305. CAST-IRON SOIL PIPE.—Cast-iron soil pipe and fittings (calked joints) shall conform to Federal Specification for Pipe and Pipe-Fittings; Soil, Cast-Iron, provided that, when approved by the authority having jurisdiction over plumbing, lighter pipe and fittings of equal quality may be used.

Sec. 306. CAST-IRON WATER PIPE.—Cast-iron water pipe shall conform to Federal Specification for Pipe; Water, Cast-Iron (Bell and Spigot and Bolted Joint).

Sec. 307. CAST-IRON SCREWED PIPE.—Cast-iron screwed pipe shall conform to Federal Specification for Pipe, Cast-Iron; Drainage, Vent, and Waste (Threaded).

Sec. 308. WROUGHT-IRON PIPE.—Wrought-iron pipe shall conform to Federal Specification for Pipe; Wrought-Iron, Welded, Black and Galvanized.

Sec. 309. STEEL PIPE.—Steel pipe shall conform to Federal Specification for Pipe; Steel, Seamless and Welded, Black and Zinc-Coated.

Sec. 310. BRASS AND COPPER PIPE.—Brass and copper pipe (I. P. S.) shall conform to Federal Specifications for Pipe, Brass, Seamless, Iron-Pipe-Size, Standard and Extra-Strong; and for Pipe, Copper, Seamless, Iron-Pipe-Size, Standard, respectively.

Sec. 311. BRASS TUBING.—Brass tubing for fixture connections and fittings shall conform to Federal Specification for Plumbing Fixtures; (for) Land Use.

Sec. 312. COPPER TUBING.—Copper tubing for use with flared or soldered fittings shall conform to Federal Specification for Tubing; Copper, Seamless (for Use with Soldered or Flared Fittings) (types K, L, and M). Copper tubing for use with flanged fittings or with silver-brazed joints shall conform to Federal Specification for Tubing, Copper, Seamless (for General Use with I. P. S. Flanged Fittings) (types A, B, C, and D).

Sec. 313. LEAD PIPE.—Lead pipe shall conform to accepted standards. (See table 313-III, pt. III.)

Sec. 314. SHEET LEAD.—Sheet lead shall conform to Federal Specification for Lead; Sheet, and shall weigh not less than 4 pounds per square foot.

Sec. 315. CALKING LEAD.—Calking lead shall conform to Federal Specification for Lead, Calking.

Sec. 316. SHEET COPPER AND BRASS.—Sheet copper and brass shall conform to Federal Specifications for Copper; Bars, Plates, Rods, Shapes, Sheets, and Strips, and for Brass, Commercial; Bars, Plates, Rods, Shapes, Sheets, and Strips, respectively, and shall be not lighter than No. 18 AWG (Brown & Sharpe gage).

Sec. 317. ZINC-COATED (GALVANIZED) SHEET IRON AND STEEL.—Zinc-coated (galvanized) sheet iron and steel shall conform to Federal Specification for Iron and Steel; Sheet, Black and Zinc-Coated (Galvanized); and shall be not lighter than the following AWG (Brown & Sharpe gage):

No. 26 for 2- to 12-inch pipe.
No. 24 for 13- to 20-inch pipe.
No. 22 for 21- to 26-inch pipe.

Sec. 318. SCREWED FITTINGS.—(a) Screwed fittings shall be of cast iron, malleable iron, or brass. Cast-iron fittings shall conform to Federal Specification for Pipe Fittings; Cast-Iron (Threaded). Malleable-iron fittings shall conform to Federal Specification for Pipe-Fittings; Malleable-Iron (Threaded). Brass fittings shall conform to Federal Specification for Pipe-Fittings; Brass or Bronze (Threaded), 125-lb.

(b) Drainage fittings shall be of cast iron, malleable iron, or brass. Cast-iron fittings shall conform to Federal Specification for Pipe-Fittings; Cast-Iron, Drainage. Malleable-iron and brass fittings shall conform to the applicable requirements of the same specification.

Sec. 319. SOLDERED FITTINGS.—Soldered fittings shall conform to American Standards Association Standard for Soldered-Joint Fittings.

Sec. 320. CALKING FERRULES.—Brass calking ferrules shall be of the best quality cast red brass of approved weights and dimensions (see table 320–III, pt. III). Iron-body ferrules shall conform to Federal Specification for Pipe and Pipe-Fittings; Soil, Cast-Iron.

Sec. 321. SOLDERING NIPPLES AND BUSHINGS.—(a) Soldering nipples shall be of red brass pipe, iron-pipe size, or of heavy cast red brass of approved weights. (See table 321 (a)–III, pt. III.)

(b) Soldering bushings shall be of red brass pipe, iron-pipe size, or of heavy cast red brass.

Sec. 322. FLOOR FLANGES.—Floor flanges for plumbing fixtures shall conform to Federal Specification for Plumbing Fixtures; (for) Land Use.

Sec. 323. PACKING.—Packing for hub-and-spigot joints shall conform to Federal Specification for Packing; Jute, Twisted.

Sec. 324. SETTING COMPOUND.—Setting compound for connecting fixtures to floor flanges shall conform to Federal Specification for Compound; Plumbing-Fixture-Setting.

Sec. 325. GASKETS.—Gaskets for connecting fixtures to floor flanges shall conform to Federal Specification for Gaskets; Plumbing-Fixture-Setting.

Sec. 326. ALTERNATE MATERIALS.—Any material other than that specified in this manual which the authority having jurisdiction over plumbing approves may be used.

CHAPTER IV. JOINTS AND CONNECTIONS

Sec. 401. TIGHTNESS.—Joints and connections shall be made gastight and watertight.

Sec. 402. VITRIFIED-CLAY AND CONCRETE PIPE.—Joints in vitrified-clay and concrete pipe, or between such pipe and metals, shall be hot-poured or cemented joints. Hot-poured joints shall be packed with approved packing and filled with an approved jointing compound at one pouring (see par. 402, pt. III). Cemented joints shall be packed with approved packing and secured with portland cement (see par. 402, pt. III).

Sec. 403. CALKED JOINTS.—Calked joints shall be firmly packed with approved packing, secured with well-calked lead, not less than 1 inch deep; and no paint, varnish, or putty shall be permitted until after the joint is tested.

Sec. 404. SCREWED JOINTS.—Screwed joints shall be made with a lubricant on the male thread only. All burrs or cuttings shall be removed.

Sec. 405. JOINTS IN CAST-IRON PIPE.—Joints in cast-iron pipe may be either calked or screwed and shall be made as required in this chapter.

Sec. 406. JOINTS BETWEEN CAST-IRON AND OTHER PIPING.—Joints between cast-iron and wrought-iron, steel, or brass piping may be either screwed or calked joints made as required in this chapter. The end of threaded pipe for calking shall have a ring or half coupling screwed on to form a spigot end.

Sec. 407. WIPED JOINTS.—Wiped joints in lead pipe, or between lead pipe and brass or copper pipes, ferrules, soldering nipples, bushings, or traps, in all cases on the sewer side of the trap and in concealed joints on the inlet side of the trap, shall be full-wiped joints, with an exposed surface of the solder on each side of the joint not less than three-quarters of an inch, and a minimum thickness at the thickest part of the joint of not less than three-eighths of an inch. Where a round joint is made, a thickness of not less than ⅜ of an inch for bushings and flange joints shall be provided.

Sec. 408. JOINTS BETWEEN LEAD AND OTHER PIPING.—Joints between lead and cast-iron, steel, or wrought-iron piping shall be made by means of a calking ferrule, soldering nipple, or bushing.

Sec. 409. JOINTS IN COPPER TUBING.—Copper-tubing joints shall be made in accordance with approved practice. (See par. 409, pt. III.)

Sec. 410. SLIP JOINTS AND UNIONS.—Slip joints and unions shall be used only in trap seals or on the inlet side of the trap, except that expansion joints of approved type may be permitted. Unions on the sewer side of the trap shall be ground faced, and shall not be concealed or enclosed.

Sec. 411. ROOF FLASHINGS.—Joints at the roof shall be made watertight by use of copper, lead, or zinc-coated (galvanized) iron flashings, cast-iron plates, or other approved materials.

Sec. 412. FLOOR CONNECTIONS.—Floor connections for water-closets and other fixtures shall be made by means of an approved brass or cast-iron floor flange soldered securely or calked to the drain pipe. The joint between the fixture and floor flange shall be made tight by means of an approved fixture-setting compound or gasket.

Sec. 413. INCREASERS AND REDUCERS.—Where different sizes of drainage pipes or pipes and fittings are to be connected, proper sizes of standard increasers and reducers shall be employed. Reduction of size of drain pipes in the direction of flow is prohibited, except as indicated in paragraph 413, part III.

Sec. 414. SUPPORTS.—Connections of wall hangers, pipe supports, or fixture settings to masonry or concrete backing shall be made with approved bolts without the use of wooden plugs.

CHAPTER V. TRAPS AND CLEAN-OUTS

Sec. 501. TYPES AND SIZES OF TRAPS.—Every trap shall be self-cleaning, shall be of the same nominal size as the drain to which it is connected, and shall conform to accepted standards. (See par. 501, pt. III.)

The minimum size (nominal inside diameter) of trap and fixture drain for a given fixture shall be not less than shown in the following table:

Fixture:	Size of trap and fixture drain, inches
Bathtubs	1½
Combination fixtures	1½
Drinking fountains	1¼
Floor drains	2
Laundry trays	1½
Lavatories	1¼
Shower stalls	2
Sinks, kitchen, residence	1½
Sinks, hotel or public	2
Sinks, small, pantry or bar	1¼
Sinks, dishwasher	1½
Sinks, service	2
Urinals, trough	2
Urinals, stall	2

For water closets and other fixtures with integral traps, the fixture drains shall be not smaller than the fixture-trap outlet. (See par. 501, pt. III.)

Sec. 502. PROHIBITED TRAPS.—No form of trap which depends for its seal upon the action of movable parts, or partitions that cannot be exposed for inspection, except in a trap integral with a fixture, shall be used for fixtures. No fixture shall be double-trapped. (See par. 502, pt. III.)

Sec. 503. TRAPS REQUIRED.—Each fixture shall be separately trapped by an approved trap placed as near to the fixture as possible or integral therewith, except that a set of not more than three fixtures such as lavatories or laundry trays, or a set of two laundry trays and one sink, may connect with a single trap, provided the trap for three fixtures is placed centrally. (See fig. 3, pt. III.)

Sec. 504. TRAP SEAL.—Each fixture trap shall have a water seal of not less than 2 inches and not more than 4 inches. (See fig. 4, pt. III.)

Sec. 505. TRAP CLEAN-OUTS.—Each trap, except those in combination with fixtures in which the trap seal is plainly visible and accessible, shall be provided with an approved clean-out plug conforming to Federal Specification for Plumbing Fixtures; (for) Land Use.

Sec. 506. INSTALLATION OF TRAPS.—Traps shall be set true with respect to their water seals and protected from freezing.

Sec. 507. PIPE CLEAN-OUTS.—Pipe clean-outs, ferrules, and plugs shall conform to Federal Specification for Pipe and Pipe-Fittings; Soil, Cast-Iron.

Sec. 508. PIPE CLEAN-OUTS REQUIRED.—Accessible clean-outs shall be provided at or near the foot of each vertical waste or soil stack and each inside leader that connects to the building drain, and at each change in direction of the building drain greater than 45°. The distance between clean-outs in horizontal soil lines shall not exceed 50 feet. Clean-outs shall be of the same nominal size as the pipes up to 4 inches and not less than 4 inches for larger pipes.

Sec. 509. CLEAN-OUT EQUIVALENTS.—Any floor or wall connection of fixture traps when bolted or screwed to the floor or wall shall be regarded as a pipe clean-out.

Sec. 510. ACCESSIBILITY OF TRAPS AND CLEAN-OUTS.—Underground traps and clean-outs of a building, except where clean-outs are flush with the floor, and exterior underground traps that are not readily accessible shall be made accessible by manholes with proper covers.

Sec. 511. GREASE INTERCEPTORS.—Grease interceptors shall be installed when required by and in accordance with the regulations of the authority having jurisdiction over plumbing.

Sec. 512. OIL INTERCEPTORS.—Oil interceptors shall be installed when required by and in accordance with the regulations of the authority having jurisdiction over plumbing.

Sec. 513. SAND INTERCEPTORS.—Sand interceptors, when installed, shall be so designed and placed as to be readily accessible for cleaning.

Sec. 514. FLOOR DRAINS.—Floor and area drains shall conform to Federal Specification for Plumbing Fixtures; (for) Land Use, where applicable.

Sec. 515. BACKWATER VALVES.—Backwater valves shall have all bearing parts of corrosion-resisting metal, and be so constructed as to provide a positive mechanical seal against backwater. The area of valve seat shall be equal to the cross-sectional area of the pipe connection.

CHAPTER VI. WATER SUPPLY AND DISTRIBUTION

Sec. 601. QUALITY OF WATER.—The quality of the water supply to each building shall meet accepted standards of purity. Development of private sources of supply shall be in accordance with approved practice. (See par. 601, pt. III.)

Sec. 602. PROTECTION OF WATER SUPPLY.—

(a) Potable and nonpotable water supplies shall be distributed through systems entirely independent of each other.

(b) Water pumps, wells, hydrants, filters, softeners, appliances, and devices shall be protected from surface water and outside contamination by approved covers, walls, or copings.

(c) Potable water-supply tanks, whether storage, pressure, or suction tanks, shall be properly covered to prevent entrance of foreign material into the water supply. (See also sec. 207.)

(d) Every supply outlet or connection to a fixture or appliance shall be protected from backflow by means of an approved air gap or backflow preventer between the control valve of the outlet and the fixture or appliance. (See par. 602 (d), pt. III.)

Sec. 603. PROTECTION FROM FREEZING.—Water pipes, storage tanks, flushing cisterns, and appliances, when subject to freezing temperatures, shall be protected. Water pipes underground shall be placed below freezing level, or shall be otherwise insulated to protect them from freezing. Interior piping shall be insulated, when necessary, for protection.

Sec. 604. SIZE OF BUILDING MAIN.—The building main, including the water-service pipe, shall be of sufficient size to permit a continuous ample flow of water to the building under the average daily minimum service pressure in the street main. The required size for each building shall be determined by the rules given in paragraph 604, part III. No building main of less than ¾-inch diameter shall be installed. If flush valves are installed, the building main shall be of not less than 1-inch diameter.

Sec. 605. Quantity of Water.—Plumbing fixtures shall be provided with a sufficient supply of water for flushing and keeping them in a sanitary condition.

Sec. 606. Size of Fixture Branches.—The minimum size of fixture branches and other supply outlets shall be as follows:

	Inch
Sill cocks	1/2
Domestic water heaters	1/2
Laundry trays	1/2
Sinks	1/2
Lavatories	3/8
Bathtubs	1/2
Water-closet tanks	3/8
Water-closet flush valves	1
Flush valves for pedestal urinals	1
Flush valves for wall or stall urinals	1/2

Sec. 607. Shut-Offs.—Accessible shut-offs with drains shall be provided on the building main and on branches for each dwelling unit and in freezing climates for each outdoor connection. Additional shut-offs may be installed.

Sec. 608. Material for Water Piping and Tubing.—Material for building water-supply pipes and tubes shall be of brass, copper, cast or wrought iron, lead, or steel, with approved fittings. All threaded ferrous pipe and fittings shall be galvanized (zinc-coated). No pipe, tubing, or fittings that have been previously used shall be used for distributing water except for replacement in the same system.

Lead piping in water-supply lines shall not be used unless it has been definitely determined that no poisonous lead salts are produced by contact of lead with the particular water supply.

Sec. 609. Relief Valves.—An approved relief valve shall be installed in each hot-water system and so located that there is no shut-off or check valve between the tank and the relief valve.

CHAPTER VII. PLUMBING FIXTURES

Sec. 701. Quality of Fixtures.—Plumbing fixtures shall conform to accepted standards. (See par. 701, pt. III.)

Sec. 702. Installation of Fixtures.—Plumbing fixtures shall be installed in a manner to afford access for cleaning. Where practicable, pipes from fixtures shall be run to the wall, and no lead trap or lead pipe shall extend nearer to the floor than 12 inches unless protected by casing.

Sec. 703. Frostproof Closets.—Frostproof closets may be installed only in compartments which have no direct access to a building used for human habitation or occupancy. The soil pipe between the hopper and the trap shall be of not less than 3-inch diameter and shall be of lead, or cast iron enameled on the inside. The waste tube from the valve shall not be connected to the soil pipe or sewer.

Sec. 704. Floor Drains.—A floor drain or a shower drain shall be considered a fixture and provided with a strainer.

Sec. 705. Fixture Strainers. — Fixtures other than water closets and pedestal and blow-out urinals shall be provided with approved strainers. (See par. 705, pt. III.)

Sec. 706. Fixture Overflow.—The overflow pipe from a fixture shall be connected on the inlet side of the trap and be so arranged that it may be cleaned.

Sec. 707. Swimming Pools. — Swimming pools shall be constructed in accordance with accepted practice. (See par. 707, pt. III.)

Sec. 708. Miscellaneous Fixtures.—Baptistries, ornamental and lily ponds, aquaria, ornamental fountain basins, and similar constructions shall have supplies thereto protected from backflow as required in section 602.

Sec. 709. Ventilation.—No plumbing fixtures shall be located in any room not provided with proper ventilation. Ventilating pipes from toilet rooms shall form an independent system.

CHAPTER VIII. SOIL AND WASTE PIPES FOR SANITARY SYSTEMS [2]

Sec. 801. Materials.—(*a*) Soil and waste piping for sanitary drainage systems within a building shall be of brass, copper, iron, steel, or lead.

(*b*) The building drain when underground shall be of cast iron.

(*c*) The building sewer shall be of cast iron, vitrified clay, or concrete.

Sec. 802. Minimum Sizes.—The minimum required sizes of soil and waste pipes, depending on location and conditions of service, shall be in accordance with the following sections and tables of this chapter and the principles, rules, and tables relating to drains and sewers in part III. (See par. 802, pt. III.)

Sec. 803. Fixture Units. — The following table of fixture-unit values designating the relative load weights of different kinds of fixtures shall be employed in estimating the total load carried by a soil or waste pipe and shall be used in connection with tables of size for waste and drain pipes in which the permissible load is given in terms of fixture units.

Table 803.—*Fixture units per fixture or group* [1]

Fixture and type of installation	Number of fixture units
Lavatory or washbasin:	
Public	2
Private	1
Water closet:	
Public	10
Private	6
Bathtub, public	4
Shower head:	
Public	4
Private	2
Pedestal urinal, public	10
Wall or stall urinal, public	5
Service sink [2]	3
Kitchen sink, private [2]	2
Bathtub, private	2
Bathroom group, private	8
Bathroom group with separate shower stall, private	10
Two or three laundry trays with single trap, private [2]	3
Combination sink and laundry tray, private [2]	3
Sewage ejector or sump pump, for each 25 gpm	50

[1] See par. 803, pt. III for fixture-unit weights not included in table 803.

[2] These fixtures and groups may be omitted in determining the total fixture units to be applied for soil pipes but the fixture-unit weights assigned must be applied for separate waste lines for groups of these fixtures.

Sec. 804. Stacks To Be Vertical.—Soil and waste stacks shall extend in a vertical line from the highest to the lowest horizontal branch or fixture branch connected thereto, except as provided for in section 806, and shall be vented in accordance with the requirements of chapter X.

Sec. 805. Size of Soil and Waste Pipes.—(*a*) Except as provided in (*b*) of this section, the total number of fixture units installed on a soil or waste stack or horizontal branch of given diameter shall be in accordance with table 805. No soil or waste stack shall be smaller than the largest horizontal branch connected thereto.

(*b*) If the total fixture units are distributed on horizontal branches in three or more branch intervals of the stack, the total number of fixture units on a straight soil or waste stack of a given diameter may be increased from the values given in table 805 within the limits of table 805(*b*)–III, part III, provided the maximum fixture units for one branch interval as computed in accordance with table 805(*b*)–III is not exceeded in any branch interval of the system.

Table 805.—*Permissible number of fixture units on horizontal branches and stacks*

Diameter of pipe (inches)	Fixture units on 1 horizontal branch	Fixture units on 1 stack
	Number	*Number*
1¼	1	2
1½	3	4
2	6	10
3 waste only	32	48
3 soil	20	30
4	160	240
5	360	540
6	640	960
8	1,200	2,240
10	1,800	3,780
12	2,800	6,000

Sec. 806. Offsets.—(*a*) A single offset, a double offset, or a return offset, with no change in direction greater than 45°, may be installed in a soil or waste stack with the stack and branches vented as required for a straight stack, provided that the total number of fixture units on such stack does not exceed one-half the limit permitted by section 805(*a*) and table 805, and no horizontal branch connects to the stack in or within 4 diameters (stack) above or below a sloping section of the offset.

(*b*) If an offset is made at an angle greater than 45°, the required diameter of that portion of the stack above the offset shall be determined as for a separate stack. The diameter of the offset including fittings shall be determined as for a primary branch, and the portion above the offset shall be considered as a horizontal branch in determining the diameter of that portion of the stack below the offset. A relief vent shall be installed in accordance with the requirements of section 1017 at the offset or between it and the next lower horizontal branch.

(*c*) An offset above the highest horizontal branch in a soil or waste stack system is an offset in the stack-vent and shall not be considered in this connection other than as to its effect on the developed length of vent.

(*d*) In case of an offset in a soil or waste stack below the lowest horizontal branch, no change in diameter of the stack because of the offset shall be required if it is made at an angle of not greater than 45°. If such an offset is made at an angle greater than 45°, the required diameter of the offset and the stack below it shall be determined as for a primary branch.

Sec. 807. HORIZONTAL AND PRIMARY BRANCHES.—(a) The required sizes of horizontal branches and primary branches of the building drain shall be in accordance with table 807, except that the permissible number of fixture units on primary branches as given in table 807 may be increased as provided for in section 807(d).

TABLE 807.—*Capacities of horizontal branches and primary branches of the building drain*

Diameter of pipe (inches)	Permissible number of fixture units				
	Horizontal branch at minimum permissible slope or greater	Primary branch [1]			
		1/16-inch fall per foot	1/8-inch fall per foot	1/4-inch fall per foot	1/2-inch fall per foot
	Number	*Number*	*Number*	*Number*	*Number*
1¼	1	....	....	2	2
1½	3	....	....	5	7
2	6	....	....	21	26
3 waste only	32	....	36	42	50
3 soil	20	....	24	27	36
4	160	....	180	216	250
5	360	360	400	480	560
6	600	600	660	790	940
8	1,200	1,400	1,600	1,920	2,240
10	1,800	2,400	2,700	3,240	3,780
12	2,800	3,600	4,200	5,000	6,000

[1] See par. 807, pt. III, for method of computing permissible number of fixture units for other slopes than those given in this table.

(b) In case the sanitary system consists of one soil stack only or of one soil stack and one or more waste stacks of less than 3-inch diameter, the building drain and building sewer shall be of the same nominal size as the primary branch from the soil stack as given by table 807, except that (d) of this section and the applicable rules in paragraph 807, part III, relating to pressure drainage may apply when the prescribed conditions are complied with.

(c) In case the plumbing system has two or more soil stacks each having its separate primary branch or has one or more soil stacks and one or more waste stacks of 3-inch diameter or larger, each soil and waste stack having its separate primary branch, the number of fixture units for a secondary branch, the main building drain, or the building sewer of a given diameter and slope may be increased from the value given in table 807 for a primary branch of the same diameter and slope to the value given in table 807(c), part III, of this manual, provided that the increase is made strictly within the principles and rules of paragraph 807, part III.

(d) In case there is no fixture drain or horizontal branch connecting directly with the building drain or a branch thereof and the lowest fixture branch or horizontal branch connected to any soil or waste stack of the system is 3 feet or more above the grade line of the building drain, the permissible number of fixture units on primary branches, secondary branches, main building drain, and building sewer, may be increased within the limits given by table 807(d), part III, provided the increases are made in accordance with the principles and rules given in paragraph 807, part III.

(e) The provisions of sections 807(c) and 807(d) shall not apply unless plans drawn to scale showing the proposed installation in detail in regard to the diameter, direction, length, and slope of the building drain and its branches and of the building sewer have been submitted to and approved by the authority having jurisdiction over plumbing.

Sec. 808. SUMPS AND RECEIVING TANKS.—All building subdrains shall discharge into an airtight sump or receiving tank so located as to receive the sewage by gravity, from which sump or receiving tank the sewage shall be lifted and discharged into the building sewer by pumps, ejectors, or any equally efficient method. Such sumps shall either be automatically discharged or be of sufficient capacity to receive the building sewage and wastes for not less than 24 hours.

CHAPTER IX. STORM DRAINS

Sec. 901. GENERAL.—Roofs and paved areas, yards, courts, and courtyards shall be drained into the storm-sewerage system or the combined sewerage system, but not into sewers intended for sanitary sewage only. When connected with a combined sewerage system, storm drains, the intakes of which are within 12 feet of any door, window, or ventilating opening, if not at least 3 feet higher than the top of such opening, shall be effectively trapped. One trap on the main storm drain may serve for all such connections. Traps shall be set below the frost line or on the inside of the building. Where there is no sewer accessible, storm drainage shall discharge into the public gutter, unless otherwise permitted by the proper authorities, and in such case need not be trapped.

Sec. 902. LEADERS AND GUTTERS.—(a) Leaders, when placed within the walls of a building or run in a vent or pipe shaft, shall be of cast-iron, zinc-coated (galvanized) wrought-iron or steel, brass, copper, or lead pipe, or of copper tubing.

(b) Outside leaders may be of sheet metal. When of sheet metal and connected with a building storm drain or storm sewer, they shall be connected to a cast-iron drain extending not less than 1 foot above the finish grade. A sheet-metal leader along a public driveway without sidewalk shall be properly protected against injury.

(c) Roof gutters shall be of metal or other materials suitable for forming an effective open channel for collecting water and conducting it to the leaders and suitable for making a tight connection with the leaders. (See par. 902, pt. III.)

Sec. 903. SIZE OF STORM DRAINS AND LEADERS.—(a) Storm drains of a building shall be of ample size to convey the estimated storm water from the roof gutters to the street sewer or other approved place of discharge without overflow and without producing dangerously high pressures in any building drain or leader. The estimated flow shall be based on the maximum expected rate of rainfall and estimated rate of flow of storm sewage from other sources. The tables in this section pertaining to leaders and building storm drains are based on the horizontal projection of the roof area, a rate of rainfall of 4 inches per hour and limited slopes as indicated in the tables. (See par. 903, pt. III, for methods of computing the requirements for conditions not covered by or in these tables.)

(b) The area drained into or by a vertical leader or a sloping leader or connecting pipe having a slope of 1/4-inch fall per foot or greater shall not exceed the values given in table 903(b).

(c) The roof area drained into a building storm sewer or into a main storm drain or any of its branches shall not exceed the values given in table 903(c).

TABLE 903(b).—*Maximum roof area for leaders*

Diameter of leader or pipe	Maximum roof area
Inches	*Square feet*
2	500
2½	960
3	1,500
[a] 3½	2,200
4	3,100
5	5,400
6	8,400
8	17,400

[a] Drainage fittings are not generally available.

TABLE 903(c).—*Maximum roof area for building storm sewers or drains*

Diameter of pipe (inches)	Maximum roof area for drains of various slopes			
	1/16-inch fall per foot	1/8-inch fall per foot	1/4-inch fall per foot	1/2-inch fall per foot
	Square feet	*Square feet*	*Square feet*	*Square feet*
2	......	......	250	500
[a] 2½	......	480	670	960
3	......	750	1,050	1,500
[a] 3½	......	1,100	1,550	2,200
4	......	1,550	2,150	3,100
5	1,800	2,700	3,800	5,400
6	3,000	4,200	6,000	8,400
8	5,900	8,700	11,900	17,400
10	9,800	15,200	19,600	30,400
12	15,900	24,700	31,800	49,400

[a] 2½-inch and 3½-inch cast-iron soil pipe and fittings and 3½-inch drainage fittings are not generally available.

(d) Roof area or drained area as applying in the preceding tables of this section shall be the horizontal projection of the area, except that where a building wall extends above the roof or court in such a manner as to drain onto the roof or court, due allowance for the additional run-off shall be made. (See par. 903(d), pt. III, for methods of computing allowance.)

Sec. 904. SEPARATE AND COMBINED DRAINS.—(a) The sanitary- and storm-drainage systems of a building shall be entirely separate, except that where a combined sanitary-and-storm street sewer is available the storm drains may connect to a combined sanitary-and-storm building drain or sewer at least 10 feet downstream from any primary branch of the sanitary system. Connections between the sanitary and storm systems shall be made at the same grade by means of a single wye fitting. (See par. 904, pt. III, for explanation of this requirement.)

(b) Up to the point of combining into one system, the sizes of the storm and sanitary branches shall be as required for separate storm and sanitary systems.

In the case of a combined sanitary-and-storm building drain or sewer, or of a branch formed by the junction of a single storm drain or sewer and a single sanitary drain or sewer when neither the storm nor the sanitary drain carries more than one-half of its allowable load as given in table 903(c), part II, and table 807(c)-III, part III, the diameter of the combined drain or combined sewer shall be at least equal to that of the larger of the two branches emptying into it, except that in no case shall a combined sanitary-and-storm building drain or building sewer be less than 4 inches in diameter. If either or both of the storm or sanitary branch drains carry more than one-half the allowable load, the combined drain or combined building sewer shall be in accordance with table 904–III and rules of paragraph 904, part III.

Sec. 905. CLOSED SYSTEM REQUIRED.—When connected with a combined sanitary-and-storm sewerage system, the building storm-drainage piping shall form a closed system with water-tight joints, except for its outlet and intake openings.

Sec. 906. OVERFLOW PIPES.—Overflow pipes from cisterns, supply tanks, expansion tanks, and drip pans shall connect with any building sewer, building drain, or soil pipe only by means of an indirect connection.

Sec. 907. SUBSOIL SUMPS.—Subsoil drains below the main-sewer level shall discharge into a sump or receiving tank, the contents of which shall be automatically lifted and discharged into the drainage system through a properly trapped fixture or drain.

Sec. 908. CONSTRUCTION OF SUBSOIL DRAINS.—Where subsoil drains are placed under the cellar floor or used to encircle the outer walls of a building, they shall be made of open-jointed drain tile or earthenware pipe, not less than 4 inches in diameter. When the building drain is subject to backwater the subsoil drain shall be protected by an accessibly located automatic back-pressure valve before entering the building sewer or drain. If such drains are connected with the sanitary sewer or with a combined system they shall be properly trapped. They may discharge to an area drain.

CHAPTER X. VENTS AND VENTING

Sec. 1001. MATERIAL.—Vent pipes or tubing shall be of cast iron, zinc-coated (galvanized) wrought iron or steel, brass, copper, or lead.

Sec. 1002. PROTECTION OF TRAP SEALS.—The seal of every fixture trap in a plumbing system shall be adequately protected by a properly installed vent or system of venting. A stack-vent, back vent, relief vent, dual vent, circuit or loop vent, or a combination of two or more of these forms installed in the manner and within the limitations specified in sections 1006 to 1012, inclusive, shall be considered as adequate protection of trap seals in the sense of this section. (See par. 1002, pt. III.)

Sec. 1003. STACK-VENTS REQUIRED.—Every soil or waste stack shall be extended vertically as a stack-vent to at least 6 inches above the highest horizontal branch and then to the open air above the roof or otherwise terminated in the open air outside the building; or the stack-vent and vent stack may be connected together within the building at least 6 inches above the flood level of the highest fixture, with a single extension from the connection to the open air.

Sec. 1004. VENT STACKS REQUIRED.—A vent stack or main vent shall be installed with a soil or waste stack whenever relief vents, back vents, or other branch vents are required in two or more branch intervals. The vent stack shall terminate independently in the open air outside the building or may be connected with the stack-vent as prescribed in section 1003, and shall connect with the soil or waste stack through, at, or below the lowest horizontal branch or with the primary branch of the building drain.

Sec. 1005. DISTANCE OF TRAP FROM VENT.—Except as provided for particular fixtures and forms of construction in sections 1010 and 1011, and excepting water closets, pedestal urinals, trap-standard service sinks, and other fixtures which depend on siphon action for the proper functioning of the fixture, each fixture trap shall have a protecting vent located so that the total fall in the fixture drain from the trap weir to the vent fitting is not more than 1 pipe diameter, and the developed length of drain from trap weir to vent fitting is not less than 2 nor more than 48 pipe diameters. A back vent or relief vent, preferably in the form of a continuous-waste-and-vent, shall be installed within these limits as may be necessary for compliance with this requirement. (See par. 1005, and fig. 13, pt. III.)

Sec. 1006. DUAL VENTS PERMITTED.—A dual vent for two fixture traps installed as a vertical continuous-waste-and-vent, or a stack-vent in a dual capacity, may be employed under the following conditions and no additional vents for the traps thus vented shall be required:

(a) When both fixture drains connect with a vertical drain or stack at the same level, and the developed length and total fall of each of the two fixture drains are within the limits given in section 1005. (See fig. 14A, pt. III.)

(b) When the two fixture drains connect with the vertical drain or stack at different levels, the difference in level of the two connections is not greater than five times the diameter of the vertical section of drain or stack, the diameter of the vertical section or stack up to and including the higher connection is not less than that required for the horizontal drain for both fixtures, the cross-section of the higher of the two fixture drains is not greater than one-half that of the vertical drain, and the developed length and total fall of each of the two fixture drains is within the limits given in section 1005. (See fig. 14B, pt. III.)

Sec. 1007. GROUP VENTS PERMITTED.—(a) A lavatory trap and a bathtub or shower-stall trap may be installed on the same horizontal branch with a back vent for the lavatory trap and with no back vent for the bathtub or shower-stall trap, provided the vertical section of the lavatory drain is of not less than 1¼-inch diameter, connects with the tub or shower-stall drain in a vertical plane, and the developed lengths of both fixture drains are within the limits given in section 1005. (See fig. 15A, pt. III.)

(b) Two lavatory traps and two bathtub or shower-stall traps may be installed on the same horizontal branch with a dual vent for the lavatory traps and with no back vents for the bathtub or shower-stall traps, provided that the horizontal branch, except the separate fixture drains, shall be at least 2 inches in diameter and the fixture drains for bathtubs or shower stalls connect as closely as practicable upstream from the vent by means of a drainage wye. (See fig. 15B, pt. III.)

(c) A lavatory trap, kitchen-sink trap, and a bathtub or shower-stall trap may be installed on the same horizontal branch, as in (a), provided the dual vent for the lavatory and sink traps is installed in accordance with section 1006. (See fig. 15C, pt. III.)

Sec. 1008. YOKE AND RELIEF VENTS.—Bathroom groups, each consisting of a water closet, lavatory, and a shower stall or bathtub with or without shower head, may be installed on a soil stack with any of the following forms of group venting:

(a) Two bathroom groups, or one bathroom group and kitchen sink or kitchen-sink-and-tray combination, may be installed in the highest branch interval of the soil stack or on a vertical yoke-vented branch not less than 3 inches in diameter with no branch vents other than the yoke vent, provided each fixture drain connects independently to the soil stack or with the water-closet drain (closet bend) in the highest branch interval and each fixture drain in all except the highest branch interval connects independently with the yoke-vented branch or with the water-closet drains (closet bends) within the limits given in section 1005. (See fig. 16, pt. III.)

(b) One bathroom group with group venting in accordance with section 1007(a) and with the horizontal branch connected to the soil stack at the same level as the water-closet drain or connected to the water-closet drain (closet bend), or a bathroom group and kitchen sink with connections to the stack in the same manner and with group venting in accordance with section 1007(c), may be installed in the same branch interval of a soil stack within the limits of permissible fixture units for one soil stack and branch intervals (sec. 805(b)), provided that a relief vent is installed from the water-closet branch drain in the third branch interval from the top and in each lower branch interval. (See fig. 19, pt. III.)

(c) Two bathroom groups with group venting in accordance with section 1007(a) or 1007(b), or two bathroom groups and two kitchen sinks with group venting in accordance with section 1007(c), may be installed in the same branch interval of a soil stack, provided a relief vent is installed for the second and lower branch intervals from the top. (See figs. 18 and 20, pt. III.)

(*d*) In all cases the relief vent required under (*a*), (*b*), or (*c*), may be a dual vent and the size shall be in accordance with section 1015. Fittings that combine the effects of two or more standard fittings in one casting may be permitted. (See also par. 1008 and figs. 13 to 20, pt. III.)

Sec. 1009. Circuit Vents and Loop Vents.—(*a*) A group of fixtures in line (battery) on the same floor or level may be installed on one horizontal branch with a circuit or loop vent connected to the horizontal branch in front of the last fixture drain, within the limits given in table 1009(*a*), provided relief vents connected to the horizontal branch in front of the first fixture drain are installed as follows:

In each branch interval, if the total fixture units installed in the branch exceeds one-half the number given in table 1009(*a*), except that no relief vent shall be required in the highest branch interval of the system or in any branch interval if the total number of fixture units on the stack above the horizontal branch does not exceed the limits for one stack given in table 805 and the number of fixtures on the circuit- or loop-vented horizontal branch does not exceed two for a 2- or 3-inch horizontal branch or does not exceed one-half the permissible number in column 2 of table 1009(*a*) for 4-inch and larger horizontal branches. A dual relief vent for two circuit- or loop-vented horizontal branches in the same branch interval may be installed.

Table 1009(*a*).—*Limits for circuit and loop venting*

(1)	(2)	(3)
Diameter of horizontal branch	Water closets, pedestal urinals, or trap-standard fixtures	Fixture units for fixtures other than designated in column 2
Inches	*Number*	*Number*
2	None	6
3	2	20
4	8	60
5	16	120
6	24	180

(*b*) The limits for circuit- or loop-vented horizontal branches may be increased to one and one-half times the values given in table 1009(*a*) for 3-inch and larger branches when relief vents are installed so that there is a relief vent inside the first fixture drain, the number of fixtures or fixture units outside the last relief vent does not exceed the limits given in columns 2 and 3 of table 1009(*a*), and the number of fixture drains between any two successive relief vents does not exceed two for a 3-inch, three for a 4-inch, five for a 5-inch, or eight for a 6-inch or larger horizontal branch.

(*c*) Two lines of fixtures back-to-back (double battery) shall not be circuit- or loop-vented on one branch, but each line may be installed on a separate branch and circuit- or loop-vented. (See figs. 21 and 22, pt. III.)

Sec. 1010. Vents for Flat-Bottomed Fixtures.—The trap and fixture drain not exceeding 2 inches in diameter of a single fixture having a relatively flat bottom at least 200 square inches of which slopes toward the outlet with a fall not exceeding ⅛ inch per foot, or the trap and fixture drain from a group of not more than three such fixtures, may be installed with a vertical section of the fixture drain not exceeding 24 pipe diameters in length at a distance not exceeding 10 pipe diameters from the trap weir, with a total length of sloping drain not exceeding 72 pipe diameters, with no back vent, provided that the fixture drain is the highest drain on the soil or waste stack or on a yoke-vented vertical section of a horizontal branch. If the total developed length of the sloping sections of the drain from the fixture to the stack-vent or relief vent exceeds 72 pipe diameters (9 feet for 1½-inch diameter or 12 feet for 2-inch diameter), a back vent to the first vertical section of the drain or a continuous-waste-and-vent relief vent at or within this prescribed maximum distance shall be installed. (See par. 1010, and fig. 23, pt. III.)

Sec. 1011. Vents for Resealing Traps.—If a resealing trap of approved design is installed for a fixture or a group of not more than three fixtures, the limits given for venting in section 1010 shall apply. (See par. 1011, pt. III.)

Sec. 1012. Fixtures at Base of Main Vent.—A group of not more than three fixtures, none of which discharge greasy wastes, may be installed on a main vent or vent stack below the lowest branch vent, provided the load does not exceed one-half the allowable load by table 807 on a horizontal branch of the same diameter as the main vent. (See par. 1012, pt. III.)

Sec. 1013. Size and Length of Main Vents.—Vent stacks or main vents shall have a diameter of at least one-half that of the soil or waste stack, and shall be of larger diameter in accordance with the limits of length and number of fixture units as given in table 1013. The length of the main vent for application with table 1013 shall be the total developed length as follows:

(*a*) From the lowest connection of the vent system with the soil stack, waste stack, or primary branch to the terminal of the vent, if it terminates separately to the open air;

(*b*) From the lowest connection of the vent system with the soil stack, waste stack, or primary branch to the stack-vent plus the developed length of the stack-vent to its terminal in the open air, if the stack-vent and vent stack are joined with a single extension to the open air.

Table 1013.—*Size and length of main vents*

Diameter of soil or waste stack (inches)	Number of fixture units on soil or waste stack	Maximum permissible developed length of vent								
		1¼-inch vent	1½-inch vent	2-inch vent	2½-inch vent	3-inch vent	4-inch vent	5-inch vent	6-inch vent	8-inch vent
		Feet	*Feet*	*Feet*	*Feet*	*Feet*	*Feet*	*Feet*	*Feet*	*Feet*
1¼	2	75								
1½	8	70	150							
2	24	28	70	300						
3	40		20	80	260	650				
3	80		18	75	240	600				
4	310			30	95	240	1,000			
4	620			22	70	180	750			
5	750				28	70	320	1,000		
5	1,500				20	50	240	750		
6	1,440					20	95	240	1,000	
6	2,880					18	70	180	750	
8	3,100						30	80	350	1,100
8	6,200						25	60	250	800

Sec. 1014. Size and Length of Stack-Vents.—Stack-vents shall be of the same diameter as the soil or waste stack, if the soil or waste stack carries one-half or more of its permissible load by table 805 or has horizontal branches in more than two branch intervals. If the soil or waste stack carries less than one-half its permissible load and has horizontal branches in not more than two branch intervals, the stack-vent may be of a diameter not less and a length not greater than required by table 1013.

Sec. 1015. Size of Back Vents and Relief Vents.—The nominal diameter of a back vent, when required, shall be not less than 1¼ inches nor less than one-half the diameter of the drain to which it is connected, and under conditions that require a relief vent for approved forms of group venting (see secs. 1007, 1008, and 1009), the sum of the cross sections of all vents installed on the horizontal branches in one branch interval shall be at least equal to that of either the main vent or the largest horizontal branch in the branch interval.

Sec. 1016. Size of Circuit and Loop Vents.—(*a*) The nominal diameter of a circuit or loop vent and the first relief vent as required by section 1009(*a*) shall be not less than one-half the diameter of the horizontal branch thus vented. Under conditions that require a relief vent (see sec. 1009) the sum of the cross-sections of the circuit or loop and relief vents shall be at least equal to that of either the main vent required or the horizontal branch. In determining the sum of cross sections for this requirement all relief vents connected to the horizontal branch may be included.

(*b*) Additional relief vents, installed in compliance with section 1009(*b*), shall be not less in diameter than one-half that of the largest fixture branch connected to the horizontal branch.

Sec. 1017. Relief Vents for Offsets.—The relief vent required for an offset, as prescribed by section 806(*b*), shall be installed either as a vertical continuation of the lower section of the soil or waste stack or as a side vent connected to the lower section of the soil or waste stack between the offset and the next fixture or horizontal branch below the offset. The size of the required relief vent shall be determined as follows:

(*a*) If the stack-vent from the upper section of the soil or waste stack is equal to that of the upper section, the relief vent shall not be smaller than the main vent of the stack system;

(*b*) If the stack-vent from the upper section of the soil or waste stack is smaller in diameter than that section, it may be the same diameter as the main vent required, in which case the diameter of the relief vent for the offset shall be equal to that of the lower section and shall be extended to the open air without reduction in size or may be connected to the main vent or stack-vent, provided the one to which it is connected is of equal or greater diameter.

If horizontal branches connect to any soil or waste stack between two offsets each offset shall be vented as required in this section.

SEC. 1018. FROST CLOSURE.—In cold climates adequate provision shall be made to guard against frost closure of vents.

SEC. 1019. LOCATION OF VENT TERMINALS.—(a) No vent terminal from the sanitary drainage system shall be within 12 feet of any door, window, or ventilating opening of the same or an adjacent building unless it is at least 3 feet higher than the top of such opening. Extensions of vent pipes through a roof shall terminate at least 1 foot above it and shall be properly flashed. Vent terminals extending through walls shall not terminate within 12 feet horizontally of any adjacent building line, shall be turned to provide a horizontal opening downward, shall be effectively screened, and shall be properly flashed, calked, or otherwise sealed.

(b) In the event that a structure is built higher than an existing structure, the owner of the structure shall not locate windows within 12 feet of any existing vent terminal on the lower structure, unless the owner of such higher structure shall defray the expenses of, or shall himself make, such alterations as are necessary to conform with the provisions of this section.

SEC. 1020. VENTS NOT REQUIRED.—(a) No vent shall be required for a leader trap, backwater trap, or subsoil catchbasin trap.

(b) No vent shall be required for the trap of a basement or cellar-floor drain or area drain, provided such drain branches into the building drain or a branch thereof at least 5 feet downstream from any soil or waste stack, the length and fall of the floor or area drain are within the limits of section 1005, the load on the building drain or any of its branches does not exceed the limits in table 807, and the building drain is not subject to backwater effects.

SEC. 1021. VENTS PROHIBITED.—(a) No back vent shall be installed within two pipe diameters of the trap weir.

(b) Except as permitted in sections 1006, 1007, 1008, 1009, and 1012, no wet vent shall be installed.

age system shall be at a temperature not higher than 140° F. Where higher temperatures exist proper cooling methods shall be provided.

CHAPTER XI. INDIRECT CONNECTIONS TO WASTE PIPES

SEC. 1101. INDIRECT WASTES.—Waste pipes from the following shall not connect directly with any building drain, soil, or waste pipe: a refrigerator, ice box, or other receptacle where food is stored; an appliance, device, or apparatus used in the preparation or processing of food or drink; an appliance, device, or apparatus using water as a cooling or heating medium; a sterilizer, water still, water-treatment device, or water-operated device.

Such waste pipes shall in all cases empty into, and above the flood level of, an open plumbing fixture or shall be connected indirectly to the inlet side of a fixture trap. Indirect waste connections shall not be located in inaccessible or unventilated cellars or other spaces. (See par. 1101, pt. III.)

SEC. 1102. SIZE OF REFRIGERATOR WASTES.—Refrigerator waste pipes shall be not less than 1¼ inches in diameter for one opening, 1½ inches for 2 or 3 openings, and 2 inches for 4 to 12 openings. Each opening shall have a trap and clean-out so installed as to permit proper flushing and cleaning of the waste pipe.

SEC. 1103. OVERFLOW PIPES.—Overflow pipes from a water-supply tank or exhaust pipes from a water lift shall not be directly connected with any building drain or with any soil or waste pipe, but shall discharge outside the building, or into an open fixture as provided in section 1101.

CHAPTER XII. MAINTENANCE

SEC. 1201. DEFECTIVE PLUMBING.—Any part of the plumbing system found defective or in an insanitary condition shall be repaired, renovated, replaced, or removed within 30 days upon written notice from the authority having jurisdiction over plumbing.

SEC. 1202. TEMPORARY TOILET FACILITIES.—Toilet facilities provided for the use of workmen during the construction of any building shall be maintained in a sanitary condition.

SEC. 1203. CONDENSATE AND BLOW-OFF CONNECTIONS.—No direct connection of a steam exhaust, boiler blow-off, or drip pipe shall be made with the building-drainage system. Waste water when discharged into the building-drain-

age system shall be at a temperature not higher than 140° F. Where higher temperatures exist proper cooling methods shall be provided.

CHAPTER XIII. INSPECTION AND TESTS

SEC. 1301. INSPECTION.—All piping, traps, and fixtures of a plumbing system shall be inspected by the authority having jurisdiction over plumbing to insure compliance with the requirements of this manual and the installation and construction of the system in accordance with the approved plans and the permit.

SEC. 1302. TESTS REQUIRED.—Every plumbing system shall be subjected to tests for tightness. The complete water-supply system of the building shall be subjected to a water or air-pressure test. The drainage system within or under the building shall be subjected to a water or air-pressure test before the pipes are concealed or the fixtures are set in place, and the sanitary-drainage and vent system shall be subjected to a final smoke or air-pressure test after the system has been completed and the fixture traps have been connected. The authority having jurisdiction over plumbing may require the removal of any plug or cap during the test to determine whether the pressure has reached all parts of the system. He may modify or change the order of any of the tests prescribed in sections 1305, 1306, and 1307, or may substitute a different test to meet special conditions, provided that the tests used are, in his opinion, as effective as those required in the sections enumerated.

SEC. 1303. NOTIFICATION FOR TEST.—(a) It shall be the duty of the plumber to notify the authority having jurisdiction over plumbing and the owner, or his authorized agent, orally, by telephone, or in writing, not less than one working day before the work is to be inspected or tested.

(b) It shall be the duty of the plumber to make sure that the work will stand the test prescribed before giving the above notification.

(c) If the authority having jurisdiction over plumbing finds that the work will not stand the test, the plumber shall be required to re-notify the authority.

(d) If the authority having jurisdiction over plumbing fails to appear within 24 hours of the time set for any inspection or test, the inspection or test shall be made by the plumber and the plumber required to file an affidavit with the authority having jurisdiction over plumbing and with the owner. The affidavit shall state that the work was installed in accordance with this manual and the approved plans and permit, that it was free from defects, and that the required tests were made and the system is free from leaks; also whether the owner or his authorized agent was present when such inspection or tests were made, or was duly notified.

SEC. 1304. LABOR AND EQUIPMENT FOR TESTS.—The equipment, material, power, and labor necessary for the inspection and test shall be furnished by the plumber, unless otherwise provided by the authority having jurisdiction over plumbing.

SEC. 1305. TESTS OF DRAINAGE SYSTEM.—(a) A water test may be applied to the system in its entirety or in sections. If applied to the entire system, all openings in the piping shall be tightly closed, except the highest opening, and the system filled with water to the point of overflow. If the system is tested in sections, each opening shall be tightly plugged (except the highest opening of the section under test) and the section shall be filled with water. In testing successive sections, at least the upper 10 feet of the next lower section shall be retested (except the uppermost 10 feet of the system) and shall have been subjected to at least a 10-foot head of water.

The water level shall remain constant without any further addition for sufficient time to inspect the entire section under test, but in no case less than 15 minutes.

(b) In place of the water test, an air test may be applied as follows: With all openings tightly closed, air shall be forced into the system until there is a uniform pressure sufficient to balance a column of mercury 10 inches in height (or 5 pounds per square inch) on the entire system or section under test. The air pressure shall be maintained on the system or section without any further addition of air for a sufficient time to determine tightness but in no case for less than 15 minutes. (See par. 1305 (b), p. III.)

SEC. 1306. FINAL TEST.—After all fixtures

have been permanently connected and all trap seals filled with water, a smoke or air test under a pressure of approximately 1-inch water column shall be applied to the sanitary system.

In the case of a smoke test, a thick penetrating smoke produced by one or more smoke machines (not by chemical mixtures) shall be introduced into the entire system through a suitable opening. As the smoke appears at the stack openings, they shall be closed and a pressure equivalent to 1-inch water column shall be applied.

Sec. 1307. TESTS OF THE WATER-SUPPLY SYSTEM.—The water-supply system shall be tested in its entirety by filling the entire system with water under a pressure of at least 100 pounds per square inch, or by applying air pressure of at least 35 pounds per square inch (70 inches of mercury column) in case the water test is not feasible or not desirable. The test in either case shall be applied for sufficient time to determine tightness.

Sec. 1308. FINAL CONDITION.—All parts of the plumbing system and associated equipment shall be otherwise tested and adjusted to work properly and be left in good operating condition.

Sec. 1309. SEPARATE TESTS PERMITTED.—Tests may be made separately, as follows:

(a) The building sewer and all its branches from the property line to the building drain.

(b) The building drain and yard drains, including all piping to the height of 10 feet above the highest point on the house drain, except the exposed connections to fixtures.

(c) The soil, waste, vent, inside leader, and drainage pipes which would be covered up before the building is inclosed or ready for completion. The test required for (b) and (c) may be combined.

(d) The final test of the whole system.

After each of the above tests has been made and proved acceptable the authority having jurisdiction over plumbing shall issue a written approval.

Sec. 1310. COVERING OF WORK.—No drainage or plumbing system or part thereof shall be covered until it has been inspected, tested, and approved as prescribed in this chapter. If any building-drainage or plumbing system, or part thereof, is covered before being regularly inspected, tested, and approved, as prescribed in this chapter, it shall be uncovered upon the direction of the authority having jurisdiction over plumbing.

Sec. 1311. DEFECTIVE WORK.—If inspection or test shows defects, such defective work or material shall be replaced and inspection and the tests repeated.

All repairs to piping shall be made with new material. No calking on screwed joints, cracks, or holes will be acceptable.

Sec. 1312. TESTS OF LEADERS.—Leaders and their roof connections within the walls of buildings, or their branches on an outside system where such branches connect with the building drain or are less than 3 feet from the wall of the building, shall be tested by the water or air test. Branches on the outside system may be tested in connection with the house drain.

Sec. 1313. OUTBUILDINGS.—If a stable, barn, or other outbuilding or any part thereof is used for human habitation, the specified inspections and tests of the plumbing system shall be made. Otherwise, all drains shall be inspected, but need not be tested.

Sec. 1314. GARAGES.—For a garage or any part of a garage the specified tests and inspections of the plumbing system shall be made.

Sec. 1315. CERTIFICATE OF APPROVAL.—Upon the satisfactory completion and final test of the plumbing system a certificate of approval shall be issued by the authority having jurisdiction over plumbing to the plumber to be delivered to the owner.

Sec. 1316. TEST OF DEFECTIVE PLUMBING.—The smoke or air test shall be used in testing the sanitary condition of the plumbing system of a building where there is reason to believe that the system has become defective. In plumbing found defective by the authority having jurisdiction over plumbing the alterations required shall be considered as new plumbing.

Sec. 1317. INSPECTIONS AND TESTS NOT REQUIRED.—No tests or inspections shall be required where a plumbing system or part thereof is set up for exhibition purposes and is not used for toilet purposes and not directly connected to a sewerage system; nor after the repairing, or the replacement by a new one to be used for the same purpose, of an old fixture, faucet, or valve; nor after forcing out stoppages and repairing leaks.

PLUMBING SYMBOLS			
Symbol	Plan	Initials	Item
————————	○	D.	Drainage Line
— — — — —	○	V.S.	Vent Line
– – – – – –	◎		Tile Pipe
—•—•—•—	○	C.W.	Cold Water Line
— — — —	○	H.W.	Hot Water Line
————————	○	H.W.R.	Hot Water Return
—✕—✕—✕—	⊗	G	Gas Pipe
••—••—••—	○	D.W.	Ice Water Supply
•••—•••—•••—	○	D.R.	Ice Water Return
⌐⌐⌐⌐⌐	○	F.L.	Fire Line
➤➤➤➤	⊕	I.W.	Indirect Waste
—I—I—	⊕	I.S.	Industrial Sewer
—\—\—	⊘	AW	Acid Waste
—○—○—	Ⓐ	A	Air Line
—○○○○—○○○○—	Ⓥ	V	Vacuum Line
←—←—←—	Ⓡ	R	Refrigerator Waste
⋈ ⋈			Gate Valves
⋈ ⋈			Check Valves
—◁CO ⋋CO	CO.		Cleanout
▢ F.D		F.D.	Floor Drain
◉ R.D		R.D.	Roof Drain
◉ REF.		REF.	Refrigerator Drain
¤		S.D.	Shower Drain
ⓖⓣ		G.T.	Grease Trap
⊢S.C.		S.C.	Sill Cock
⊢G		G.	Gas Outlet
⊢VAC		VAC.	Vacuum Outlet
⊢Ⓜ⊣		M	Meter
⊡			Hydrant
H.R.		HR	Hose Rack
H.R.		H.R.	Hose Rack-Built in
L		L.	Leader
Ⓗᵂᵗ		H.W.T.	Hot Water Tank
Ⓦₕ		W.H.	Water Heater
Ⓦₘ		W.M.	Washing Machine
Ⓡв		R.B.	Range Boiler

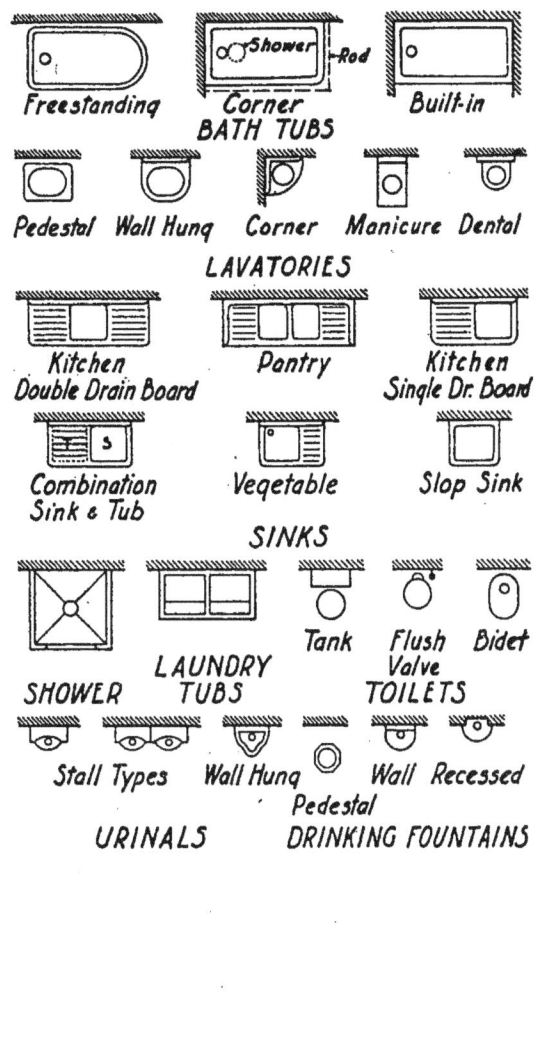

FIGURE 1.—*Standard plumbing symbols.*

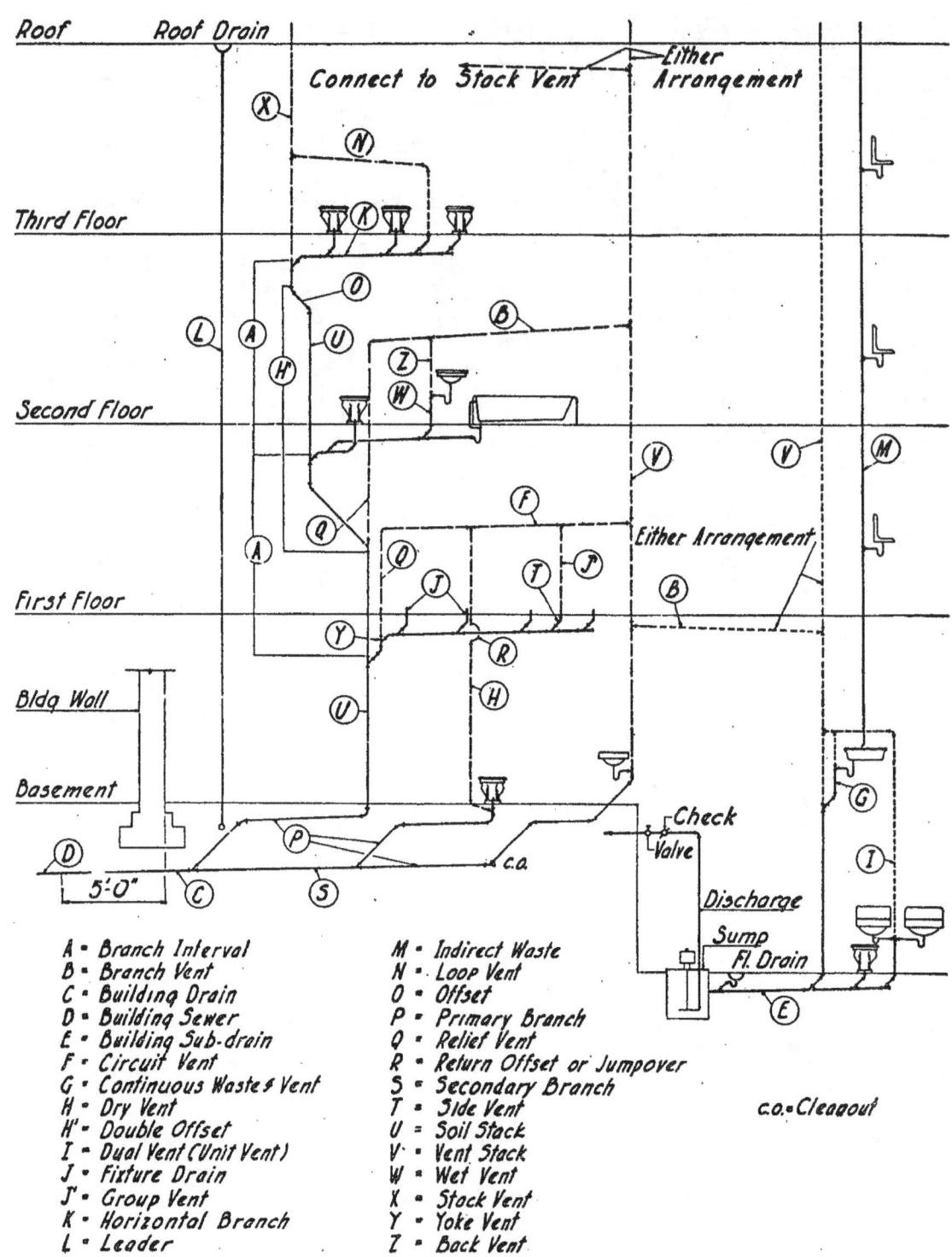

FIGURE 2.—Illustration of definitions.

www.ingramcontent.com/pod-product-compliance
Lightning Source LLC
Chambersburg PA
CBHW082205300426
44117CB00016B/2672